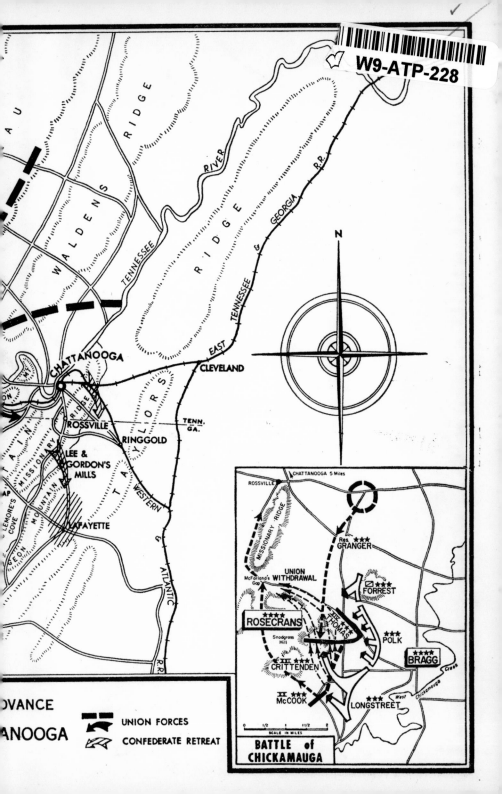

BATTLE of CHICKAMAUGA

UNION FORCES
CONFEDERATE RETREAT

STORMING OF THE GATEWAY

Chattanooga, 1863

Other Books by FAIRFAX DOWNEY

History

CLASH OF CAVALRY: THE BATTLE OF BRANDY STATION, JUNE 9, 1863
THE GUNS AT GETTYSBURG
SOUND OF THE GUNS
INDIAN-FIGHTING ARMY
DISASTER FIGHTERS
OUR LUSTY FOREFATHERS
HISTORY OF DOGS FOR DEFENSE
HORSES OF DESTINY
DOGS OF DESTINY
CATS OF DESTINY
MASCOTS
GENERAL CROOK, INDIAN FIGHTER
FAMOUS HORSES OF THE CIVIL WAR

Biography

THE GRANDE TURKE; SULEYMAN THE MAGNIFICENT
BURTON, ARABIAN NIGHTS ADVENTURER
RICHARD HARDING DAVIS: HIS DAY
PORTRAIT OF AN ERA, AS DRAWN BY C. D. GIBSON

Historical Novels, Juveniles

WAR HORSE
DOG OF WAR
JEZEBEL THE JEEP
CAVALRY MOUNT
THE SEVENTH'S STAGHOUND
ARMY MULE
TRAIL OF THE IRON HORSE
A HORSE FOR GENERAL LEE
THE SHINING FILLY

Humor and Light Verse

A COMIC HISTORY OF YALE
FATHER'S FIRST TWO YEARS
WHEN WE WERE RATHER OLDER
YOUNG ENOUGH TO KNOW BETTER
LAUGHING VERSE (edited)

STORMING OF THE GATEWAY
Chattanooga, 1863

By FAIRFAX DOWNEY

DAVID McKAY COMPANY, INC.

New York

MANUFACTURED IN THE UNITED STATES OF AMERICA

VAN REES PRESS • NEW YORK

To

DR. JAMES C. HAZLETT

Guide over the battlefields, counselor on cannon,
and faithful friend

TO WHOM IT MAY CONCERN

The Company of Military Collectors & Historians, through its Reviewing Board, takes pride in sponsoring this book and in recommending it as a graphic and absorbing account of one of the most significant campaigns of the Civil War. Outstanding as a thoroughly researched logistical study, it is enlivened with the personal narratives of individual fighting men from generals to privates, all treated with insight and facility. It is a definite contribution to the military literature of the 1861–1865 period.

HAROLD L. PETERSON
President

REVIEWING BOARD
Colonel Harry C. Larter, Jr., USA (Ret.)
Francis A. Lord
Lee A. Wallace, Jr.
Henry I. Shaw, Jr., *Editor in Chief*

OFFICIAL
[Signed] HENRY I. SHAW, JR.

Foreword and Acknowledgments

The Civil War armies in the West, both Union and Confederate, considered themselves neglected for the East, as undoubtedly they were. Priority in arms, ammunition, and equipment was given the East. Official and public attention centered on the struggle for Richmond and Washington. There were exceptions such as Lincoln's abiding concern for the loyalists of Tennessee. But essentially it was, of course, the demands of over-all strategy, realization that the war could not finally be won in the East alone, that raised the West to rightful equality. Conviction came with two great Union achievements: the capture of Vicksburg, opening the Mississippi River, and the Chattanooga campaign, which flung wide the gateway to the southeast for Sherman's march to Atlanta and the sea.

Historians as well long scanted the western theater, and only recently has the pendulum begun to swing toward it. This book on the Chattanooga campaign, following others on Gettysburg and Brandy Station, may be offered as an instance of the trend.

As with the earlier works, I have devoted chapters to the background and preliminaries of the culminating battles—to the setting for operations, to the character of the commanders and of the units they led, and to their arms and the manner of their use. Thus, it seems to me, the tale of how they met the test of battle—those gallant men of a war whose centennial we are about to commemorate—can best be told. Also, as in previous books, appendixes are added to serve the same purpose.

Considerable use has been made of accounts by men who fought in the campaign and of those by other first-hand witnesses. Among the latter was War Correspondent Benjamin Franklin Taylor. His book, *In Camp and Field,* with its classic reporting of the Battles of Lookout Mountain and Missionary Ridge, has demanded frequent quotation. Although like a good newspaperman he kept himself in the background, it seems fitting to summon him back to take the bow that is his due. He was forty-four, thickset, of medium height, smooth-shaven, and quiet in manner, when he came to the camps around Chattanooga to cover the war for the *Chicago Evening Journal.* He had taught school and served as the paper's literary editor.

Ben Taylor was excruciatingly shy. He had rather risk gunfire than ask questions [writes Louis M. Starr in *The Bohemian Brigade*]. Effusive at times, at others unabashedly sentimental, Taylor yet managed to write of the war with more power, more subtlety and depth of understanding than any of his colleagues, or, for that matter, than most who have tried it since. His battle dispatches, "dim and imperfect pictures taken by the flash of great guns," are as uneven as the figure suggests, and so with his essays on camp life. Taylor indulged in flights of fancy; the flag was ever streaming forth in his battle prose; many were the allusions to the deity, his tributes to "our brave lads." Yet there is implicit in his work a personal sense of the terrible grandeur of the war, illuminated again and again by imagery. The poet in him kept the whole drama in mind. His Missionary Ridge and Lookout Mountain have a rolling majesty about them that honors the victories they describe.

The idea of this book came from my friend, the late D. Sidney Rollins, of Newport, New Hampshire. Acquaintance through him with his Dartmouth classmate, John S. Fletcher, greatly furthered the project. Mr. Fletcher, head of a Chattanooga law firm, lives on Lookout Mountain, where I spent a memorable evening in his home. My research owes much to him, his family, and Dr. Gilbert E. Govan and Professor James W. Livingood of the University of Chattanooga. Once more I am deeply indebted to the military knowledge of Colonel Harry C. Larter, Jr., who checked my entire manuscript. This book's dedication is acknowledgment to Dr. James C. Hazlett, expert on Civil War ordnance. Grudging neither his time nor the loan of books from his library, Dr. Hazlett was my companion on a tour of the battlefields, where we were accompanied by our wives, not only tolerant of but participating in our preoccupation with military history. Rock L. Comstock, Jr., historian of the Chickamauga-Chattanooga National Military Park, proved a "Rock of Chickamauga" for me in his guidance of a tour of the battlefields and with valuable comment on my battle chapters. I drew often on the weapons lore, unstintedly given, of Harold L. Peterson, collector and historian, and on the advice of my son-in-law, Lieutenant Colonel William A. Knowlton, Armor. Stephen Sears, of *American Heritage,* was most helpful on illustrations.

Again I am grateful to my editor, Kennett L. Rawson, and Mrs. Douglas Ryan, of the David McKay Company, and to my literary agent, Oliver G. Swan, of Paul R. Reynolds & Son. As for all my books, my wife, Mildred Adams Downey, served as critic, secretary, and typist, undismayed even by the tasks of index and bibliography.

An author can only attempt to express his thanks to the libraries on which he depends and to their kind staffs. Chief sources of my reference were the libraries of Dartmouth College and Yale University, the New York Public Library, and that of the University Club of New York City. I am grateful to *Ordnance, Army,* and to *Civil War Times* for permission to reprint chapters, which appeared in those magazines, and to all who granted permissions for the use of quotations.

FAIRFAX DOWNEY

West Springfield
New Hampshire

Contents

Illustrations

xiii

ILLUSTRATIONS IN THE TEXT

MAPS

STORMING OF THE GATEWAY
Chattanooga, 1863

There was no more formidable theater of operations in the Civil War than that around Chattanooga. Chattanooga was the gateway to the East.

— Henry Steele Commager, *The Blue and the Gray*

Chattanooga's location made it one of the most important cities in the South.... By holding Chattanooga the Confederates could threaten the Ohio River and could prevent a Union penetration of the southeastern part of the Confederacy. If the Union armies pushed through Chattanooga, they would be in position to attack Savannah, Ga., or even Richmond from the rear.

American Military History, 1607–1953

As the capture of Vicksburg cut the Confederacy in two on the line of the Mississippi, so the victory at Chattanooga cut in two the remainder of it on the line of the Alleghenies.

— John Fiske, *The Mississippi Valley in the Civil War*

The occupation of Chattanooga by the Union Army cut the Confederacy asunder.

— Michael Hendrick Fitch, *The Chattanooga Campaign*

CHAPTER 1

The Mountain

Clouds hovered over Lookout Mountain in waning November of the year 1863. The glory of its fall foliage had faded, but a hint of haze hanging in the air silvered the forests that clothed it—oak and pine, sourwood and dogwood and black gum, hickory and tulip trees. When that haze thickened into mists and fog, the clouds appeared to have descended to robe all the mountainsides in white.

Massive, precipitous, the mountain seemed the boundary wall of the world to one who scanned it,[1] and in actuality for the space of those autumn days it was the border of a nation divided. On it and around it were entrenched and encamped 150,000 men under arms, determined to hold or to break over that mighty barrier.

Through the chill nights soldiers in gray on the summit and slopes and blue-clad troops at the base warmed themselves at little blazes, "the watch-fires of a hundred circling camps." Those twinkling dots of light and the dancing signal torches on the pinnacle outlined the vast bulk of the mountain. It was as if it had borrowed the stars to limn it against its dark background, as it would the clouds to cloak it.

By day the grandeur of the mountain was awe-inspiring, both for the men of the South from the vantage of its heights and for those of the North who stared up at it from the valley of the Tennessee River. Its lofty peak, rising 1,500 feet above the plain—2,100 feet above sea level—granted glimpses of four states—Georgia, North Carolina, and Alabama besides its native Tennessee. The Blue Ridge of Virginia loomed beyond vision, as did smoky Carolina ranges where lifted King's Mountain, long famed by battle,[2] a destiny now about to be shared by Lookout.

You cannot get out of sight of Lookout [wrote a war correspondent for the Union]. Go where you will within all this horizon, yet, turning southward, there frowns the mountain. It rises like an everlasting thunder-storm that will never pass over. Satan might have offered the kingdoms of the world from that summit. Seen dimly through the mist, it looms up with its two thousand feet and recedes, but when the sun shines strongly out it draws so near as to startle you, and you feel as if you were beneath the eaves of a roof whence drips an iron rain.[3]

Palisaded by its forest, battlemented by its rocky escarpment, the mountain was a great natural castle for the Confederates. It was "a dark shield" held before the eyes of the enemy, its peak a watchtower commanding all the countryside. At its northern base the Tennessee River formed a moat and wound on to coil half around Chattanooga. Over the city the mountain stood as sentinel or menace, as a medieval stronghold guarded or threatened the towns and villages below it. Across the valley to the east stretched the castle's outer works: Missionary Ridge, a third or less as high as the mountain but formidable naturally and rendered more so by successive lines of entrenchments. Although the citadel fell, these outer defenses, stoutly defended, might still be maintained. Three gaps breached them, sally ports or posterns in a wall five miles long. Their passage might be denied as adamantly as by a portcullis clanging down to close a gateway.

Such was the fortress of the mountains, garrisoned by the Gray, beleaguered by the Blue. There has been no more spectacular setting for combat since men have fought for high ground—since the first hilltop was stormed—since armies clashed where

> The mountains look on Marathon,
> And Marathon looks on the sea.[4]

In lordly contemplation the mountains confronted one another. Lookout, Signal, Raccoon, narrow Missionary, and the rest. "Mountains looking at each other," the Cherokee had called them long ago, bestowing a name. Fernando de Soto and his Spaniards had gazed upon them in 1540, and they had echoed to shots of the French and Indian Wars. The long hunters knew them. Canoemen peered up at them from the Tennessee, grateful for its 900-mile-long waterway, though its sinuous curves, compelled by the mountains, lengthened their journey, and rapids and whirlpools in the gorges forced portages.

Now these crags were about to reverberate to the cannonading and musketry of the battles around Chattanooga, with the little city in the river's bend the gage of combat. The mountains were proscenium, wings, and backdrop, and finally the stage itself, the theater of warfare, and never in history has the term more vividly applied. For actors and for audience—directing generals, troops not immediately engaged, and war correspondents—every move save one was as plainly visible as from a front-row seat.[5] As if the impressive setting were not enough, Nature would provide superlatively dramatic stage effects: an eerie eclipse of the moon; the mists and fogs that lowered a curtain before the struggle on Lookout and won it the name of "The Battle Above the Clouds."

Here in the autumn of 1863 the twain, East and West, *did* meet. For the possession of this ground had attained such high strategic value that for a time Washington and Richmond were all but forgotten as the first prizes of war. By one accord the western forces of the Union and the Confederacy were reinforced from the east in mass movements of troops by railroad in the large-scale use of which, for that purpose, the Civil War pioneered.

Tough "Jayhawkers" of the Armies of the Tennessee and of the Cumberland skeptically and sourly watched the arrival of "paper-collar and kid-glove soldiers" of the Army of the Potomac. "Bull Run," the Westerners jeered. "Fall back on your straw and fresh butter." "All's quiet on the Potomac." So, given the pick of arms, ammunition, and equipment,[6] these easterners had won a three-day fight at Gettysburg and halted invasion, had they? How did that stack up against months of floundering through the swamps around

Vicksburg and the storming of the blazing batteries of the town on the high bluff to win the Mississippi River for the Union? In turn the Potomac men stared disdainfully back at the westerners, scoffing at them as "backwoodsmen," undisciplined and unmilitary; "except for the color of their uniforms they looked exactly like the Rebels." "There were times, indeed, when it seemed that the Union soldiers disliked each other more than they disliked the Confederates." [7]

Across the lines "butternuts" of the Army of Tennessee as dubiously observed the detrainment of a corps from the Army of Northern Virginia, admittedly battleworn but surely less ragged and rugged. These newcomers bore laurels of Manassas, Fredericksburg, and Chancellorsville, and upon them lay the glamour of service under Robert E. Lee and Stonewall Jackson. Let them learn now that bloody Shiloh and a score of odds-on fights in the West were more than names, faintly heard.[8]

Such are the jealousies and fierce pride of veterans; they would find an echo eighty years later in the rivalry between the armies of the European and Pacific theaters in World War II. Certainly one of the most memorable features of the Chattanooga campaign was the discovery by East and West in each other of the same stanch fighting qualities. Under the shadow of Lookout Mountain a comradeship was cemented. After the war it would merge men who had worn the blue and the gray as they fought side by side in their country's future conflicts.

The armies of the West dropped their often secondary role and came into their own when Union conquest of the Mississippi and Confederate stalemate in Pennsylvania inevitably shifted the seat of warfare to the mountain fastness of Chattanooga.

It was the centre of great lines of railroad radiating in every direction to the Mississippi, the Ohio, the Atlantic Ocean, and the Gulf of Mexico. Situated at the end of that huge mountain defile known as the East Tennessee, in the heart of a region which some have called the American Switzerland, it guards the only avenue by which Virginia can be approached directly from the southwestern states. Its possession by a Federal army would practically isolate Virginia and North Carolina on the one hand, and lop off Mississippi and Alabama on the other; and by opening the way into the interior of Georgia would throw what was left of the war entirely into the Atlantic region. Its possession by the Confederates gave them control of eastern Tennessee, enabled them easily to move reinforcements between Virginia and the West, and was a perpetual menace to middle Tennessee and Kentucky.[9]

One wedge had split the Confederacy north and south when the fall of Vicksburg opened the Mississippi River. It was the moment now to attempt to hammer another through Chattanooga deep into the southeast, and that effort, if successful, must toll a knell for the seceded states.

Besides its paramount importance for strategic maneuver, the region loomed large because of its abundance of the sinews of war—for its rich crops of wheat, corn, and hay—for beef and pork—"an abundance of all good things the Yankee 'vandals' had not reached, with no end to come. No wonder that the rebels are making a desperate effort for the recapture of this country. We are in their very granary and without it they cannot live," wrote a Wisconsin artillerymen.[10] Provisions from the farms of East Tennessee had been supplying not only the Confederate forces in the vicinity but were shipped to others. When those supplies were cut off, followed by the ravages of Sherman's march to the sea and Sheridan's raids through Virginia's fertile Shenandoah Valley, the pace of the Southern armies, "marching on their bellies" in the Napoleonic maxim, was fatally slowed.

And here lay the Confederacy's last considerable reserve of horses and mules in this fine breeding country for riding and draft animals. Already it has been whittled down to a narrowed compass by Northern victories in Kentucky, Missouri, and western Virginia. By this period the Old Dominion and the Deep South had been scoured for mounts and teams until not many were left beyond essential farm animals. Most Texas mustangs were too small for military use. Lose Tennessee, and the Gray cavalry, artillery, and wagon transport would be further crippled, with the Blue's correspondingly strengthened.

As much as for the conquest of a seceded state, this campaign was designed as a rescue expedition. Tennessee had left the Union by vote of its legislature but by no means by the will of all its people. The mountain folk, mostly small farmers, were loyal, detesting and distrusting the wealthy planters and slaveowners. In the bitter border strife of the first years of the war they suffered for their allegiance. Their homes and farms destroyed, they were forced to flee to Kentucky, where many enlisted in the Union Army, or to hide deep in the mountains. An earlier plan for an invasion to march to their relief had had to be canceled, but Abraham Lincoln had never forgotten them. Wherever they lay in the power of the enemy, a nation's faithful must be freed, an obligation inherent in the preservation of the Union, taking precedence over the ending of Negro slavery. The flags carried up Lookout Mountain and the slopes of Missionary Ridge bore among the honors inscribed on their folds an invisible legend, *Noblesse oblige.*

The East Tennessee campaign matched any in the East as a fascinating study in command. Here stars on the shoulder straps of officers, numbers of them battle-wise veterans of the Mexican and Indian wars, brightened or were tarnished, increased or vanished. Upon the failure of Rosecrans after a beginning of high promise, Lincoln at last found his general in Ulysses S. Grant. Furthermore, the God of Battles now bestowed on the Union three other first-rate commanders with the emergence of Sherman, Sheridan, and Thomas. "Fighting Joe" Hooker came West and redeemed his sobriquet forfeited at Chancellorsville. Although some corps leaders fell short, able generals of division and brigade upheld them.

Generals don't die; they only get relieved. Thus sardonically remarked the lower ranks. That was not true, particularly in this war, where casualties among general officers were notably high, and some leaders undoubtedly would have preferred death in action to suspension from command with all it implied. Rosecrans had a counterpart in the Confederacy's Braxton Bragg. The latter squandered his brilliant victory at Chickamauga, the former's downfall, and let slip an opportunity that would never come again. In this theater Longstreet, Lee's balky war horse at Gettysburg, became again the spirited, willing charger of earlier fields. Here a fighting Irishman, Pat Cleburne, proved himself one of the South's finest combat commanders as he had before and would again until a fatal bullet found him a year later. Two dashing leaders of horse, "First with the Most" Forrest and "Fighting Joe" Wheeler, on terrain generally unfavorable for mounted operations, outrode and outfought the Federal cavalry as definitely as had their comrades of the arm in the East until Brandy Station.

The great captains and the men they led—their monuments, dotting the 8,190 acres of the splendid Chickamauga and Chattanooga National Military Park, commemorate them and their deeds, marking the scene of two of the most courageous charges in history when the slanted banners, falling and rising again, climbed Lookout Mountain and Missionary Ridge. There stand their arms—rifles, revolvers, and sabers in museums—the cannon in the fields and on the high ground where they were manned in several of the war's most striking artillery actions. These weapons, wielded by men fighting for their beliefs, vividly bring back across a century the epic conflicts of those autumn days when flame spurted from muzzles, gleaming bayonets thrust, and Parrotts, Napoleons, and howitzers woke thunderous echoes in the crags.

Gone are the veterans. There bugles blow and drums roll no more. No longer waves signal flag or torch from the peaks. The guns are silent. Inscribed shafts and plaques speak for soldiers who have marched on. A greater monument, immemorially preceding them, more grandly proclaims their undying valor—the Mountain.

CHAPTER 2

"For I Am a Man Under Authority, Having Soldiers Under Me"

Sixteen years before armies marched and countermarched through the Cumberland ranges, the curtain had risen in another mountainous theater of warfare. The *mise en scène* of the conflict with Mexico would prove so reminiscent to its veterans in the Chattanooga campaign that many of them may well have thought: Over such ground have I fought before. In the palisades of Lookout Mountain they must have seen another walled Chapultepec and in Missionary Ridge the heights of Buena Vista. Eighteen sixty-three was the second act of the drama of 1847, with many actors reappearing, though some had changed costume with their allegiance and wore gray instead of blue. Its continuity is especially notable in the development of and interplay among four of its cast of characters:

Captain Braxton Bragg, 3rd U.S. Artillery. West Point, Class of 1837. Later Commanding General, Army of Tennessee, C.S.A.

Lieutenant George H. Thomas, Bragg's Battery. West Point, 1840. Later commanding XIV Corps, Army of the Cumberland, U.S.A.

Colonel Jefferson Davis, Mississippi Rifles. West Point, 1828. Resigned but returned to the service for the Mexican War. Later Secretary of War, U.S.A.; then President of the Confederate States of America.

Lieutenant Ulysses S. Grant, Infantry. Acting Quartermaster. West Point, 1843. Resigned 1854 but returned to serve in the Civil

War. Later commanding Union armies in the West; then General in Chief, Armies of the United States.

A dour, difficult, punctillious man was Captain Bragg of Alabama. His martinet efficiency had made his flying battery one of the best in General Zachary Taylor's army in northern Mexico. Uniforms smart, guns, caissons, harness, and the hides of horses clean and shining, its mounted drill was a thing of beauty, and it did him proud in battle.

Brother officers in other units often found him as hard to get on with as it was, so they declared, for him to get on with himself. Once he commanded a company at a post where he was detailed as quartermaster in addition to his other duties. As company commander he submitted a requisition for supplies that, as quartermaster, he declined to endorse. In his first capacity he reapplied with reinforced reasons and in his second role again refused to issue. Thereupon he referred the correspondence to the post commander. That officer took an astounded look at the sheaf of papers and exclaimed: "My God, Mr. Bragg, you have quarreled with every officer in the army, and now you are quarreling with yourself!" [11]

Toward militia units his battery supported, the attitude of Bragg, the Regular, was overbearing and contemptuous. They responded with dislike that intensified to hatred. Militamen were suspected of placing under his cot a fused shell that exploded just as he lay down to rest. The cot was shattered and tent walls shredded, but Bragg picked himself up unharmed.

Buena Vista wrote his name in history and upon a future artillery center [12] when he galloped his flying battery into action at a crucial moment. General Taylor's order, "Double shot your guns and give 'em hell!" was obeyed by blazing volleys of canister that helped break a Mexican charge about to overwhelm the American line. The aura of that day's victory clung to him through an interval of peace and on into the greater war that followed.

It was Bragg's tragedy and the South's, when he became her sixth ranking general, that the years had dulled the dash and decisiveness of the crack artilleryman of the War with Mexico. Dyspepsia and migraine headaches further soured his disposition. General Bragg was even harder to get on with than Captain Bragg. He was still the martinet, a "ferocious disciplinarian" who mercilessly sent his own soldiers to face firing squads for violations of military law.[13] Increasingly subordinates began to mistrust a commander prone to shift all blame for any defeat onto them. A veteran's competence and inborn aggressiveness, those were still his; he squandered both by his inability to follow success through or redeem failure. Barren victories and lost opportunities mounted on his record: Perryville, Murfreesboro or Stone's River, and finally Chickamauga.

Yet the stars of a lieutenant-general still sat firmly on Braxton Bragg's shoulder straps when he marched his army toward the little city in the Tennessee River's bend. But "the stars in their courses fought against Sisera."

A playwright or novelist would have been accused of license in making George H. Thomas a lieutenant of Bragg's Battery in Mexico. The Civil War sequence seems too pat. The one-time subordinate, a Virginian, remains loyal to the Union instead of following his seceding state. It happens that in one of the great battles of the West he commands a corps facing the army led by his former captain. Thomas's gallant and stubborn stand, with two other Federal corps largely routed, prevents defeat from turning into disaster. Yet such is is the truth of history, sometimes stranger than fiction.

Deliberate—"slow" by self-accusation—tenacious, Thomas's characteristics as a young officer were ingrained and enduring. "Old Slow Trot" was one of the nicknames he would pick up, along with "Old Reliable." Once in battle, he fought it up to the hilt. In the bitter street combat for Monterrey he brought the gun of his section into action in a narrow alley, blasting away at a Mexican barricade. Heavy enemy fire from the front and bullets from the housetops above, "as if bushels of hickory nuts were hurled at us," began to cut down his crew. Ordered to withdraw, Thomas would not retreat until he had given the foe a parting round and battered back a charge. Then he, surviving cannoneers, and infantrymen heaved the piece up and out of its alley trap, limbered, and saved it.

Bragg, who would subsequently see Thomas perform a similar feat with a corps instead of a cannon, wholeheartedly praised his conduct in Mexico. "No officer of the army," he stated in a recommendation of Thomas for an appointment, "has been so long in the field without relief, and to my personal knowledge no one has rendered more arduous, faithful and brilliant service." [14] Such acclaim would be magnified when the national spotlight beat on Thomas as a Union general.

... If you exalted George Henry Thomas to a very lofty niche [wrote a war correspondent], you may just leave him and History will keep him there forever. I do not assert that he saved the Army of the Cumberland, but I believe he did; that the salvation was not a lucky blunder, but the result of brains as well as guns; that it was a disposition of force to defeat the enemy's design, struck out with a rapidity so wonderful and a wisdom so masterly that a month of mathematics would not have materially modified the adjustment. It was a stroke of what, for the want of a better name, we must call genius. Not one of those men that draws his sword every time he bids you good morning, General Thomas is, perhaps, the most modest. Combining the energy, resolution, and tenacity of the soldier with the simple manners of a gentleman, he can handle a corps and make a hammer or an anvil of it at will, and yet he is one of the few in the Cumberland Mountains who does not believe he could handle the Cumberland army....

Not scrimped anywhere, and square everywhere—square face, square shoulders, square step; blue eyes with depths in them, withdrawn beneath a pent-house of a brow, features with legible writing on them, and the whole giving the idea of massive solidity, of the right kind of a man to "tie to." [15]

Thus Thomas was described after his epic stand on September 20, 1863, covering the disorganized retreat of the rest of the Union Army. It was what he might have been expected to do, his former commander in Mexico may have ruefully reflected when he failed to reap the victory he had won. By a final touch of dramatic irony

Thomas, not Bragg, took a title from the battle, "The Rock of Chickamauga."

Coincidence again stretched forth a long arm when Colonel Jefferson Davis led his Mississippi Rifles into Mexico. It chanced that the Mississippians and Bragg's Battery were frequently in action together through the campaign. Davis was a former Regular. Bragg could not complain of his fighting quality or that of his regiment, state unit though it was.

The mutual confidence and comradeship of a smooth-working infantry-artillery team met their greatest test at Buena Vista. Under a terrific Mexican onslaught the Rifles stanchly held the center until lancers threatened the American rear. Davis fell back and reformed his regiment into a V. The splendidly uniformed lancers, riding down from the mountains, had looked "too pretty to shoot" to the Mississippians, who forgot their mock compunctions as they were charged. From the sides of the V volleys mowed down the horsemen rushing into it, but other squadrons galloped forward to press an attack that could scarcely have been withstood. Before it could be delivered, Bragg's Battery and other guns whirled up, unlimbered, caught the enemy cavalry in a deadly crossfire, and shattered them. As the artillery changed position to meet the main frontal assault, cannoneers glanced back. The Mississippi Rifles, behind their colonel, wounded but firm in his saddle, were marching back into battle to their support.

So was cemented "that military friendship between Jefferson Davis and Braxton Bragg which was to have such a fateful bearing on the fortunes of the Confederacy." [16] Inevitably Davis was swayed by it when as President of the Confederate States and Commander-in-Chief of their armies he gave Bragg command in the West. At the same time he warned his general:

You have the misfortune of being regarded as my personal friend, and are pursued, therefore, with malignant censure by men regardless of truth, and whose want of principle to guide their conduct renders them incapable of conceiving you are trusted because of your known fitness for command and not because of friendly regard.[17]

The judgment a regimental colonel had formed of an artillery captain remained unshaken. To the President directing armies it seemed an estimate as valid as when he had made it. Humanly it was apparent to neither man that he was filling a role beyond his capacity. In the East, Davis's exercise of the command function was tempered and transmuted by the genius of Robert E. Lee. The more remote theater in the critical autumn of 1863 was confidently left in Bragg's hands. Evidence, piling up prior to the East Tennessee Campaign that Bragg was unequal to his key post, failed to shake the President's stubborn loyalty to his favorite commander, his comrade-in-arms of Mexico.

Chattanooga, to paraphrase Wellington on Waterloo and Eton, was lost of the battlefield of Buena Vista.

Ulysses S. Grant, the reluctant West Pointer, the infantry officer in Mexico, still disliking the army and so bored with his detail as quartermaster that he took to nipping whisky in the solitude of his tent, a habit that would grow and force his resignation from the service six years later.

Only moments of high excitement redeemed the war for him, and he sought them out, quitting duties behind the lines. For this brief study two especially apposite episodes will suffice.

At Monterrey, Lieutenant Grant volunteered to carry an order for more ammunition for a battery whose supply was almost exhausted. Men remembered both his daring and his superb horsemanship as he rode across the enemy's front. On the instant that a long line of muskets leveled and flamed, Grant at a headlong gallop swung down along his horse's offside Indian fashion. A storm of lead swept close above the vacant saddle, and rider and mount, unhit, were out of range before another volley could be fired. The battery whose ammunition was replenished as a result of Grant's ride was Bragg's.

In the storming of Mexico City, Lieutenant Grant, who had been

making notes on artillery, put them into practice. He helped manhandle a mountain howitzer up into a church belfry. Deadly fire,
poured down on rooftop snipers and enemy massed behind street
barricades, cleared a passage that could otherwise have been forced
only at the cost of considerable casualties. A curious reversal in days
to come would see cannon on more commanding heights, on the
slopes of Lookout Mountain and Missionary Ridge, manned against
Grant but not so effectively as by the quartermaster of 1847.

Captain Sam Grant drowning in drink the peacetime monotony
of a Pacific coast fort. An apparent end to his army career under
that stigma, "for the good of the service." The Civil War volunteer,
drilling a home-town company but failing of election as one of its
officers. Then, nevertheless, appointed colonel of another regiment
and whipping that undisciplined unit into shape. At Shiloh a
general, the same dogged, obstinate fighter he would always be,
taking heavy losses as he would so often later, but this time to such
public indignation that he barely escaped a second forced resignation.

Fort Donelson besieged and yielded, and his initials triumphantly
spelled out as "Unconditional Surrender" Grant. Victory at Vicksburg. A short, untidy soldier leads the long blue columns at Chattanooga—and on to Appomattox.

Grant and Bragg and Thomas. Like the centurion of St.
Matthew's gospel, men under authority and exercising it. They who
wore the blue must ultimately answer to Lincoln, Secretary of War
Stanton, and "Old Brains" Halleck, the Chief of Staff. Wearers of
the gray responded to the remote, and finally in this campaign to
the immediate control of Jefferson Davis. Meanwhile on the field
of maneuver and in combat the leaders bore on their own shoulders
the dreadful responsibility of command.

How that heavy burden is carried, a cause, and the lives of many
soldiers at stake—what manner of men sustain its weight—with these
a battle study is primarily concerned.

Generals who fought at Chickamauga and Chattanooga formed
as notable a group as the Civil War assembled in any theater. Their

roll in that autumn of 1863 lacked only a few of the outstanding commanders. None of those charged with the defense of the Union at first raised the nation's hopes higher than William S. Rosecrans, commanding the Army of the Cumberland.

A trained soldier, West Point, 1842, he had resigned to enter business but rejoined the army in 1861. Like McClellan, he had the gift of winning troops' devotion. "Old Rosy" they affectionately nicknamed him and sang:

> Old Rosy is our man,
> Old Rosy is our man,
> He'll show his deeds, where'er he leads.
> Old Rosy is our man.

Victories in Virginia and as commander of the Army of the Mississippi had proved his flair for strategy and his willingness to join battle. His was a leadership that inspired men to fight their utmost as at Corinth, when his regiments in desperate hand-to-hand combat broke a fierce Confederate assault. He came to the valiantly defended redoubt to praise them, sweeping off his hat and declaring that he must stand bareheaded in the presence of the brave. No wonder "Old Rosy" was their man.

A record of unbroken successes lay behind him when he took command of the Army of the Cumberland. Halleck prodded him to move before he was ready, threatening to relieve him. Rosecrans telegraphed a curt refusal and added that if the judgment of a general on the ground were not trusted, he ought to be relieved. "Old Brains" backed down, and Rosecrans launched the Chattanooga campaign in his own good time.

At Roman triumphs men were stationed along the streets to mingle insults and disparagement with the plaudits of the crowd for a victorious general lest the fates, envious of his glory, retaliate. There were few skeptics or doubters to perform such a service for Rosecrans when he marched toward Chickamauga Creek.[18] None yet questioned whether he gave enough personal supervision to his line of battle—if he did not leave too much to subordinates—

whether, besides winning victories, he could meet a more severe test of generalship and cope with disaster on a stricken field.

Rosecrans' chief of staff was James A. Garfield, efficient and energetic but "rather too democratic and academic to become a typical soldier." One of the brigadiers, John Beatty, characterized his politician's affability when he noted in his journal that Garfield gave him a grip suggesting, "Vote right, vote early." Yet the chief of staff, while a politician, was not also a political general of the Butler or Sickles stripe. The campaign would prove to be a stepping-stone for him; he left the army toward its close for a seat in Congress. No bullet was marked with his name in the war, but an assassin's would kill him when he was President of the United States.

The Army of the Cumberland assembled four diverse corps commanders. That two were equal to their tasks and two were not indicates the delicate balance at Chickamauga, with the needle swaying between defeat and debacle.

Thomas has already been mentioned. The Reserve Corps was led by General Gordon Granger, West Pointer and Mexican War veteran, "a profane, bearded, rough-hewn regular-army type from the old days." [19] He was a fighter, the sort of general who marches to the sound of the guns with or without orders—the kind, too, who in the heat of battle cannot always resist taking personal part as when he turned cannoneer at Missionary Ridge and was brusquely ordered by Grant to attend to his command. On the debit side were Thomas L. Crittenden and bluff, hearty Alexander McD. McCook. Beatty [20] described them scathingly: the former as a good drinker who knew how to blow his own horn; the latter, he said, had a "weak nose that would do no credit to a baby" and his grin "excites the suspicions that he is either still very green or deficient in the upper story." West Pointers both, who had led divisions with some success, they were unequal to handling corps in the crisis at Chickamauga, and there their stars faded.

History singled out one of the division commanders: little, hot-tempered Phil Sheridan. That temper of his was under better control than in West Point days when he almost bayoneted the cadet sergeant who reprimanded him. The bowlegged cavalryman-to-be was still leading infantry. One cannot resist speculating what he might have done with the cavalry in the Chattanooga campaign had it been under his command instead of that of others who were outfought by Bedford Forrest's and Joe Wheeler's Gray horsemen. But Sheridan must wait a little longer for the great role he would fill as head of the Cavalry Corps of the Army of the Potomac.

Leading reinforcements from that army to the West, Joseph Hooker surely welcomed the miles between him and Chief of Staff Halleck in Washington and their running feud. Still more welcome was a chance to wipe out the blot of Chancellorsville on his record. After that battle his nickname of "Fighting Joe," which he had always secretly deplored as grandiloquent, had seemed worse than bombast—a contradiction. For him Lookout Mountain loomed like the beacon of another opportunity.

Given a choice—not his to make but Halleck's—Hooker would never have selected the XI as one of the two corps he took westward. It was the XI, surprised and routed by Stonewall Jackson, that Hooker could blame for the loss of Chancellorsville, although the defeat was his ultimate responsibility. Nor would that corps have elected to have continued under its own commander, O. O. Howard. Its largely German-American personnel considered him no reincarnation of Frederick the Great and was irked by the religious Howard's reputation as a great biblical soldier. It had not fought well under him either at Chancellorsville or Gettysburg. Howard possessed ability and was a brave man; he led rallies clutching the colors beneath the stump of an arm he had lost at Fair Oaks. By the same token the German-American was a good soldier. Here was a misfit of a commander and command that a change might have corrected to the advantage of both.

Finally, to join Grant and Sheridan and complete the mighty trio that would win the war for the Union, William Tecumseh Sherman brought parts of two corps from the Army of the Tennessee. Reddish-haired "Cump" Sherman, his temper as quick as his decisions. The soldier who called war hell and fought it to fit the name. When the Chattanooga campaign forced open the gateway to the southeast, it would be his lot to march through it to Atlanta and the sea.

In the wings stood Ambrose Burnside, holding the city of Knoxville, which ranked a close second to Chattanooga as a key point of the campaign—Burnside, who passed his whiskers down to posterity in reverse as sideburns. "He was a rather large man physically, about six feet tall, with a large face and a small head, and heavy side-whiskers," Charles A. Dana wrote. "He was an energetic, decided man, frank, manly, and well educated. He was a show officer—not that he *made* any show; he was naturally that." When given command of the Army of the Potomac, Burnside had the chance of greatness thrust upon him. He could not rise to it and relinquished the post as willingly as he had reluctantly assumed it. But though for a time he considered abandoning Knoxville, he managed to hold that block to Confederate rail transport and for that he deserved the gratitude of the Republic.

During the battle in East Tennessee, as elsewhere, Union or Confederate commanders could look through their field glasses and in the opposite lines sight an old friend, a West Point classmate, or a fellow veteran of the War with Mexico—or someone who was all three. Such recognition was possible in a war where generals were often at the fighting front or close to it; if it were not visual, a leader would usually be known as soon as his unit was identified. Frequently action was dictated by a commander's knowledge of his adversary's characteristics and capabilities.

At Chickamauga, Lieutenant General James Longstreet, C.S.A., was once so far forward that he rode into a group of enemy pickets. Only the darkness of woods, concealing the gray of his uniform, saved him from capture. It had earlier been reported by Federal intelligence that he had brought Bragg reinforcements from the Army of Northern Virginia. Union leaders knew they were up against a hard-hitting professional. How he would act depended upon his opinion of a superior's orders. If he approved, he would deliver a smashing assault or make a stubborn stand. Orders contrary to his judgment exacted slow and reluctant compliance. Lee at Gettysburg had suffered grievously from his obstinacy and delays.

Now Longstreet was present by his own will and as a result of his advice. Aware of the theater's importance, he had urged that Bragg be strengthened from Virginia to crush Rosecrans, or Vicksburg would be followed by a march through Georgia that would wreck the Confederacy. He had agreed to serve as one of Bragg's corps commanders or, so he plainly hinted, to supersede him. What might have happened had not Jefferson Davis ignored the hint is one of the fascinating "ifs" of military history.

Before Longstreet left to join Bragg, Lee had urged him, "Now, General, you must beat those people in the West." And Longstreet had answered: "If I live; but I would not give a single man of my command for a fruitless victory."[21] Yet such a sacrifice, many times multiplied, was to be his destiny.

West with Longstreet came John B. Hood, the bold, rash soldier, all but indestructible. In an Indian fight of 1857 he had received a wound that left him partly incapacitated for two years. He lost an arm at Gettysburg. Before he had wholly recovered, he was back in action with his Texans at Chickamauga, and there his right leg was so badly mangled that it had to be amputated. With an artificial limb, the gift of his division, he rode back into battle through the rest of the war.[22]

Two other doughty warriors were Pat Cleburne, born in County Cork, Ireland, on St. Patrick's Day, archtype of the Fighting Irish as his valiant defense of Missionary Ridge would prove; and little Joe Wheeler, the dashing cavalryman whose raids cut Federal communications and supply lines. "Fighting Joe" became one of four Civil War general officers to serve again in the War with Spain. Leading a cavalry division in Cuba, he revived the past with his shout at Las Guasimas, "Come on, boys, we've got the damnyankees on the run!" Among the able veterans was William J. Hardee, who fought by the book, having written it: *Hardee's Tactics,* adopted as an army text.

The long list of officers who did not get on with General Bragg was swelled by the campaign. D. H. Hill was one of those who

signed the petition for Bragg's removal after Chickamauga. He paid
for it when President Davis refused to send in his nomination as
lieutenant general to the Senate; also by relief from his command,
although he was later given back his old division. Mutual distrust
existed, too, between Leonidas Polk and Bragg. The former had
resigned soon after graduation from the U.S. Military Academy,
where he led a "praying squad," to enter the Episcopal ministry
and become a bishop; then, when the war began, exchanged clerical
black for Confederate gray. In bravery Polk followed the tradition
of the medieval soldier-bishops; he would die in battle. As a general
he lamentably failed. Polk had such stanch advocates as able
Colonel Sorrel, who wrote of him:

Of commanding presence and most winning address, he served
with distinction and renown. While suffering at the hands of Bragg
treatment unjust and harsh, he on the other hand had won to himself the abiding affection and confidence of all officers and men whom
he commanded.

History does not sustain such praise, and Bragg undoubtedly
regarded Polk as his evil genius, for he failed, of course, to realize
that that malign spirit was strongest in his own character. After
Chickamauga Bragg relieved Polk from command. But President
Davis for once refused to support his old friend and ordered the
bishop-general reinstated.

Longstreet, Hill, Polk, and still more. After the first day's battle
at Chickamauga their mistrust of Braxton Bragg mounted high.
The Civil War offers no other such striking example of forfeited
faith. George B. McClellan's repeated failures to seize opportunities
steadily lost him the confidence of his officers, though never of his
troops, and there are no few instances of minor commanders tried
and found wanting. But the condemnation of Bragg, in which so
many of his top commanders combined and which they declared
in his presence before President Davis, is unique. Yet with one
general only did it flame into absolute insubordination.

Nathan Bedford Forrest was the ablest cavalryman the war produced in the opinion of Lord Wolseley, the noted British soldier.

From boyhood on, he had the daring and iron courage he would later display on so many battlefields. He rode fractious horses, unsaddled and unbridled. With revolver and bowie he beat off four men who had killed his uncle; with a knife alone he faced down an angry mob about to lynch a man in jail. As a youngster he volunteered in the War with Mexico, but his unit was not sent to the front. Enlisting as a private in 1861, he rose rapidly to a generalcy. "First-with-the-Most" Forrest, they called him, "The Wizard of the Saddle." His hell-for-leather combat leadership, as skillful as it was intrepid, got him several wounds, with twenty-nine horses killed under him. A tough man to tangle with, Bedford Forrest—not only for the enemy but for General Bragg.

It was Forrest's note to Bragg, urging him to complete the Federal rout at Chickamauga and press on rapidly to Chattanooga, that aroused the latter's ire. Promptly Bragg ordered the cavalryman to turn over his command to Wheeler. Forrest's reaction, a violent letter, by no means assuaged a rage more towering then his six-foot-two stature. He rode to headquarters, accompanied by his chief surgeon, Dr. J. B. Cowan. Bursting into the tent, Forrest refused the General's proffered hand and delivered a blast that probably never has been surpassed as a white-hot defiance of a superior officer.

I am not here to pass civilities or compliments with you, but on other business. You commenced your cowardly and contemptible persecution of me soon after the battle of Shiloh, and you have kept it up ever since. You did it because I reported to Richmond facts, while you reported damn lies. You robbed me of my command in Kentucky and gave it to one of your favorites—men that I armed and equipped from the enemies of our country. In a spirit of revenge and strife, because I would not fawn upon you as others did, you drove me into West Tennessee in the winter of 1862, with a second brigade I had organized, with improper arms and without sufficient ammunition, although I had made repeated applications for the same. You did it to ruin me and my career. When, in spite of all this, I returned with my command, well equipped by captures, you began again your work of spite and persecution, and have kept it up; and now this second brigade, organized and equipped without

thanks to you, or the government, a brigade which has won a reputation for successful fighting second to none in the army, taking
advantage of your position as commanding general in order to
further humilitate me, you have taken brave men from me. I have
stood your meanness as long as I intend to. You have played the
part of a damn scoundrel, and are a coward; and if you were any
part of a man, I would slap your jaws and force you to resent it.
You may as well not issue any more orders to me, for I will not
obey them, and I will hold you personally responsible for any
further indignities you endeavor to inflict upon me. You have
threatened to arrest me for not obeying your orders promptly.
I dare you to do it, and I say to you that if you ever again interfere
with me or cross my path it will be at the peril of your life.[23]

Under that torrent of wrath Bragg sat dumfounded. It was as
sudden and cataclysmic as the shell that had exploded beneath
his cot in the War with Mexico.

He realized that in his stormful mood Forrest acknowledged no
accountability to law, civil or military, human or divine, as he
stood there towering above him, launching at him this fierce denunciation, and emphasizing each expression of contempt with a quick
motion of the index finger, which he thrust almost into Bragg's
face. The general did not utter a word or move a muscle of his face
during this shower of invective from his brigadier. The scene did
not last longer than a few minutes, and when Forrest had finished
he turned his back sharply upon Bragg and stalked out of the tent
toward the horses. As they rode away, Dr. Cowan remarked, "Well,
you are in for it now!" Forrest replied instantly, "He'll never say
a word about it; he'll be the last man to mention it; and, mark
my word, he'll take no action in the matter." [24]

He was right. Bragg took no official notice of the incident. It was
the fuming Forrest who pressed the bitter quarrel to the top, facing
President Davis with still another dilemma. Davis, unwilling to
lose one of his best cavalry leaders, managed to solve the problem
by persuading the far from unwilling Forrest to accept a command
in another sector of the West.

With such dissension smoldering in this campaign even before its outset and flaming up in its midst, the cards were stacked against the Confederate Army.

"Write me one word that will best describe American command as you have studied it in all the wars since the American French and Indian wars," someone once asked Douglas Southall Freeman. Without a second's hesitation the great military historian set down the word, "Character." Then he added two other essentials of leadership: Know your job. Take care of your men.[25]

It is delicately balanced and it has many facets, this relationship between commander and commanded. Successful leaders in all wars have been born with its knowledge or learned it readily or the hard way. How they must be father or older brother to uncertain, frightened recruits—to youngsters in the ranks, and there were so many of them in the 1860's, down to boys in their early teens. Toward the older men "to be with them and yet not of them." Wise is the new lieutenant who is quick to be taught by his veteran sergeants and treats them with that measure of deference they deserve. The essentials of impartiality and just enforcement of discipline were particularly important in the Civil War, begun under the pernicious system of election of regimental and company officers by their men.

Know your duties, though it means, as it did for John Beatty and other officers fresh from civilian life, sitting late in a tent studying manuals by candlelight. Competence breeds confidence, and its companions are care and compassion and courage. Before men he leads into battle the officer, like the color-bearer, must not falter.

Rank has its privileges, in the old army phrase. It has also its penalties: its heavy responsibilities. For those who shoulder them ably the reward is great: the respect, the affection, and the willingness of their men to follow wherever they lead. At Chickamauga, Lookout Mountain, and Missionary Ridge many officers won that reward, and, if they survived, cherished the memory of it all their lives.

Well led or ill led, the Blue and Gray divisions and brigades, the battalions and the companies—an array like that of Lars Porsena, summoned east and west and south and north—marched that fall of 1863 into the Georgia woods and the valleys and mountains of Tennessee.

CHAPTER 3

The Volunteers

"I've Got Three Years to Do This In" is the title of an army bugle march, referring to the enlistment term. It might have been sounded as a warning during the Chattanooga campaign, for time was running short. The period of service for which the volunteer regiments had signed in 1861 (after the ending of the ninety-day folly) would expire in 1864.[26] There was no enlistment for the duration of the war, no effective draft law.[27] Whether a soldier joined up again was a matter of his own choice.

Had the campaign reached a winter stalemate and been deferred until spring, the Union forces in the West would have faced the same problem Grant then met when he took over command in the East: depleted ranks, bounty jumpers, hired substitutes, and resentful draftees—malingerers and the unfit—a flood of desertions. But through the crucial autumn of 1863 the hard core of veterans still served on.

"Three years of war had created on both sides veteran soldiers who were the equals of any army of any time.... From now on in this war, the veteran is going to make every engagement decisive, and the Civil War might be said to begin in 1863."[28]

Faithful men, war-weary and homesick, many bearing the scars of wounds, re-enlisted in sufficient numbers [29] for the North to continue to overbalance the South's veteran man power, now dwindling alarmingly.

In the western armies a company that had re-enlisted to the extent of three-fourths of its numbers (this was the percentage required if a regiment was to keep its old number and its organizational status) would parade through the camps, fife and drum corps playing and everybody cheering; the example was contagious and led others to sign up.[30]

They were still the Umpteenth Volunteer Infantry from their state and they were proud of it and the flag they followed, and they deserved to be.

When they put down their names for another hitch, they grumbled bitterly that they had done their share and it was high time they were spelled. Regardless, they "re-upped," and the proportion willing to stick and finish the job proved vital to the war's issue. But for them the victories at Chattanooga might have been won in vain.

The title of volunteer was to persist in U.S.V. insignia in the war with Spain, thereafter disappearing, though there would always be many men who offered to serve in their country's armed forces. In both world wars equitable and effective administration of the draft successfully merged the conscripted with the volunteer. By then divisions wore numbers as high as those of regiments in the Civil War, and regiments far higher ones. State contingents continued to exist, sometimes solidly: New England's Yankee Division or 26th, the Rainbow or 42nd, a composite from various states; New York's 7th and 69th Regiments. However, state names began to vanish in designations, except parenthetically, in the great armies of the twentieth century.

Something of value was lost, inevitable though the change was, fitting as it was that national replace regional pride. State ties of the sixties were closer, as witness the great majorities that followed their birth states in supporting the Union or seceding from it. In that respect the conflict is more aptly called the War Between the States than the Civil War or the War of the Rebellion. Georgians or Iowans and the rest, they fought for the Confederacy or the United States but often primarily for hearth and home.

The Chattanooga campaign, with the armies in the West reinforced from the East, was extraordinary as a mighty muster of the states. It was the Stars and Stripes or the Bonnie Blue Flag that rallied men in blue or gray when the heights were stormed or defended. Yet blazoned on the former banner was often the name of the state of the regiment that carried it. And in the stand of colors beside the latter's red field with its blue St. Andrew's cross might wave the palmetto banner of South Carolina or the lone star of Texas.

No drafted contingent vitiated the ranks of the Army of the Cumberland. Its regiments were mostly from Ohio, Indiana, Illinois, Michigan, Kentucky, Wisconsin, and Minnesota, with two from Missouri, one from Kansas, and several of Tennessee loyalists; the East was represented by five from Pennsylvania. There was one brigade of Regulars.[31] They, too, were volunteers but never received the enlistment or re-enlistment bounties paid other components. Between them and state troops sometimes arose antagonism similar to that of the western and eastern armies, and there were lively fights. "We're as good as Regulars," the volunteers asserted, and they often were, but by and large the latter plainly admired the former. On the other hand, a Regular battery, for instance, whose ranks were thinned by casualties, was glad to accept and absorb men from state infantry units who offered to join it. Since Regulars were recruited from all parts of the country, they lacked regional cohesion, for which was substituted an espirt de corps, inherited from the past and carried on to breed the Old Army of post–Civil War years.

The heavy contribution of the Midwest to the Union cause was indicated by the high numbers of some of the regiments in the campaign: the 125th Ohio, the 128th Illinois, the 101st Indiana.

Cumberland units and those of the other armies, North and South, took pride not only in the state of their origin but from characteristics and differences lending individuality and hence promoting morale. From their records—the battle names on their colors. From a commanding officer who was able or colorful or both. From a sergeant, as brave as he was tough, or their bands and drummer

boys. From physical characteristics such as tallness; there were so
many tall men in the 21st Wisconsin that it was called a regiment
of walking liberty polls. From marching ability. From smart appearance or hard-bitten swagger or some small variation in uniform
that set them apart.[32] From foreign blood of which they still strove
to be worthy although they had become patriotic Americans. Several Wisconsin regiments were almost solidly Scandinavian. Colonel
Hans C. Heg commanded the 15th—Norwegians, Swedes, and Danes
—with almost every other man answering to the name of Ole.
Companies were called St. Olaf's Rifles, Oden's Rifles, the Norway
Bear Hunters. The Dane Guards and the Scandinavian Guards
were companies of the 3rd Wisconsin. A corporal in the 4th Wisconsin was Norwegian-born Knute Nelson. Before he was twenty-
one he had completed three years of service. He would become
governor of Minnesota and United States senator.

The Confederate Army also "had three years to do this in," three
years and a little more. Most of its original enlistments had been
twelve-month instead of nine-month men. Hence the terms of those
who rejoined thereafter were expiring in the spring of 1864.
A draft law, preceding the Union's, had been passed by the Confederate Congress in April of 1862, covering all male whites, not
legally exempt, between the ages of eighteen and thirty-five, a limit
later extended to forty-five. From the outset the same troubles beset
the South as the North. A rush to enter the exempted classes, hired
substitutes, buying out of the service for $500 (a privilege allowed
those with religious scruples), a swelling stream of desertions.[33]
When President Davis tried to plug some of the law's loopholes, he
inspired, at least, a versifier.

> Oh, weep not, conscript, weep not,
> Old Jeff has called for thee.
> A soldier Congress makes you,
> A soldier you must be.
> Make up your mind
> To stand in line,
> And quake not at the Yanks,

> To shoot your gun
> And call it fun,
> . And for life return your thanks.[34]

Yet volunteers continued to come forward south of the Mason and Dixon's line as north of it, in spite of the same war weariness, homesickness, and misgivings. When terms ran out, the Gray camps saw scenes similar to the Blue's.

A favorite device of officers to inspire pledges to further service was the assembling of men for dress parade, addressing them in patriotic vein, moving the flags a few paces up ahead, and then asking those who were willing to re-enlist for the duration of the war to step up to the colors. When the lead was taken, whether by few or many, the impulse for all to follow suit was usually overwhelming.[35]

The 20th Tennessee Regiment Volunteer Infantry was one of the many that emphasized the Volunteer in its title. Its antipathy toward drafted men was expressed in lampooning verses by Captain Albert Roberts of Company A. Curiously he chose to parody a familiar poem of the day, "I Am Dying, Egypt, Dying," by the Union brigadier, William H. Lytle, who would be killed at Chickamauga by a sharpshooter's long-range shot.

> I'm conscripted, Smith conscripted,
>   Ebb the subterfuges fast,
> And the sub-enrolling marshals
>   Gather with the evening blast;
>
> Let thine arms, O Smith, support me.
>   Hush your gab and close your ear,
> Conscript grabbers close upon you,
>   Hunting for you far and near.
>
> Though my scarred, rheumatic "trotters"
>   Bear me limping short no more,
> And my shattered constitution
>   Won't exempt me as before;

> Though the provost guard surround me,
>   Prompt to do their master's will,
> I must to the "front" to perish,
>   Die the great conscript still.[36]

Finally, Roberts concluded, it was not enemy fire but "bust-head whiskey" that finished off the conscript.

South or North, not a few conscripts, once they were called up, served gallantly. Of such were the true "hardship" cases, men who would have come forward of their own accord had not family or other imperative obligations prevented.

Yet it was the volunteers who had freely joined the colors—who so often re-enlisted when their terms expired—it was they who bore the brunt and wore their title like the badge of honor it was.

CHAPTER 4

"*This Is the Arsenal*"

Many of the guns men fought with at Chickamauga and Chattanooga came from Springfield Arsenal, flowing out in a stream of weapons that commenced in the early days of the nation. When Longfellow scanned the tiers of racked muskets and rifles—

> ... From floor to ceiling,
> Like a huge organ, rise the burnished arms ...

the poet longed for a millennium when the need of the famous armory would vanish.

> Peace! and no longer from its brazen portals
> The blast of War's great organ shakes the skies!

But that day seemed dim and distant in the 1860's. The demands for Springfield's products were greater than ever, and the arsenal could not begin to meet them. Manufacture of rifled muskets to replace smoothbore muskets had started some twenty years before the Civil War. However, quantities of the older type were still on hand, with a serious shortage of the superior weapon.[37]

An effective arm, the Springfield rifled musket. It could kill at 1,000 yards, its extreme range, and was accurate at from 300 to 500 yards. In the hands of a steady veteran it was capable of firing three rounds per minute. Thus it set the stage for a new era of warfare. There were still the point-blank volleys of Fontenoy—"Gentlemen of France, fire first." Civil War riflemen still heard versions of

33

Bunker Hill's "Don't fire till you see the white of their eyes." Lines
in blue and gray still charged, though they paused as they came
on to blaze away at ranges previously unheard of. But now it was
bloodier work then ever against a well-entrenched enemy, sighting
along rested barrels, and for every charge driven home there were
scores that were blasted back, stumbling over their dead and
wounded in retreat.

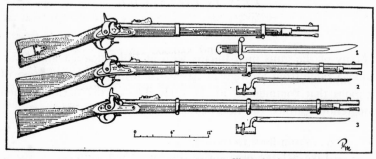

Illustration by Robert L. Miller, from
Notes on Ordnance of the American
Civil War, 1861–1865 *by Harold L. Peterson.*

1. U.S. Harper's Ferry rifle, Model of 1855. 2. U.S. Springfield rifle-
musket, Model of 1861. 3. Enfield rifle-musket. The bayonet for each is
also shown.

As yet cannon generally lacked the power to help or hinder
decisively [38]—either by demolition or by the killing power of their
ammunition, except for canister. Those spreading balls sprayed from
muzzles were deadly, but their range was short: scarcely better than
600 yards. Infantrymen from a safe distance or from the flanks
picked off the gunners and dropped the horses. The rifle, weapon
of "The Queen of Battles," was king.

So the Springfield, models of 1855, 1861, or 1863, reigned, and it
held sway on both sides of the front. For the Arsenal's guns were
turned against the Union it served. Upon secession the Confederacy armed itself with 235,000 stands of arms from Federal armories, stocked chiefly from Springfield, in its territory. Stonewall
Jackson captured 13,000 small arms at Harper's Ferry, where rifles
had been made since 1803. Victorious battlefields yielded the South

many more; Chancellorsville alone, 20,000. At Chickamauga the Confederates claimed to have taken 15,000 small arms and 51 cannon.

For both South and North existing supplies were far from sufficient, as regiment after regiment joined the colors and the armies burgeoned. As a result European arms markets enjoyed a tremendous boom. Agents for the Union and Confederacy—and dealers who sold to both—bought all sorts of weapons at high prices. Foreign governments, which had been rearming their troops with more modern guns, were delighted to be rid of castoffs. They exported 180,000 obsolete muskets and 550,000 rifles of varying types and bore sizes. The conglomeration of calibers equaled that of the Revolution. Frequently soldiers could not use each other's ammunition, and wagons were forced to carry five or more different kinds of cartridges.[39]

The Austrian (170,000 purchased) guns were especially detested. Out of one consignment of 3,000 only 500 could be used. . . . The Belgian guns were worse, if possible, than the Austrian. They were of uneven caliber, some had crooked barrels, and many of the locks were out of repair. The soldiers called them "pumpkin slingers" and pronounced the crooked barrels able to shoot around hills. Finally the barrels were so brittle as to be easily broken into pieces. The Vincennes rifle was described as having an irregular bore causing the bullets to fit too tight and then too loose. The locks were of soft iron, the bayonets impractical, and the rifling shallow and useless.

As an example of the varied assortment of arms employed, Iowa troops in the first year of the war were equipped with Austrian muskets, Spencer carbines, Sharp carbines, Colt revolvers, navy revolvers, Whitworth rifles (English), Colt revolving rifles, Minié rifles, besides some of the other varieties of less known weapons.[40]

Best of the importations was the English Enfield rifle of which 428,000 were bought, mostly by the Confederacy. Enfields were .577 caliber but could use the issue .58 ammunition for a few shots before fouling. Springfields also possessed a certain amount of bore tolerance. Because of powder fouling, sometimes after as few as twenty-five shots, one battalion commander drew ammunition of two calibers whenever possible: .58 to be carried in the top of cartridge boxes and used when the piece was clean; .57 in the bottom for use after fouling.[41]

But Springfields and Enfields, good arms though they were, remained single-shot muzzle-loaders. How their nine-step loading was accomplished, as it usually was with such comparative smoothness and speed in the heat of battle, is a marvel.[42] Seize the cartridge, prescribed the manuals. Bite off its paper top—pour the powder into the barrel—ram down the ball—remove the old percussion cap from the nipple—take a new one from the pouch and press it down. Even so a fast man could manage as many as three rounds per minute. The powder, which ringed mouths weirdly with dark circles, became a sort of war paint. Some units deliberately elaborated by streaking their whole faces and advancing to action whooping like Indians.

Single-shot muzzle-loading rifles, as provided with the new form of ammunition, with which most of the Civil War was fought, were a great advance. But the breechloader and its corollary, the repeating rifle, were far greater ones.

Breech-loaders had been known for centuries. Two made during the reign of Henry VIII were exhibited in London during the 1860's and found to be remarkably like the contemporary Snider rifle. The breech-loading rifle of a British officer named Patrick Ferguson was used to good effect at Brandywine in 1777. An American named John Hall patented a breech-loading rifle in 1811, and in 1825 two companies at Fortress Monroe were armed with it and liked it.[43]

But manufacture, hampered by prejudice and the lack of precision machine tools to solve various problems such as gas escaping at the breech, had been halted before the Mexican War.

Enter now the great obstructionist, General James W. Ripley, Chief of Ordnance. It can be fairly said that the Union could have won the war far earlier but for Ripley. Stubbornly, with hidebound aversion to progress, he rejected the breechloader, the repeater, and other advances in weapons long and adamantly. Had the Federal Army been equipped with them at the outset, the Confederacy, asserted one of its generals, would have been defeated within a year.[44]

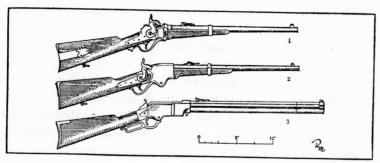

Illustration by Robert L. Miller, from Notes on Ordnance of the American Civil War, 1861–1865 *by Harold L. Peterson.*

1. Sharps carbine. 2. Spencer carbine. 3. Henry rifle.

Yankee inventors persistently proffered promising working models, notably the Sharps and the Spencer. Christian Sharps's single-shot breech loader was approved in 1860 but not put into Government production. Its rate of fire was from eight to twelve rounds per minute, its range up to 1,400 yards. Ripley curtly dismissed it as "a new fangled gimcrack." Also in 1860 young Christopher Spencer came forward with the first successful breech-loading repeater. A loading tube containing seven rim-fire metallic cartridges, caliber .54, was inserted into its stock, and the rounds levered into the chamber. Sights graduated to 800 yards, it spat a stream of lead—fourteen shots per minute. A trooper could carry ten extra loaded tubes, making seventy more rounds readily available. This was the carbine (made also as a rifle) that the Confederates called "the new gun the Yankees loaded Sunday and fired all week."

Ripley rejected the Spencer, too, as liable to break down under field conditions; but it was buried in sand and still functioned. It took Abraham Lincoln himself, supported by such able subordinate ordnance officers as A. B. Dyer and Stephen V. Benét, to break the obstructionist's blockade. Ripley was forced to order 10,000 Spencers in 1861, but it was an appallingly long time before they and later supplements were put into the hands of troops. Obstinate opposition to advances in weapons told a tragic story, one recorded before and since,[45] a story whose sequel is victory or defeat—life or death for many thousands.

It is significant to this study that Spencers were first officially tried out in the field by the Army of the West on June 24, 1863. A little later Buford's cavalrymen used them tellingly to hold up the Confederate attack on the first day of Gettysburg. In the West, Rosecrans had approvingly witnessed the trial and requested a consignment of Spencers. Ripley, still dragging his feet, sent them, but so slowly that they arrived too late for Chickamauga.[46]

Meanwhile repeating arms commanded a premium among western troops. Some officers bought repeaters for their commands with personal funds. Companies and regiments pooled their pay, and individual soldiers emptied their pockets, to buy the superior arms their government failed to furnish. "I got a Henry rifle—a 16 [sic] shooter," an infantryman jubilantly noted in his diary. "I gave 35 dollars—all the money I had for it. I am glad I could get it. They are good shooters and I like to think I have so many shots in reserve." [47] A Federal major who served in the Chattanooga campaign declared: "Every man felt confident that with his new Spencer he was good for at least any two rebs in Dixie," adding, "We think our Spencers saved us, and our men adore them as the heathen do their idols." [48] Such was the high worth to morale of the repeating rifle, so long withheld. One shot rapidly multiplied by seven. Seventy more in ready reserve. Might of firepower such as the English archers at Crécy knew when they loosed their swift flights of arrows against the French chivalry—power excelled only by repeating rifles and by the machine gun, the latter available but inexplicably so little employed in the Civil War.

Privately purchased or issued, the repeaters heavily weighted the scales in favor of the Union from mid-1863 onward. That was particularly true of Spencers, with which the cavalry was increasingly armed. One brigade was fortunate enough to have them (an earlier acquisition) at Chickamauga. General J. T. Wilder had signed a note for the money to buy them for his Lightning Brigade, the men promising to reimburse him on pay day (a pledge they were about to keep when the Government stepped in and supplied the funds). Those three regiments of mounted Illinois infantry defended Alexander's Bridge with their new weapons. There the impact of their storm of fire accounted for a repulse in the hard-pressing Confederate attack. Longstreet's advance across an open field withered under their blast.

While they lived, the startled Confederates heard a new and terrible sound, not the familiar volleying of muzzle-loaders, rattling and rolling and dying away like the intermittent crash of brick walls in a fire, but a steady roar, a torrent of fire and lead. They had run up against Spencer repeating rifles of Wilder's Lightning Brigade. And as Wilder's men worked their Spencers in the woods, they saw a strange sight: the head of the column, as it was pushed on by those behind, appeared to melt or sink into the earth, for, though continually moving, it got no nearer. The Rebels broke and fell back, were rallied and pushed forward, and at last found shelter in the drainage ditch—until a pair of Federal 10-pounders scoured its length with double-shotted canister.[49]

Wilder remembered with a shudder that "they fell in heaps, and I had it in my heart to order the firing to cease to end the awful sight. One could have walked for two hundred yards down that ditch on dead rebels without touching the ground."

Firepower and man power and, behind them, the power of industry and material resources—they foretold the outcome of the conflict. For the South valor, fostering a belief in invincibility, was not enough. Valor could be and was matched. Not so the sinews of war. "The North set a new record for iron production in every year of the war except the first. Much the same overwhelming disparity held true for almost every kind of industry." [50] Confederate shortages, inevitable considering the small number of arms works,

other manufacturies, and material scarcities, were intensified when
the sea blockade became effective. It was not long before public
documents in state libraries began to be used for cartridge papers,
and sash weights and irons and candlesticks were contributed or
commandeered for metals.

The armory and battlefield captures and the foreign purchases
already mentioned, considerable though they were,[51] could not
suffice. Neither could guns, percussion caps, and powder, fore-
sightedly bought from munitions plants in the North from 1859
until an embargo was clamped down on April 19, 1861. The able
Confederate Chief of Ordnance, General Josiah Gorgas, was compelled to draw on every source from shotguns to the shops of cross-
roads gunsmiths.

Besides the Enfields, a small but valuable importation was the
Whitworth rifles, notable for accuracy and long range like the same
firm's breech-loading cannon; both had hexagonal bores and ammunition. The rifle, caliber .451, had "enormous penetration" and
proved accurate in tests up to and beyond 1,800 yards. Queen
Victoria fired it at Wimbledon in 1860, hitting the bull's-eye one
and one-half inches from the center at a range of 400 yards.[52] A
Confederate sharpshooter's Whitworth, equipped with telescopic
sights, killed Union General Lytle at Chickamauga at 800 yards.[53]
General Cleburne armed a company of thirty sharpshooters with
Whitworths and other makes of outstanding rifles.

Lack of breechloaders and repeating rifles played a large part in
the destiny of the Lost Cause. The South made some of the former
in South Carolina and Richmond, but they were often defective
because not gas tight. Others, using a metallic, self-primed cartridge,
were manufactured at Nashville and later at Atlanta. Repeaters
were beyond Confederate facilities. The thrill of capturing a Spencer
from the enemy quickly dissolved in bitter frustration; when its
ammunition was exhausted, it had to be discarded. Toward the end
of the war the Confederates devised machinery to make cartridges for
captured Spencers, but it came into use too late. Again and again,
as in Longstreet's attack at Chickamauga, the Gray ranks would
melt away before lethal torrents of lead.

They kept their rifles clean, for malfunction as a result of a dirty or clogged bore might forfeit life, and they burnished barrels to make a smart appearance. Sunlight flashing on polished metal could betray a regiment's advance, but the art of camouflage was little regarded. During the Chattanooga campaign the 1st Tennessee's guns were inspected and required to be "as bright as a silver dollar." Its officers and noncoms counted contents of cartridge pouches; for each missing round a soldier was fined twenty-five cents and stood extra duty.[54]

After all it was the Minié bullet, named for its French inventor—the soldier's "minnie ball"—that had made the rifle really effective. Of elongated shape, the bullet was hollowed at its base to which was fastened the paper-covered powder cartridge. Gases of the exploded charge forced the lead into the rifling, insuring a snug fit, and the bullet was driven through the spiraling grooves, which imparted its true, rotating flight. A soldier usually carried forty rounds, a weight of seven pounds, in his pouch. For a long battle he would be issued extra ammunition to stuff in his pockets. The impact of the "minnie ball" on Civil War history is as memorable as the wounds inflicted by its soft lead were dreadful.

Fixed bayonets glittered like the gun barrels. Some manuals omitted instruction in the bayonet, but George B. McClellan had published one, translated from a work by a French fencing master, following his foreign tour in 1852.[55] The future Union general, then a cavalry captain, praised the bayonet in his preface:

There is an instance on record of a French grenadier who, in the battle of Polotsk, defended himself, with the bayonet, against the simultaneous attack of ten Russian grenadiers, eight of whom he killed. In the battle of Sanguessa, two soldiers of Abbé's division defended themselves, against twenty-five Spanish cavalry, and, after having inflicted several severe wounds, rejoined their regiments without a scratch. At that period there was little or no regular instruction in the bayonet.

Although Civil War hospital records show the treatment of few bayonet wounds, the effectiveness of the arm should not be alto-

gether discounted. The infantryman was equipped with it and knew
how to fix it. While he may have received little training in its use,
the menace of cold steel in a charge was undeniable. If a lunge
missed, there remained the savage butt stroke. And the rifle-attached
variant of the *arme blanche,* the sword, was the weapon of last resort
when ammunition was exhausted. Among the instances of spirited
and telling use of the bayonet is the counterattack by the 9th Ohio
against an assault by South Carolina troops at Snodgrass Hill on the
second day of Chickamauga.

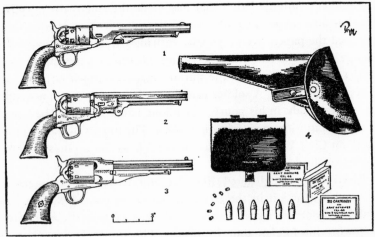

Illustration by Robert L. Miller, from
Notes on Ordnance of the American
Civil War, 1861–1865 *by Harold L. Peterson.*

1. Colt Army revolver. 2. Colt Navy revolver. 3. Remington Army revolver. 4. Holster and cartridge box with packets, .44-caliber cartridges,
and percussion caps.

Holstered revolvers—the Army and the Navy Colt six-shooters
were the favorites—hung at the hips of officers, cavalrymen, and,
infrequently, of artillerymen, who should have been regularly armed
with them for defense of an overrun battery. The officer's sword was
more a symbol of leadership than an arm. Increasingly the cavalryman left his saber in its scabbard and depended on his carbine and
revolver. Artillerymen packed away sabers issued them in the battery

wagon or strapped them to the limbers as encumbrances. For a fight in the gun position rammer staffs and trail handspikes were preferred.

Chattanooga adds a footnote to the curious case of the machine gun. War Correspondent Taylor saw ten of them there in the armament of the Union Army. They were probably the J. D. Mills model, which President Lincoln had dubbed "Coffee Mill Guns" because their ammunition hoppers looked like those on coffee-bean grinders. Rosecrans had requisitioned some, and this lot may have been a delayed delivery.[56] Taylor, after watching a demonstration, his imagination shuddering at the lethal effect their fire could have, added to their name, calling them "The Devil's Coffee Mills." He watched one of them fired in demonstration. "It was tick, tick, tick, sixty to the minute, as fast as you could think." But if any use of them was made in action, research has failed to disclose it. The correspondent's article furnishes clues to the neglect of the machine gun. He described it as "an implement that might do tremendous execution in skirmishing were it not as liable to get out of order as a lady's watch." And he added:

Soldiers do not fancy it. Even if it were not liable to derangement, it is so foreign to the old, familiar action of battle—that sitting behind a steel blinder and turning a crank—that enthusiasm dies out; there is no play to the pulses; it does not seem like soldier's work. Indeed they regard it much as your genuine man-of-war's man is apt to look upon the creeping, low-lying mud turtles of Monitors, when, shut up in an iron box, he remembers with a sigh the free decks and upper air broadsides of his dear, old stately ship-of-the-line, whose "fore-foot" lifts grandly on the waves as if she were going up a sea-green stairway, and who shakes her splendid plumage as if she were ready to fly.[57]

There it was—the nostalgic affection for the old and tried and familiar that many a soldier and sailor has felt—resentment at the submergence of war's pomp and panoply by grim, deadly efficiency. It prevailed before the days when one of Shakespeare's knights denounced "villainous salt-petre" and "vile guns"—when chivalry branded artillery as the artifice of Satan—on through the dropping of the first atomic bomb. It partly explains the attitude and actions of General Ripley and others like him. And, save for isolated instances, it swept the machine gun off the stage of the Civil and Indian wars.[58]

So from historic Springfield, from Richmond's armories, and from the rest poured forth the arms with which men in blue or gray fought in the Georgia woods, in the valleys, and on the mountains of Tennessee—fought to storm or defend the gateway to the Southeast.

> The bursting shell, the gateway wrenched asunder,
>   The rattling musketry, the clashing blade;
> And ever and anon, in tones of thunder,
>   The diapason of the cannonade.[59]

CHAPTER 5

"The Diapason of the Cannonade"

When Confederates rolled rocks down the slopes of Lookout Mountain and Missionary Ridge upon the assaulting enemy, they were using an early form of artillery. From the force of gravity the catapult had taken over; then gunpowder and the cannon. In the western battles of 1863, as for centuries before, men marched to the sound of the guns. Smoke billowed across Chickamauga Creek and curtained the Georgia woods. From flaming muzzle or bursting shell it thickened the mist of the Battle Above the Clouds where field guns fired down from the heights, as from towering battlements, and were answered by siege and light pieces from the valley.

They had come rumbling into action, those Blue and Gray batteries, a gallant sight behind their streaming guidons. One hundred and fifty-five officers and enlisted men, if they had their full quota, which they infrequently did. Captain, lieutenants, sergeants and corporals, cannoneers and drivers, buglers, guidon-bearer, and artificers. Six to four guns, twice as many caissons, and limbers for all. Behind lumbered battery and forge wagons. One hundred and fifteen horses, saddle and draft, carrying riders or keeping traces taut. Each six-horse gun or caisson team pulled a weight running up to 3,800 pounds, including the ammunition and the cannoneers seated on the chests. Miring mud and jutting underbrush seldom halted them. Through narrow forest trails they sped, men and horses whipped and battered by branches. They jolted over miserable roads, or vestiges thereof, or rough ground where there were none at all. The toughest going was ascending a mountain incline, drivers

45

bent low over pommels and urging on their pairs, climbing like cats. Or sliding down the steep descents, with sturdy wheelers bracing back mightily against the breeching, and cannoneers crouching forward on the chests in dread of those crushing pounds of metal and wood behind them. Finally the bugle blast for action sounded, trails were unhooked and dropped, unlimbered carriages whirled to the rear, and the guns spoke.

"They spoke a powerful language." Crews swarmed around them, ramming powder charge and projectile or fixed round into muzzles while the vent was thumbed lest smoldering grains from a previous load ignite the new one and blow off the rammer's arms. Cannoneers primed, gunners sighted. "Fire!" and lanyards jerked, pieces leaped back in recoil, and shells soared through a wreath of flame and smoke to burst among the enemy. And there was none who manned the guns who would not echo that boast of the Pennsylvania battery: "In our eyes no branch of the service was equal to the artillery."

In tones of thunder the Napoleons, the Parrotts, the three-inch ordnance and James rifles, and the howitzers spoke at Chickamauga and Chattanooga. For the North there had been cannon enough at the beginning. In 1861 the supply of smoothbore pieces, unlike that of small arms, had been adequate. Provision of artillery kept pace with batteries trained to man it through a war which was primarily the infantryman's, a war in which the Union Army was issued 7,892 cannon in contrast to more than 4,000,000 small arms.[60] By 1857 the Government had adopted the Napoleon, a bronze, smoothbore gun-howitzer, a 12-pounder (so called from the weight of the solid ball it fired). Named after the French Emperor Napoleon III, this light (some 1,230 pounds) fieldpiece became the artillery work horse of the Civil War. It of course lacked the range, accuracy, and penetrating power of rifled cannon, but it stood unmatched for the type of warfare it met: for close fighting in the woods and for the defense of entrenched positions; above all for the lethal blasts of canister, single, double, and triple charges, it delivered at ranges descending from 600 yards to point blank. And the bronze Napoleon, unlike iron guns, seldom burst.

Tredegar and other Confederate foundries began turning out Napoleons on the designs of former United States ordnance officers who had joined the South.[61] Those products, however, were inferior to the Northern-made, battlefield captures of which were eagerly sought. Through such trophies, arsenal seizures, and manufacture the Confederacy kept comparatively well supplied. It was the increasing shortage of horses for the teams that was finally crippling.

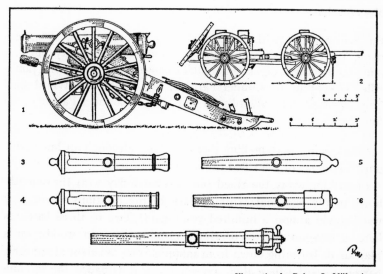

Illustration by Robert L. Miller, from
Notes on Ordnance of the American
Civil War, 1861–1865 *by Harold L. Peterson.*

1. Napoleon gun-howitzer, 12-pounder, Model of 1857. 2. Caisson and limber for Napoleon. 3. 6-pounder gun, Model of 1841. 4. 12-pounder howitzer, Model of 1841. 5. 3-inch Ordnance rifle, Model of 1861. 6. 10-pounder Parrott rifle. 7. 12-pounder Whitworth breech-loading rifle.

Approval of Napoleons by artillerymen and the high command of both sides carried through the war. A gunner in Lumsden's Confederate battery remarked that the Yankees boasted that "with their 3-inch rifles they could hit the top of a barrel at a mile, but just let them get within a thousand yards, and we'll outshoot them every time with our Napoleons." In General Grant's March, 1864, reorganization of the army, numbers of batteries armed with rifled cannon were issued Napoleons in their place.

Along with the Napoleons rolled other makes and calibers whose variety was exceeded only by that of shoulder and hand guns. Many a battery was armed with two types, the disadvantage of carrying the two sorts of ammunition somewhat countered by the opportunity to use one type of gun or the other in a mission for which it was better suited. As to the complexity of armaments, Birkhimer observes that:

the field artillery with Rosecrans' army, February 8th, 1863, was made up of thirty-two 6-pounder smooth-bores, twenty-four 12-pounder howitzers, eight 12-pounder smooth-bores, twenty-one James rifles, thirty-four 10-pounder Parrotts, two 12-pounder Wiard steel guns, two 6-pounder Wiard steel guns, two 16-pounder Parrotts, and four 3-inch ordnance guns." [62]

Smoothbores were making their last bow, although an impressive one.[63] The day of the rifled cannon had dawned.

In striking array the rifled pieces stand today with the smoothbores in the National Military Park in the positions where they were fought almost a hundred years ago.[64] Two or three batteries here, a two-gun section or single cannon there—in woods, on a plateau, or frowning down from summits. You can sight along their barrels toward where their targets lay and visualize the circumstances when the iron or steel rifles [65] were telling as they dropped their shells at a distance and with precision Napoleons could not equal. There stand the Parrotts with their characteristic iron jackets shrunk on over the breech, giving them their sturdiness—Parrotts that had poured forth from the West Point foundry—the 10- and 20-pounder fieldpieces, the 30-pounder siege guns. Yonder are ranked trim 3-inch ordnance rifles (sometimes called Rodmans), always effective but especially favored by horse artillery. Six-pounders, their bores enlarged to 12-pounder dimension and rifled on the James method, lift their now-mute muzzles.

Ghostly cannoneers seem to pat the stubby barrels of the 12- and 24-pound howitzers. Smoothbores like the Napoleon but not so

PRINCIPAL CHARACTERISTICS OF SMOOTHBORE AND RIFLED
ARTILLERY USED IN THE CHATTANOOGA CAMPAIGN

	Bore diameter (inches)	Material	Length of tube (inches)	Weight of tube (pounds)	Weight of projectile (pounds)	Weight of charge (pounds)	Muzzle velocity (ft. per sec.)	Range at 5° elevation (yards)
SMOOTHBORES								
Models of 1841-44								
6-pounder gun	3.67	bronze	60	884	6.10	1.25	1,439	1,523
12-pounder howitzer	4.62	"	53	788	8.90	1.00	1,054	1,072
24-pounder howitzer	5.82	"	65	1,318	18.40	2.00	1,060	1,322
12-pounder mountain howitzer	4.62	"	32.9	220	8.90	0.50	650	900
Model of 1857								
12-pounder Napoleon	4.62	"	66	1,227	12.30	2.50	1,440	1,619
RIFLES								
10-pounder Parrott	3.00	iron	74	890	9.50	1.00	1,230	1,850
3-inch Ordnance (Rodman)	3.00	"	69	820	9.50	1.00	1,215	1,830
20-pounder Parrott	3.67	"	84	1,750	20.00	2.00	1,250	1,900
12-pounder James	3.67	bronze	60	875	12.00	0.75	1,000	1,700
12-pounder Blakely	3.40	steel and iron	59	800	10.00	1.00	1,250	1,850
30-pounder Parrott	4.20	iron	136.00	4,200	29.0	3.75	1,250	2,200

—Peterson: *Notes on Ordnance of the American Civil War*

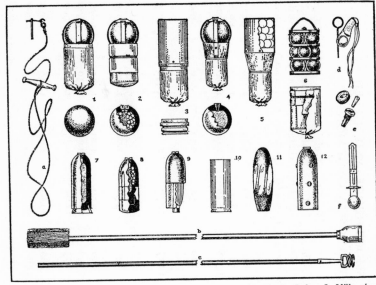

Illustration by Robert L. Miller, from
Notes on Ordnance of the American
Civil War, 1861–1865 *by Harold L. Peterson.*

Artillery ammunition and accessories: Smoothbore ammunition— (1) solid shot with fixed round having protective paper cap in place; (2) spherical case with fixed round for gun; (3) canister for gun, fixed-round canister sabot; (4) common shell, fixed round for howitzer; (5) canister fixed round, showing contents; (6) grapeshot and separate cartridge. Ammunition for rifles—(7) cutaway view of Parrott shell; (8) cutaway view of Hotchkiss case shot; (9) Schenkl case shot with papier-mâché sabot; (10) Hotchkiss canister; (11) Whitworth bolt; (12) shunt or studded shell for Armstrong and Blakely rifles. Accessories— (a) friction primer and lanyard; (b) sponge and rammer; (c) worm for clearing bore; (d) vent pick and thumbstall; (e) Bormann fuse and paper fuse with metal fuse plug; (f) pendulum sight.

popular and of shorter range, their charges of spherical case (shrapnel) and canister were nonetheless deadly within their limits. Crews were fond of them because of their light weight, less heavy by one third than the Emperor's namesakes.[66] With tired artillerymen it counted to have a lighter piece to manhandle into position that teams could not reach or an exposed spot where the horses would have been vulnerable to enemy fire.

At Chickamauga are emplaced two of the four mountain howitzers, which comprised part of the armament of Captain Eli Lilly's 18th Indiana Battery. Officers who observed their fire in that battle were convinced of their effectiveness at short range.[67] Models of 1836 or 1841, those short-barreled pieces had been employed in the Mexican and Indian wars.[68] Light (the tube weighed only 220 pounds and the carriage 180), they could be drawn on wheels or disassembled and packed on mules or horses. Muleback transportation sometimes gave trouble, as in the case of a mountain battery with Jackson at Port Republic. The long-eared carriers rolled on the ground to rid themselves of their loads, and gunners were occupied more with controlling them than with delivering fire on the enemy. Derisive infantrymen asked whether the guns were to fire the mules, or the mules the guns.[69]

Lilly's wheeled howitzers were not in action during the mountain fighting around Chattanooga. Disuse of those on hand, under conditions for which they were developed (along with failure to provide more), is as strange as neglect of machine guns. Although their range at five degrees of elevation was only 900 yards, their transportability was a matter of first import. There were points on Lookout and Missionary Ridge where they could have served most efficiently, where they could have been put in positions defying placement of heavier pieces, just as U. S. Grant and his men had heaved one up into that Mexico City belfry. And canister blasts from a battery of mountain "hows," had they been included in escorts of the Union wagon trains, could have handily beaten off some of the damaging raids of Joe Wheeler's Gray cavalry.

But although mountain howitzers were lacking on the heights, there were artillerymen like that crack gunner officer, Colonel E. Porter Alexander, C.S.A., who ingeniously handled the cannon they had. Alexander, who had come West with Longstreet, stationed his battalion on Lookout and fought daily with a:

vicious little battery on Moccasin Point, almost directly under us. This battery had nearly buried itself in the ground under high parapets, and fired up at us like a man shooting at a squirrel in a tree.[70] We propped our trails high up in the air to depress the muzzles, and tried to smash our opponents into the earth with solid shot and percussion shell; but we never hurt them much, and when we left the mountain, they were still as lively as ever.[71]

Also at Chattanooga and again at Knoxville Alexander rigged four howitzers as mortars to drop shells behind parapets and search out spaces sheltered from direct fire.

To accomplish this, skids were prepared inclined at an angle of forty-five degrees, one end resting on the ground and the other on a horizontal pole supported about 6 feet from the ground on forked posts. The axle of the howitzer was run up on these skids, raising the wheels in the air one each side of the skids, and leaving the trail on the ground between them, until the pieces had an elevation of about 60 degrees.

With the range regulated by the amount of powder used (charges had to be diminished at high elevations), the system worked nicely and gave very fair mortar practice, the Colonel declared.[72]

Seen through a poet's eyes, the guns took on attributes their crews sensed though few could express them. War Correspondent Taylor, scanning the array of ordnance at Chattanooga, wrote: [73]

There are "Parrotts" with their long, black shafts, "reinforced" at the breech, like a trooper's trousers. There are bright "Napoleons" brisk and spiteful, twelves, twenty-fours, thirty-twos, and so on up.[74] Here is a sturdy fellow that growled at Stone River; there a grim one that roared at Shiloh; yonder, a "Columbiad" made at Memphis. Do you see those pairs of immense wheels? They are not mill-wheels, but only the carriages of siege-guns. If it blows at all in this roomy kennel, it must literally "blow great guns." Those rows of carts with the black boxes and the convex covers are not young bakers' wagons gone into mourning, as you might think, but only battery forges, the blacksmith's shops of Mars' own fiery self. And so we have seen thunder "in the original package."

Here and there on the battlefields, companioning the guns, rise little black pyramids of the round shot that fed them. They mark the headquarters of generals or spots where they were killed or mortally wounded. Greater tokens of artillery's might are the shells and their fuses—percussion and time, the latter cut to explode the projectile in flight at a desired moment. Look at the shell Henry Shrapnel of the Royal Artillery devised as early as 1784 and you can imagine the death and destruction its cone of scattering balls spewed forth when it burst over a target. Through the Civil War it was called spherical case; later it bore its inventor's name. Deadly, too, was the fragmentation of other types of shells, and deadliest of all at close range were the shotgun-like blasts of canister balls.[75]

Shot and shell, familiar objects to artillerymen, inspired Correspondent Taylor no less than the cannon that hurled them when he visited the ordnance stores of the Army of the Cumberland.

If you are given to glowing words, be dumb; if there be any fire in your eye, be pleased to shut it while here, among kegs and barrels of the fine black grain that sows fields with death; among boxes of cartridges without end; among rows of canister; among nests of shells, out of which shall be hatched a terrible brood; among cases of every species of irritable combustible known to war; among clusters of the grape that presses the wine of life out; in the midst of death in every form that flies. Sentinels stand aside, doors unbolted and unbarred swing open, a gush of cool air meets you, the shutters are thrown open, and the treasures of the magazine are revealed. Wooden boxes of four colors, boxes, boxes, everywhere—olive, red, black and white. Be seated upon that olive box; it contains nothing but solid shot, or, perhaps, percussion shell. In the red, you will be sure to find spherical case-shot; in the white boxes, canister; and in the black, that diabolical chronometer, time-shell. Take your choice of a seat and be happy. Look through a glass magnifying about sixty times at an old-fashioned clock-weight, and you will see pretty nearly such a thing as stands there at your right, and which happens to be a hundred-pound "Parrott" shell. A dull affair to look at, but give it a ration of nine pounds of powder and a good range, and it will "make" four miles in twelve seconds at a cost of ten dollars, and possibly something else that it would puzzle you to enter in a cash-book. Those little round coops, about the size of a lantern, with wooden top and bottom and two wire rings between, contain, as you see, a cluster of nine such grapes as vine-dresser never cultivated.[76] They together weigh eighteen pounds, and by that handle you can swing them about like a dinner-pail. Give a twenty-four-pound gun six pounds of powder and one coop, and that cluster will make nine terrible and deadly lines of flight. We are not well out of the fruit business, for there are thousands of long tin cans, looking home-like and harmless enough to hold the best berry God ever made, and that you put up for next Christmas. They are twenty-five-pound canisters, filled with shrapnel, five dozen musket-balls, and packed in, like "Isabellas," with sawdust, as if they were something to "keep." Driven from a thirty-two with eight pounds of powder, your fruit-can goes to pieces, and the bullets scatter as if from a tremendous, wide-mouthed basket.

And here we are pleasantly walking where sleeps an earthquake; making each other hear where slumbers a voice that could shake these everlasting hills. Ah, what a flash of lightning or a glowing coal could do for all this! That is not a potash-kettle you have sat down upon—it's a shell! [77]

"A battery seen is a battery lost," ran a maxim of World War I. Enemy observers, directing the fire of cannon with improved range, precision, and mechanism, could by instant communications from their posts launch a salvo of shells at a fleeting target and smash it. In the Civil War batteries seldom went unseen, although they took concealment when they could in the edge of woods or behind crests. Sometimes they were dug in, protected by parapets. Far more often they fought in the open, firing over the heads of their infantry or, as frequently, in line with them or ahead of them. Indirect fire, that is fire on a target unseen from the gun, with sights laid on an aiming stake and angles calculated therefrom, was little used in the 1860's.

Crews manned cannon lacking the gun shields and aprons of latter days. Every man was exposed, especially the swabbers and loaders who must run to muzzles and turn their backs on attacking enemy to load and swab. Artillery's only defenses were such supporting infantry as it might have and its own mobility. Batteries could call up the limbers and shift position or retreat, providing that all the horses were not shot down in the maneuver. Even with most of a six-horse team dead or crippled and cut out of the traces, there is record of two or even one of the surviving animals gallantly managing to pull the gun to safety. With all horses gone, cannoneers time and again dragged the pieces back by prolonge ropes, halting to slam a round back into pressing pursuit, then hauling the guns back again under the momentum of their recoil.[78]

Overrun by an assault before they could escape, valiant artillerymen fought it out in the battery position. Officers and sergeants swung sabers. Those lucky enough to have revolvers blazed away. Cannoneers jabbed and flailed with the only weapons they usually had: rammer staffs and trail handspikes. Stone's River, Chickamauga, Lookout Mountain, and Missionary Ridge—like many another battle of the war—all saw desperate stands by Blue or Gray artillery around cherished pieces they would count it a disgrace to lose. Not until Korea would as much close combat among the guns be waged again.[79]

In truth mighty feats of arms are recalled by the cannon in the Chickamauga–Chattanooga National Military Park and by the bronze bas-reliefs of artillery in action on their battery monuments. They stand silent but no less eloquent, whether they mount their perpetual guard in the Georgia woods or in the small reservations on Tennessee heights, hemmed in by suburban houses. Even the pair on Missionary Ridge, whose muzzles stare straight at the windows of a home, now blocking their field of fire, seem to speak their part. "Hence we once dealt death to enemies."

General James Barnett, Chief of Artillery of the Army of the Cumberland, used to make those feats vivid when in after years he illustrated the campaign by moving miniature cannon about on maps.[80] Other veterans chronicled deeds in battery histories, remembering the autumn days when "the artillery's roar, reverberating through the valleys and from the mountains, made a deep and impressive sound as though the whole country was in convulsion."[81]

It was then, as always, a proud thing to have manned the guns.

CHAPTER 6

Your Move, General

In the gambits that were preliminaries to the final Chattanooga campaign, the generals of armies shifted their pieces and their pawns forward and backward on a wide board that covered six states. The war-chess comparison seems especially apt, since one of the pieces actually was a bishop. Leonidas Polk, a classmate of Jefferson Davis at West Point, then head of an Episcopal diocese, now led a Confederate corps.[82] Other corps commanders may be termed the kings, responding promptly or slowly to a master's hand or, isolated, usurping his seat. There may even be said to have been a queen, Mme. Turchin, wife of a Russian-born Union officer whose command she competently took over when he was ill.[83] Those horse-headed pieces, the knights, were embodied by cavalry, frequently in play, and castellated rooks symbolized the strong points.

When the generals made their moves, it was at times by their own decision, on other occasions under an electrical impulse: the telegraph from Washington and Richmond. Such remote control was not always satisfactory to the statesmen. Despite the distance, travel to the western theater was considered necessary in the military service. President Davis or War Secretary Stanton and his assistant, Charles A. Dana, arrived to breathe down the generals' necks and make suggestions, or, more often, issue orders.

Summer, 1862, and Chattanooga, the gateway, was any man's to seize and hold. The Federals frittered away time mending an unneeded railway line. Bragg got there first and had his sally port for an invasion of Kentucky. Except for a slashing cavalry raid by the

56

incomparable Bedford Forrest, Bragg gained little from his opportunity. A Union army met him at Perryville on October 8 in a
sanguinary collision in which nearly 5,000 men were killed and
wounded on each side. Enough drive remained in the Gray attack
to have carried on through, but it was not sufficient in the opinion
of General Bragg. He retreated southeasterly into east Tennessee
through Cumberland Gap and thence back to Chattanooga.

Now the city in the river bend was beginning to take its place as
the Richmond of the West. Bragg moved out to defend its approaches, as Lee had so often staved off the enemy from the capital.
Marching northward, he drew up his lines at Murfreesboro.

Meanwhile Jefferson Davis had journeyed to Chattanooga and
thence proceeded to Bragg's headquarters. There, exercising his
prerogative as commander-in-chief, he made a momentous decision.
One-fourth of the Army of Tennessee would be detached to
strengthen Confederate forces in Mississippi against Grant's menace
at Vicksburg. While Bragg must have protested the diversion of so
much of his strength, "of no present value" to the other front in the
opinion of General Joseph E. Johnston, there was no alternative to
compliance. Then, and bitterly so later, Braxton Bragg could not
but have resented his being deprived of 10,000 men, which would
throw the odds against him at the Battle of Murfreesboro. It was all
the less tolerable since it was done by order of his old comrade of
the Mexican War who so often supported him. "Yea, mine own
familiar friend, in whom I trusted . . . has lifted up his heel against
me."

Thirty miles north of Murfreesboro, the Union Army of Major
General William S. Rosecrans stood poised at Nashville for a countermove. The General rested on his October laurels, won at Corinth,
where, inflicting double the loss he took, he had battered back Van
Dorn, a victory taking considerable pressure off Grant, besieging
Vicksburg. But Rosecrans, for all of Chief of Staff Halleck's prod-
ding, refused to leave Nashville until more than a month passed.
More laurels could wait. He wanted rations and would not stir
until he had filled his wagons with a generous supply. Then,
secure in the knowledge that his army was marching on its stomach

in the Napoleonic tradition, he broke camp, considerately waiting till the day after Christmas. By slow stages over muddy roads, with the advance guard skirmishing, it took the column three days to reach Murfreesboro.

The armies clashed east of the town, for which the Confederates named the battle, and across Stone's River, the Union's title for it. The conflict, opening December 31, 1862, was "one of the most obstinately contested and bloody of the war, in proportion to the numbers engaged." Northern casualties mounted to 13,249 killed, wounded, and missing out of a strength of 45,000; the South lost 10,266 out of 38,000 in action.

The battle in various respects was a preview of Chickamauga, with most of the same commanders displaying the same qualities. Rosecrans and Bragg testing each other's mettle, and neither quite resolving the test. McCook routed and Thomas standing rocklike. The fiery Sheridan, fighting his division to the hilt till its ammunition was gone, then resorting to the bayonet. Bishop-General Polk, giving reason for doubt that it had been wise to ask him to doff surplice for uniform. Hard-hitting, stanch Pat Cleburne. The same valiant rank and file in gray or blue, charging each other's cannon whose thunders were so deafening that the men snatched cotton from bolls in the fields and stuffed it in their ears.

By the day's end the Federals had not quit the field, but it had been a near thing for them, and they were hurt worse than the enemy. That night Rosecrans, his uniform stained with blood—that of an aide who, riding at his side, had been beheaded by a cannon ball—called a war council. Thomas napped until the word "retreat" roused him; then he came awake and stated flatly, "This army can't retreat," and that settled it.

But Bragg had fully expected to see no bluecoats but dead ones in the vicinity next morning. He had telegraphed Richmond, "God has granted us a happy New Year." Even when he woke to find the Army of the Cumberland still facing him, he spent the next twenty-four hours combining Thanksgiving and New Year's Day and to no better purpose. On January 2 he tardily resumed the battle. A Yankee Pioneer, E. S. Buck, abandoned pick and shovel for musket and plunged with his brigade into the desperate fighting that would inspire him to pen an "Epick."

> ...Hip; Hip; Huzza, just see them run.
> Come on, brave Pioneers.
> I never shall forget that hour,
> The ground all stained with blood,
> While hundreds of our dying men
> Lie weltering in the mud.

> Again we drove the Butternuts
> And took a Rebel Flag,
> The Banner of that tory band,
> The god of General Bragg... [84]

It was the Federal artillery that put a resounding period to the battle. From across the river massed batteries, fifty-eight pieces, firing a hundred rounds a minute, delivered one of the most magnificent concentrations of the war. That storm of shell shattered a Gray charge, strewing the field with 2,000 of the flower of the Army of Tennessee.

Surgeons were busy among the thousands of wounded. Here, as on many another field where the casualties were heavy, the doctors were swamped by far more injured than they could adequately care for, yet they did their utmost.

At the call of patriotism and mercy, the surgeons had left their practices and donned uniforms of blue or gray. What if many of them never had been to medical school but had simply been serving apprenticeships in the offices of older physicians? There was desperate need of them, whatever their skill. As late as mid-1863 Union losses from disease and infection were two and a half times greater than the losses on the battlefield itself.

The reasons for this were in the hospitals themselves. One of the the more famous Federal doctors often sharpened his surgical knife on his boot during an operation, and threaded his suture needle after moistening the silk in his mouth. Antiseptic surgery was unknown. Surgery was performed on germ-laden tables, and unsterilized sponges were used. Shrapnel and bullet wounds were explored with dirty fingers, and preventive vaccinations were unknown. Chloroform and ether were used, but the hypodermic syringe, the clinical thermometer, sterilized bandages, rubber gloves, first aid packets, and Xrays were unknown. There was no scientifically proved foundation for field sanitation, and first aid, where rendered, was a desperate and uncertain procedure. Medical care could be no better than medical science from which it stemmed. In spite of the strenuous efforts to improve it by commanders and medical men, crowded conditions made hospitals a focal point for the spread of contagious diseases.[85]

Medical corps, under the inadequate organization of the first years of the war, could not cope with their task. The appalling record of Second Bull Run, when out of the 4,000 Federal wounded 600 still remained on the battlefield, exposed to rain and scorching sun, a week later, was gradually improved. At Gettysburg, where 1,100 ambulances were in service, all the Union wounded and Confederate injured left behind at the retreat had been picked up and attended within twelve hours after the battle was over. Conditions, somewhat better still at Chattanooga, because of evacuation by hospital trains, were still far from ideal by modern standards.

Taylor pictured the scenes on battlefield and in hospitals when surgeons operated on the dreadful wounds inflicted by soft lead "minnie" balls and shell fragments—how the doctors rolled up sleeves and opened cases "filled with the terrible glitter of silver steel," as the casualties commenced to arrive.

They begin to come in, slowly at first, one man nursing a shattered arm, another borne by his comrades, three on an ambulance, one on a stretcher; then faster and faster, lying here, lying there, waiting each his terrible turn. The silver steel grows cloudy and lurid; true right arms are lopped like slips of golden willow; feet that never turned from the foe, forever more without an owner, strow the ground. The knives are busy, the saws play; it is bloody work. . . . "My God!" cried a surgeon, as, looking up an instant from his work, he saw the mutilated crowds borne in; "my God, are *all* my boys cut down!" . . .

Medical Department, United States Army, 1861–65. Left to right: Surgeon; contract surgeon; nurse with patient; hospital steward.

Not a whimper, nor a plaint. Only once did I hear either. An Illinois lieutenant, as brave a fellow as ever drew a sword, had been shot through and through the thighs, fairly impaled by the bullet—the ugliest wound but one I ever saw. . . . He had just been brought over the mountain; his wounds were angry with fever; every motion was torture; they were lifting him up as tenderly as they could; they let him slip and he fell, perhaps six inches. But it was like a dash from a precipice to him, and he wailed out like a little child, tears wet his pale, thin face, and he only said, "My poor child, how will they tell her?" It was only for an instant; his spirit and his frame stiffened up together, and with half a smile he said, "don't tell, boys, that I made a fool of myself!" The Lieutenant "sleeps well," and alas, for the "poor child"—how did they tell her? [86]

Among the surgeons of the Cumberland and other armies were some who were faithless and callous like the one who ordered his horse and went on a pleasure ride when two hundred wounded were waiting his attention. The great majority were dedicated men. No less so were the few, overworked women nurses such as "Mother" Mary A. Bickerdyke, Annie Wittenmyer, and others. They cut red tape and commandeered supplies, and when a fierce storm blew down hospital tents at the foot of Lookout Mountain, they rescued the helpless wounded.

Bragg's heavy losses at Murfreesboro convinced him that he had had more than enough fighting for the time being. A Union versifier stated the case for him with a jubilant stanza.

> But Rosey knew a thing or two,
>   And made him quick knock under,—
> Gave him to feel the true-edged steel,
>   Mid storms of Yankee thunder.
> Says Bragg, "I'm sad: my cause is bad,
>   And so, to save my bacon,
> I will retreat, and save defeat;
>   For Rosey can't be taken." [87]

Leaving Murfreesboro to the Army of the Cumberland, Bragg withdrew to Tullahoma. He had lost far more than a railroad station on the approach to Chattanooga—the faith of many of his officers and enlisted men. As one of his own staff testified: "By this time General Bragg's corps commanders, as well as their subordinates down to the regimental rank and file, scarcely concealed their want of confidence in him as the commander of the army." [88]

So fatal a forfeit may be redeemed by the opposite of conduct that yielded it, though neither by indulgence nor severity of discipline. Bragg's strict enforcement of the latter continued. Before the Battle of Murfreesboro a private of the 6th Kentucky had attempted to desert after refusal of permission to visit his widowed mother, who wrote she needed him sorely. He was caught and sentenced to be shot. When Bragg refused a petition to commute the punishment to a lighter one, the soldier died before a firing squad. "Surely," wrote one of his comrades, "clemency might have been used in this case with good effect." [89]

The instance, no isolated one, was of course justified by the rules of war, and in the Army of Tennessee under Bragg's command mercy did not temper justice. The General at Tullahoma was offered some caustic comment on his actions. Meeting a Tennessee mountaineer, the commander reined in his horse and asked the man if he did not belong to Bragg's army.

"Bragg's army?" came the reply. "He's got none; he shot half of them in Kentucky, and the others got killed up at Murfreesboro." [90]

The General laughed and rode on. But it was no laughing matter.

In the Union Army discipline was less stringent. General Beatty watched the punishment of a soldier who had run away at the Battle of Stone's River. The culprit, his head shaved, was drummed out of camp, sentenced to confinement in a military prison for the duration of the war. "I could not help pitying the poor fellow," Beatty remembered, "as with carpetsack in one hand and hat in the other he marched crestfallen through the camps, to the music of the 'Rogue's March.'" [91]

> Poor old soldier,
> Poor old soldier,
> Tarred and feathered and sent to hell
> Because he wouldn't soldier well.

Death and oblivion, believed Beatty, would have been less severe and infinitely more desirable. However, that sentiment might not have been shared by the soldier or by a firing squad detailed to shoot him or by comrades drawn up in ranks to witness the execution.

ROGUES' MARCH

Winter and spring, 1863. Cold and rain and mud while the armies waited out nearly six months for good marching and fighting weather. By March there was an indication it had come. The Pioneer Brigade was ordered to strike its big tents and turn them in.

In their place it was issued small shelter ones which the men derisively called dog tents or pens and placarded accordingly.

PUPS FOR SALE

RAT TERRIERS   BULL PUPS HERE   DOGHOLE NO. 1

SONS OF BITCHES WITHIN   DOGS   PURPS

General Rosecrans and staff, while riding by one day, were greeted with a tremendous bowwow. The boys were on their hands and knees, stretching their heads out of the ends of the tents, barking furiously at the passing cavalcade. The general laughed heartily and promised them better accommodations.[92]

The queen on the chessboard was in motion again. Mme. Turchin continued to flaunt the regulations against military personnel in the field being accompanied by women. Let others keep homefires burning, not that determined wife, "a fine-looking, intelligent, and a thoroughly womanly woman." When the armies began to stir, she led some efficient foraging parties through the countryside. And she would not be far from her brigadier, "the Mad Cossack," at Chickamauga and following battles.[93]

Cavalry kept flashing across the board. Before the winter stalemate ended, Rosecrans found it necessary to dispatch a brigade to Georgia to counter Gray horsemen who had been raiding his supply lines. Forrest harried it. Using the old trick of marching his 500 men again and again in a seemingly endless column past the enemy's view, he deluded the whole brigade of 1,600 into surrender. Later, tables were turned when Confederate General John H. Morgan led his cavalrymen into Kentucky, crossed the Ohio River, and threatened Cincinnati. Blue troopers bottled him up, capturing him and most of his command.

Chancellorsville and Gettysburg kept the spotlight on the East until, with the ending of the latter battle, it suddenly shifted westward. Grant had taken Vicksburg at last. The Mississippi was open, and the Confederacy cut in twain.

A little earlier, on June 24, Rosecrans had marched from Murfreesboro to assail Bragg at Tullahoma. About the same time General Ambrose E. Burnside advanced from Cincinnati to storm Knoxville. Both the latter general's seizure of an important railroad center and the former's brilliant strategy in outwitting Bragg were to be overshadowed by the fall of Vicksburg. Yet the two events also set the board for the finale at Chattanooga.

Tullahoma, southeast from Murfreesboro on the railway, was a second line of defense for Chattanooga. Bragg had thrown up strong fortifications around the town and manned them with 45,000 fine troops. Rosecrans had 60,000, far too slim odds for a successful assault on formidable entrenchments. Maneuvers to force the enemy out of his position seemed the answer. Old Rosy's skillful planning of them marked the apex of his career. He feinted toward the right in the direction of Shelbyville, drawing a Gray countermove. Then he swing to the left toward Manchester, threatening to cut the railroad south of Tullahoma and assault the Confederate redoubts in the rear. Bragg, taken by surprise and completely baffled, pulled out and did not halt his retreat short of Chattanooga. At small cost, without a pitched battle—no more than skirmishes—Rosecrans had achieved his objective.[94]

It was top strategy, its execution as notable as its conception. The marches that accomplished it were made in unseasonable, drenching downpours of rain, turning roads into quagmires and rivulets into torrents that had to be forded thigh-deep. In squelching boots, wet to the skin day and night, infantrymen plodded on through the mud, or tailed on to ropes and heaved to help the guns and supply wagons up the slippery grades. But Tullahoma was theirs at last, and they had the great news that Vicksburg had fallen. Bragg was in full retreat, and the way to Chattanooga was open.

In this short campaign [comments Steele in *American Campaigns*, I, 440], Rosecrans made the first use in the Civil War of the kind of flank or turning movements afterwards successfully employed by Sherman in the Atlanta campaign. Such movements constituted a favorite method of Napoleon in offensive mountain warfare; that is the method by which the attention of the enemy in position at a gorge or upon heights is occupied by one force, while another turns his position and gains or threatens his rear by a different pass.

Occupying the Confederate camp, Yankee soldiers gathered around their fires and toasted their departed opponent with some unknown minstrel's lay, "Bragg a Boo."

> Dear General Bragg, here's to your health,
> With Secesh script to swell your wealth;
> Your coat of arms, when Fortune deals,
> We trust will bear a pair of heels.

> CHORUS

> Then, shout, boys, shout! The foe is put to rout,
> And Bragg a Boo and Morgan, too,
> Have started on for Dixie.
> Hey, ho! We've laid them low.
> Secesh are blue as in-di-go.[95]

Once more the wires from Washington throbbed with orders to get moving. August 16, 1863, and Rosecrans marched again.

The most direct approach to Chattanooga was by the left through Therman and over Waldron's [Walden's] Ridge, a spur of the Cumberland Mountains named after a hardy pioneer of a century ago. But Rosecrans had two good objections to that road. One was that it would carry him far from the railway, with a long wagon-haul over steep and dangerous roads; the other was that Bragg fully expected him to come that way in spite of its difficulty. The alternative route was by the right through Bridgeport and Stevenson and over the mountains of northern Alabama and Georgia. This would keep Rosecrans near to the railway and to his depot of supplies which he was just establishing at Stevenson, but it necessitated moving through a country so difficult that Bragg did not believe he would dare attempt it. A series of parallel mountain ranges, hard to climb and penetrable only through narrow defiles, stood in his way.[96]

THE CHATTANOOGA THEATER

Immediately in front was the first great barrier in the advance movement—the Cumberland Mountains—a lofty range of rocks dividing the waters flowing into the Cumberland and the Tennessee Rivers. The range rises far to the north and extends to the south-west into Alabama. North of Chattanooga the mountains are much bolder, more difficult to cross, with almost sheer declivities on each side.

Beyond the main range, in the direct road to Chattanooga, running south, flows the Sequatchie River through the valley of that name, formed by another range jutting off slightly to the east from the main range, and between it and the Tennessee River. This spur is known by the name of Walling's [Walden's] Ridge. It abuts close on the Tennessee in precipitous rocky bluffs.

South of the Tennessee, and separated from the mountain ranges north by this river, are the two ranges known as Sand and Lookout Mountains. The northern extremity of the former is called Raccoon Mountain. Here the river cuts its channel as a great chasm through these mountain ranges, so sharply defined that the masses abut directly upon the water in heavy palisades of rock.

The tops of all these mountain ranges are of poor soil but generally with considerable timber; rough, with but few roads, and these almost impassable for wagons and nearly destitute of water. The western slope of Sand Mountain reaches nearly to the Tennessee River. Between this latter range and Lookout Mountain is Lookout Valley with the creek of that name flowing through it into the Tennessee a short distance below Chattanooga. This valley is also known as Wills Valley, and at that time was traversed by a railroad branching from the Nashville road at Wauhatchie, terminating at Trenton.

Beyond this was Lookout range, 2,400 feet above the sea, with almost perpendicular sides, heavily wooded and with little water, abutting abruptly on the Tennessee, some two miles south of the town, with only three practical wagon roads over it—one close to the river, one at Johnson's Crook, and the third at Winston's Gap, twenty-six and forty-two miles respectively south of Chattanooga.

To the east of Lookout Mountain is Chattanooga Valley with the town at the head of it and the creek of that name flowing through, with Dry Creek as a branch emptying its waters into the Tennessee just south of the town. Beyond this to the east is Missionary Ridge, and parallel to it and just beyond is Chicakamauga Valley, with the creek of that name running through it emptying into the river above Chattanooga, formed by East, Middle, and West Chicka-mauga Creeks, uniting with Pea Vine Creek between the latter two as a tributary. Chattanooga and West Chickamauga Creeks have a common source in McLemore's Cove, which is formed by Pigeon Mountain on the east, jutting to the north as a spur of Lookout Mountain, with the latter on the west, Missionary Ridge running out as it enters this cover. The wagon road from Chattanooga to Rome, known as the La Fayette road, crosses Missionary Ridge into Chickamauga Creek at Lee and Gordon mills, thence to the east of Pigeon Mountain, passing through La Fayette some twenty-two miles south of Chattanooga; it then continues on to Summerville, within twenty-five miles of Rome, and so on to the latter place.

Beyond these ranges is Taylor's Ridge, with a number of lesser ranges between it and the Atlanta Railroad, running through Dalton. Both Pigeon Mountain and Taylor's Ridge are very rough mountain ranges, with but few roads, and these only through gaps. At Dalton is the junction of East Tennessee with the Atlanta Railroad, in the valley of the headwaters of the Coosa River, which valley is here some ten miles wide and is the great natural passageway into East Tenneseee from the South.[97]

So the Army of the Cumberland faced and dared the mountains, crowned by mighty Lookout. Force a passage, and the prize was Chattanooga, the gateway to final victory.

As long as we held it [a Confederate general was to confess to a Union war correspondent],[98] it was the closed doorway to the interior of our country. When it came into your hands, the door stood open, and however rough your progress in the interior might be, it still left you free to march inside. I tell you that when your Dutch general Rosecrans commenced his forward movement for the capture of Chattanooga we laughed him to scorn; we believed the black brow of Lookout Mountain would frown him out of existence; that he would dash himself to pieces against the many and vast natural barriers that rise all around Chattanooga; and that then the northern people and the government at Washington would perceive how hopeless were their efforts when they came to attack the real South.

The mountains swallowed the long blue columns—horse, foot, and guns. Thomas's XIV Corps, Crittenden's XXI, McCook's XX, Granger's Reserve. Creaking wagons loaded with ammunition enough for at least two battles and with twenty-five days' rations. A lumbering bridge train with pontoons to span the Tennessee if they reached it. If they did—if they attained the river's north bank— they would still be considerably west of Chattanooga, and passage of another high mountain barrier must be forced before they could storm the town.

Now and then Confederate cavalry pickets loomed up on the heights above the advancing columns. Invariably they melted away, leaving the path clear. A determined defense of one of the passes might have made of it another Thermopylae. But there was no Leonidas in the Army of Tennessee save Bishop-General Leonidas Polk, and neither he nor another repeated history with a Spartan stand.

Bragg had pulled General Simon Bolivar Buckner out of Knox- ville to reinforce him. Now Burnside had seized and held that railroad town as a blockade to Confederate reinforcements from the East through it, and the side-whiskered general became an ever- present menace on Bragg's flank. And once again Bragg fell victim to Rosecrans' masterly strategy. Not only had the latter taken the unexpected route, but his feints and advances on several widely separated points would further deceive Bragg and, by threatening his communications, force him either to abandon his position or give battle on equal terms.

September, 1863, and, the great passage accomplished, Blue divisions mounted the crest of Sand Mountain. A soldier of the 104th Illinois looked down on an unforgettable spectacle spread out before him.

Far beyond mortal vision extended one vast panorama of mountains, forests and rivers. The broad Tennessee below us seemed like a ribbon of silver; beyond rose the Cumberlands, which we had crossed. The valley on both sides was alive with the moving armies of the Union, while almost the entire transportation of the army filled the roads and fields along the Tennessee. No one could survey the grand scene on that bright autumn day unmoved, unimpressed with its grandeur and of the meaning conveyed by the presence of that mighty host." [99]

Meanwhile the appearance of Bragg's retreating army in Chattanooga had thrown the town into turmoil. Headlined *The Rebel: THE CRISIS IS UPON US.*

Refugees from Middle Tennessee arrived continuously, and their desperate search for local shelter and transportation farther South to supposed safety added to the confusion. . . . Some of the residents with railroad connections were able to secure cars in which they set up housekeeping. They refugeed in these caravans, keeping in advance of the armies by moving whenever they could secure a locomotive. A bank vault was emptied to serve as a bombproof.[100]

Suddenly the enemy was at hand. Colonel John T. Wilder, a fine figure of a man looking every inch the dashing leader he was, brought his Lightning Brigade of mounted infantry down Walden's Ridge. Daylight of August 21 revealed them on the hills across the river.

The Lightning Brigade was perhaps the most remarkable unit in the Army of the Cumberland. It was originally composed of the 17th and 72nd Indiana Infantry, with the 92nd, 98th, and 123rd Illinois later added. Wilder, its enterprising commander, frustrated by the forays of Forrest's, Wheeler's, and Morgan's cavalry, determined to mount his doughboys to cope with the enemy. He put it to a vote of his men, which was aye, but he started them on quiet, convalescent nags to prevent a change of mind. Then the brigade began to raid the countryside for good mounts. Besides yields from barns and pastures, it found them hidden in woods and caves. One fine animal was discovered concealed in a lady's back parlor. The raids netted a total of some 2,000 horses, plus mules for the wagons, all without expense to the Government. Saddles, hard to come by, were improvised from blankets and gun straps. There were no stirrups; a man could not mount with full equipment but had to have it handed up after he had vaulted aboard his steed.

No forage was drawn until the spring of 1863; the brigade supplied itself from the farms of Southern sympathizers. Coal was confiscated for the farriers' forges, and wagons rebuilt from wrecks scattered along the road. When saddles and cavalry uniforms finally were issued, Wilder's men stripped the yellow stripes from the breeches and jackets of the latter. They were not cavalrymen but mounted infantry and proud of it.

Wilder spent his own money, later reimbursed, to buy invaluable Spencer repeaters for his command, which also boasted some unconventional armament.

Each man carries a hatchet with a handle two feet in length,— whence they have acquired the *sobriquet* of "The Hatchet Brigade." Their hatchets are described as handy and effective both in bivouac and in fight. Every teamster, cook, and extra-duty man in the brigade is a negro, and every white is an effective soldier in the ranks. The colonel is a firm believer in the friendship and good will of the negroes.[101]

They became good horse soldiers, those mounted infantrymen of the Lightning Brigade, living up to their name throughout the Chattanooga campaign, and their accompanying artillery was as good as they were.

As Wilder's horsemen approached the river, the Colonel snapped an order to his battery commander. The guns unlimbered to open fire on Chattanooga, the town of which Wilder would become a postwar mayor.

Captain Eli Lilly saluted and turned to his 18th Indiana Battery. His expert gunners laid their 3-inch rifles on two steamboats at the Chattanooga wharf, sank one of them and damaged the other. Promptly the defenders retaliated, blazing back with nineteen guns, mostly 12-pound howitzers and rifled 6-pounders. Only their big 32-pounder could make the range. One of its projectiles sheared off a leg of an Indiana corporal and killed four horses. Lilly kept on shooting. His 3-inchers threw shells directly into embrasures of parapets protecting the opposing artillery and dismounted its guns. By day's end he had silenced every battery that had opened on him.[102]

The attack, spearheaded by Wilder, was a ruse to make Bragg believe that it was the forerunner of the Union Army's main assault to be delivered there from upstream on the north side of the Tennessee. It was a completely successful deception, and the crossings below Chattanooga were left virtually unguarded. Rosecrans thrust the bulk of his forces at the river in the vicinity of Bridgeport and Caperton's Ferry, Alabama, and Shellmound, Tennessee. Although there were not enough pontoons in the train for two bridges to span the stream, high and swollen by the rains, trestles, rafts, and improvised boats eked them out. Blue regiments, breaking step, poured across the swaying, bobbing avenues of planks. Wheels rumbled as artillery drivers and wagoners, quieting nervous teams, urged them across the narrow bridgeways.

Brushing aside light opposition, the Army of the Cumberland had passed safely over by September 4. The Confederate left was turned. Communications and the supply line from Atlanta, along with all other railroads to Chattanooga, would shortly be severed. General Bragg was in imminent danger of being boxed in by Rosecrans on the west and south, by Burnside on the north and east.

Bragg had been reinforced by Buckner's Corps of 8,000, and two divisions (9,000 men under Generals John C. Breckinridge and W. H. T. Walker), with 2,500 more to follow from Mississippi. His urgent appeals to Richmond would bring Longstreet's Corps from the Army of Northern Virginia to his aid. Despite additional troops,

Chattanooga potentially was a trap. On September 8 he evacuated the town, concentrating his army behind Pigeon Mountain, its front and flanks covered by cavalry.

Let the Yankees have Chattanooga. The town or its approaches might soon prove to be as deadly a trap for them.

CHAPTER 7

Jaws of a Trap

Once more the mountains filled their varied roles in this campaign they dominated. As before, they were barriers and natural ramparts. Their wooded sides were mighty screens until their peaks were gained. And now the gaps, which pierced them and made them passable for marching armies, provided a new potential. They became entrances to a trap.

Lookout, Missionary Ridge, and easternmost Pigeon Mountain, all stretching southwesterly from Chattanooga and the Tennessee-Georgia line, reared upward as the snare's walls. They could be penetrated by a number of gaps, including Rossville, Steven's, and Winston's. Yet none of those means of passage was close to another, and the two extreme ones, Rossville and Winston's, were so far separated that the flanks of a force, advancing through them and intermediate ones, would be forty miles apart.

The Confederate Army of Tennessee, after its retreat from Chattanooga, concentrated behind Pigeon Mountain near LaFayette, Georgia. There it awaited reinforcements from the East and the enemy's next move. When Longstreet's Corps arrived, Bragg, with close to 70,000 men, could meet the Federals on better than even terms. Meanwhile, he protected his communications, lay in ambush, and baited a trap for the Army of the Cumberland.

Bragg used as a lure his favorite technique of pretended deserters. If it worked, the loss of a number of good men would be worth while. The General sent them off singly and by twos and threes to make their way into the Union lines—men intelligent enough to play their part convincingly and as willing to face the possibility of a slow death in Yankee prison camps as a fast one on the battlefield. Bragg was in full retreat, the "deserters" reported. They told their captors that the Confederacy was done for, and so far as they were concerned, the rest of the war could go hang.

Another retreat by Bragg was amply credible—Murfreesboro and Tullahoma and Chattanooga again. Rosecrans swallowed the stories and issued marching orders. His decision to go forward was both good tactics, from the viewpoint of pressing a reputedly demoralized foe, and good policy. He had frequently been condemned by the War Department for being as unconscionably slow in moving as Charles II declared he was a-dying. The fault lay in his acting on no better information than the questionable yarns of deserters and in failure (in which Bragg shared) to make adequate reconnaissance.

Each commander seemed to be more ignorant concerning his adversary's movements than was generally the case in the campaigns of this war; this ignorance was the chief cause of the mistakes. The country was so rugged and wooded, and so lacking in roads and good trails, that it was impossible for the cavalry to do first rate reconnaissance. Yet it should seem that the cavalry ought to have been able to do better work than it did. In fact, if we except the work of Minty's cavalry brigade and Wilder's mounted infantry, the cavalry operations of this campaign do not appear to have been as good as we find in many other campaigns of the war. More fault can be found with the Confederate cavalry than the Federals, mainly because its strength was greater. Bragg had 14,260 troopers, while Rosecrans had only 9,842. It should seem that Wheeler and Forrest ought to have met the Federal columns as soon as those columns got across the Tennessee, and, by holding the mountain passes, ought to have delayed their progress many days. Time was of great importance to Bragg—a few more days would have brought him four more of Longstreet's brigades and Alexander's battalion of artillery. The trouble with Bragg's cavalry at this time was the lack of unity in its command. It consisted practically of two corps under separate commanders, Wheeler and Forrest, with no single cavalry general commanding them as a body.[103]

So in the camps around Chattanooga bugles blew and drums rolled. Little Billy Birch of the 2nd Minnesota expertly wielded his sticks, remembering how proud he had been when he donned a blue uniform and slung this drum of his back in 1861. He was small and had not been fifteen then. The regiment wouldn't take him without parental consent, but his patriotic persuasion of his father had been so irresistible that the two of them joined up. Billy, a full-fledged drummer, marched south with K Company "to do or die for my country if need be." Now he was a veteran, trudging toward a creek called Chickamauga.[104] Over in the 22nd Michigan Johnny Clem listened to the other lads rattle away without regret for his own drum, smashed by a shell at Shiloh. A fighting man now, he shouldered his cut-down musket and fell into ranks.

Four fine corps took the road. McCook's XX, as the right wing, marched toward Alpine by way of Winston's Gap, covered by cavalry. Thomas's XIV in the center advanced by the Trenton-LaFayette road. Crittenden's XXI, on the left, detached a brigade to garrison Chattanooga and moved forward by the Ringgold road, headed by Minty's and Wilder's horsemen. Granger's Reserve Corps remained in support, a good distance to the rear.

Only by such division could swift pursuit of a fleeing enemy be achieved. To have massed the command and funneled it through one of the gaps would have occasioned a considerable delay, which in all probability would permit the escape of the quarry.

Strategy is in part the art of outguessing an adversary. But the guesses must be good ones. When they are based on unwarranted and erroneous assumptions, they can prove fatal. General William S. Rosecrans, the hitherto-brilliant strategist, made his choice and put it to the hazard.

The Army of the Cumberland opened up and spread out like a gigantic blue fan, its segments about to be stripped and separated by the mountain passes. The General, whose grasp held the handle, would find that fan hard to close.

Braxton Bragg was standing fast. Another withdrawal, he was well aware, would be a retreat straight into personal oblivion.

He lifted up his eyes unto the hills and found more hindrance than help. They had played him false once when Lookout screened the Union Army that had driven him from Chattanooga.

It is said to be easy to defend a mountainous country [he grumbled,] but mountains hide your foe from you, while they are full of gaps through which he can pounce on you at any time. A mountain is like the wall of a house full of rat-holes. The rat lies hidden at his hole, ready to pop out when no one is watching. Who can tell what lies hidden behind the wall? [105]

Yet now the mountains seemed to be serving him well. He could play the cat at the ratholes. Two enemy columns were emerging from the gaps, apparently in complete ignorance that he was lying in wait for them behind Pigeon Mountain. So much his cavalry scouts told him. He did not know that a third column, McCook's Corps, was headed toward Summerville whence it could encircle his left flank. However, that force, the southernmost, was distant. Before it could either menace him or, lacking any good connecting roads, support its comrade corps, they could be dealt with separately and destroyed. Seldom have the gods of war offered a general a more magnificent opportunity.

General Braxton Bragg, C.S.A. gave his commanders their orders. March through the Pigeon Mountain gaps. Strike and crush Thomas. Then swing on Crittenden and smash him.

Once more the clock must be turned back seventeen years to the War with Mexico—to Captain Bragg, U.S.A., with three lieutenants his loyal and admiring subordinates.

George H. Thomas, as has been previously mentioned, was presently facing his former battery commander across the lines. Another subaltern, John F. Reynolds, who, like Thomas, had become an able Union general, had been killed at Gettysburg. Enter now the third lieutenant of Bragg's Battery, D. H. Hill, recently appointed lieutenant general, C.S.A. "It was a strange casting of lots," he reflected, "that three [of the four] messmates of Corpus Christi should meet under such strange circumstances at Chickamauga." [106]

Hill confessed that he went west with high hopes to take over a corps in the army of his leader of Mexico, whom he had not since seen. Those hopes fell at their first meeting. To Hill, Bragg was:

silent and reserved and seemed gloomy and despondent. He had grown prematurely old since I saw him last, and showed much nervousness. His relations with his next in command (General Polk) and with some other of his subordinates were known not to be pleasant. His many retreats, too, had alienated his rank and file from him, or at least had taken away that enthusiasm which soldiers feel for a successful general, and which makes them obey his orders without question, and thus wins for him other successes. The one thing that a soldier never fails to understand is victory, and the commander who leads him to victory will be adored by him whether that victory has been won by skill or by blundering, or by the awkward use of overwhelming numbers.[107]

Disillusionment and infection with the prevailing distrust of the commanding general were quick to seize on D. H. Hill. His conduct and that of Polk, Buckner, and others in the forthcoming critical situations were extraordinary in any disciplined army. Those subordinates were guilty of disregard of or delay in obeying orders, behavior that justified their summary relief from command. Explanations they gave boiled down to the fact that they considered their judgment better than Bragg's. The spirit of unquestioning obedience of the Light Brigade at Balaklava—"Theirs not to reason why"—would have told a different story on the eve of Chickamauga.

Be it said in justice to General Bragg that he saw his opportunity when the Federal columns poured through the gaps, and he tried to take it. He issued the proper orders, orders whose fulfillment should have won striking successes considerably deferring ultimate Union triumph in the war. That Bragg, "that fate-haunted soldier," had himself sown the deadly seeds of disloyalty that balked him does not exculpate the failure of his subordinates.

Action and counteraction crowded fast on each other in those emergency-fraught days of early September. Rosecrans' three columns were pressing forward speedily. By the tenth McCook's Corps was at Alpine. Thomas was thrusting through Steven's Gap, his spearhead, Negley's Division, probing into Dug Gap of Pigeon Mountain. Crittenden was at Chickamauga Creek on the Ringgold road. Heads of both the latter columns collided with Gray cavalry. Opposition was tough enough to indicate that these were more than stands by bodies of horsemen covering an army's retreat. Here were the advance guards of an army about to attack.

Bragg had dispatched his orders on the evening of the ninth. Polk was to send Hindman's Division to cut off Negley's advanced spearhead in McLemore's Cove. Hill was directed to rush Cleburne's Division through the gaps to join Hindman in the destruction of the isolated Union command.

Hindman was in position to attack on the tenth, but there was no sign of Hill's men. That commander reported that he had been unable to get through the gaps, blocked by felled trees—it would take twenty-four hours to clear the way, and besides Cleburne was sick. Bragg then urgently ordered Buckner to march his corps to Hindman's support. By afternoon Buckner was on the ground. There were now three Confederate divisions poised to overwhelm the lone Union one, not three miles away and still without any support that could reach it in time.

No attack was launched. Buckner and Hindman believed they had a better plan, which they sent back by courier to headquarters while they rested on their arms. Bragg refused their proposal. (His official report contains no hint of the fireworks its receipt must have set off.) He repeated his orders and hurried more troops to the scene. But it was too late then, and the chance had vanished. Negley had seen his danger and hastily retreated on Thomas at Steven's Gap.

Opportunity loudly knocked again. Crittenden had divided his corps, marching two divisions toward Ringgold and one to Lee and Gordon's Mills. Once more, on the twelfth, General Bragg dictated tragically futile orders. Polk's Corps was to strike Crittenden's one division at the Mills. The result of a swift descent by a corps upon a single division could be predicted.

At eleven o'clock that night Polk astoundingly reported that he had taken a strong position for defense and requested that he be heavily reinforced. Bragg pointed out the Bishop-General's already greatly superior strength, yet promised the support of Buckner's Corps, to be on hand soon after the assault Polk was now commanded to make at dawn on the thirteenth.

"You must not delay attack for his arrival," Bragg wrote, "or another golden opportunity may be lost by the withdrawal of our game." [108]

Bragg and Buckner reached the field on the morning of the thirteenth to find Polk still holding his "strong position for defense" and nothing else. During the night the lone Union division had slipped away and reunited with Crittenden's other two beyond Chickamauga Creek. Bragg's report expressed his emotions mildly with the phrase, "again disappointed," but his pent-up ire was rising to the point where it could not much longer be contained. Upon Polk's next dereliction, Bragg would relieve him and prefer charges against him of failure to obey the lawful commands of a superior officer.[109]

In the preliminaries to Chickamauga and the battle itself the speech of Shakespeare's Cardinal Wolsey might be accusingly reversed by Bishop Polk. Had I but served my general with half the zeal I served my God . . .

D. H. Hill, who had also failed to attack as ordered—the general who had reported it would take twenty-four hours to clear a blocked gap—would enter the lists with a postwar article: [110]

As the failure of Bragg to beat Rosecrans in detail has been the subject of much criticism, it may be well to look into the causes of failure. So far as the commanding general was concerned, the trouble with him was: first, lack of knowledge of the situation; second, lack of personal supervision of the execution of his orders. No general ever won a permanent fame who was wanting in these grand elements of success, knowledge of his own and his enemy's condition, and personal superintendence of operations on the field.

But in the case of both ordered but undelivered attacks, Bragg does not appear to have been ignorant of situations but well aware of them and their opportunities. Must a general see personally to the execution of his orders? The answer is: yes, if his subordinates mistrust him. And the corollaries are: one fit to command does not earn the distrust of those under him, or if he does, refuses to tolerate them and continue them on duty.

At last General Rosecrans became aware of the deadly peril into which he had flung his divided columns. Twice had trap jaws begun to close on two of them and only by rare luck had they remained unsprung. Couriers galloped to McCook with urgent orders to close on Thomas. McCook marched on the night of the thirteenth by way of Valley Head and by the seventeenth had concentrated his corps at the eastern end of Steven's Gap. Awaiting him, the corps of Thomas and Crittenden stood fast. The Army of the Cumberland, not yet united and passed from the offensive to the defensive, covered the roads to Chattanooga.

It still was not too late for a master stroke by the Confederate Army. But General Bragg had relapsed into his hesitant role, brooding in black pessimism. Although he heavily outnumbered Thomas and Crittenden combined, let alone separate, and those corps had not yet been joined by McCook, he did not strike. He let the precious days, from the thirteenth to the eighteenth, flit by while he waited for the arrival of reinforcements under Longstreet from the East.

CHAPTER 8

The Iron Horsemen

People who gathered at railroad stations to watch the trains go through were given an especially stirring spectacle that fall of 1863. It was an epochal sight: the first two long-distance, mass movements of troops by rail in history—a landmark in the annals of warfare. Mighty marches, Xenophon's anabasis and the rest, receded more dimly into the past. Hard-riding invasions by Mongol cavalry and other hordes faded in retrospect, along with feats of transportation by sea, lake, and river. The tread of marching men, the thud of hoofs and rumble of wheels, the beat of oar and propeller—all these would still sound and in due course merge into the roar of truck and airplane motors. But at the moment the Iron Horse was the new-crowned king of military transportation.

For now both armies in the West, first the Confederate, then the Union, were being reinforced from the East, and only by railway could it be accomplished in time to tip the scales of battle one way or the other.

The Civil War was the first war in which railroads were extensively used for the transportation of large bodies of troops and great quantities of supplies.

Masters of construction and of destruction, the railroaders called themselves, and well deserved the title on both counts. The name of the Union's engineering genius, General Herman Haupt, led all the rest. Superimposed upon a West Point background was a civilian career that had distinguished him as "perhaps the foremost railroad construction engineer in the world." His coworker and successor, General D. C. McCallum, also possessed high ability, while the accomplishments of their opposite number in the Confederacy, Major Frederick W. Sims, were all the more remarkable because of the dearth of lines, equipment, and materials that confronted him. The South's network of railroads was far scantier than the North's. Numbers of the engine drivers on Southern lines were transplanted Northerners. When they were suspected of slowdowns or causing breakdowns, armed guards were put aboard to ride in the cabs behind them. Without any manufactory of locomotives and but one small mill capable of making rails, it was forced to depend upon the rolling stock within its borders at secession and on captures. And Southern tracks, once the Yankees got at them, were thoroughly wrecked by such methods as Haupt's portable machine, which twisted rails into spirals. On the other hand, if the Rebels had damaged their own lines before an enemy advance, Haupt's men carried tools to straighten rails.

General Bragg, already reinforced from Mississippi and Knoxville, was about to receive a fresh accession of strength. Amends were to be made for the 10,000 men taken from him before Murfreesboro.

No sooner had the news of the evacuation of Chattanooga reached Richmond than the Confederate Government put forth its utmost energies in support of Jefferson Davis's favorite commander. General James Longstreet—a host in himself—was detached from Lee's army, with the two fine divisions of Hood and McLaws, and sent in all possible haste to reinforce General Bragg." [111]

That action and the events that led to it bristle with military "ifs." If Bragg had not been weakened prior to Murfreesboro, might he not have decisively gained that battle and never have been forced to abandon Chattanooga? With the town on the Tennessee firmly in his grasp, need he have pulled Buckner's Corps away from the important railroad center of Knoxville? Could it not have been successfully defended against the chronically underconfident Burnside? Even after such speculations had been canceled by *faits accomplis,* might Confederate arms have triumphed in the balance of the campaign if the positive, hard-driving Longstreet had, in accordance with his hint, superseded in command the vacillating Bragg, whose path henceforth was to be spiked by the thorns of lost loyalties?

However, the die was cast. Orders were written in Richmond, General Lee concurring as to the necessity of redeeming the gateway to the southeast, though it would cost him for a time the services of one of his best commanders and corps.

Bugles sounded "The General" at Orange Court House, Virginia, and veterans packed equipment. Infantrymen gathered scanty belongings in a holiday spirit; they were going to ride, not walk. Artillerymen entraining later were faced with manifold chores. Inspecting teams, requisitioning scarce horseshoes, and putting the blacksmiths to work. Pulling and shoving balky nags up ramps and into boxcars. Manhandling the guns and carriages onto flats and making them fast with chocks, blocks, and battens. Busier still were quartermaster and ordnance officers, seeing to the provision of rations and ammunition and calling for details to load them. But worries and tribulations hung heaviest over the heads of the railroad people.

A tremendous task was demanded of the resourceful Major Sims and his assistants. With all secrecy and speed possible, they must schedule and put through rail transportation for some 7,000 troops with animals and supplies for a trip of 900 miles. Now that Knoxville lay in enemy hands (but for that road block the movement could have been made via Lynchburg, Bristol, and Knoxville in an estimated four days), the distance had been almost doubled and the time element dangerously stretched. Longstreet must now be routed via Richmond, Wilmington, Augusta, and Atlanta. Sixteen different lines were involved. Lack of connecting links, varying track gauges, and unbridged rivers would force troublesome and time-consuming transfers. And the job must be done with equipment inadequate from the outset of the war and much of it irreplaceable because of the South's lack of manufacturing facilities. By the summer of 1863 the condition of rolling stock and rails ranged from poor to decrepit. Achievement under such handicaps stands high among logistical triumphs in any war.

Never before [recalled Longstreet's Chief of Staff, Moxley Sorrel] were so many troops moved over such worn-out railways, none first-class from the beginning. Never before were such crazy cars—passenger, baggage, mail, coal, box, platform—all and every sort, wobbling on the jumping strap-iron—used for hauling good soldiers.[112]

All the discomforts—crowding, exposure, jolts, transfers—counted not at all to the veterans of the Army of Northern Virginia. For them much of the trip was like a long parade down a home-town main street, and not a blistered foot in a carload. Most of the soldiers aboard hailed from parts of the Carolinas and Georgia they traversed. Home folks lined the tracks to cheer them through, waving flags and handkerchiefs. There was an abundance of pretty girls, blushing at appreciative whoops that ran the length of a train. Men in closed cars, jealous of outsiders' better view, chopped out sidewalls to get into the act, putting railroad equipment into considerably worse shape. But no matter, it held together, and there were bright memories to be carried into battle. Tears shed as the trains passed went unseen. And though the gladiators' farewell, *Morituri te salutamus,* was invisibly chalked on every car, the cheering men waving back gave no hint of it.

Only at night was the passage tinged by the somber. Mrs. Mary B. Chesnut, a general's wife, saw a train roll by and wrote in her diary:

At Kingsville (S.C.) on my way to Camden, I caught a glimpse of Longstreet's Corps going past. God bless the gallant fellows; not one man intoxicated, not one rude word did I hear. It was a strange sight. What seemed miles of platform cars, and soldiers rolled in their blankets lying in rows with their heads all covered, fast asleep. In their gray blankets packed in regular order, they looked like swathed mummies. One man nearby was writing on his knee. He used his cap for a desk, and he was seated on a rail. I watched him, wondering to whom that letter was to go. To his home, no doubt. Sore hearts for him there!

A feeling of awful depression laid hold of me. All these fine fellows going to kill or be killed, but why? A word took to beating about my head like an old song, "The Unreturning Brave." When a knot of boyish, laughing young creatures passed, a queer feeling of sympathy shook me. Ah, I know how your homefolks feel. Poor children! [113]

Advance elements had left Orange September 8 and would detrain near Ringgold, Georgia, on the eighteenth. Infantry having been given precedence, Alexander's battalion of artillery, marching to Petersburg, did not entrain until late in the afternoon of the seventeenth. It covered the 225 miles to Wilmington in fifty-eight hours—changed cars and ferried across a river—reached Kingsville, South Carolina, 192 miles, in twenty-eight hours—changed trains again. Thence it traveled 140 miles to Augusta, 171 miles to Atlanta, and 115 miles to Ringgold, arriving at 2 A.M., September 25. It had traversed a total of 843 miles in seven days and ten hours.

The artillery came too late for the Battle of Chickamauga, fought on the nineteenth and twentieth. Longstreet himself was not on the ground until late on the nineteenth and for the crucial fight on the following day had available from his own corps only three of Hood's brigades and later two of McLaws's. The Knoxville railroad block, compelling the long detour, had played a fateful part.

"This delay," wrote a Union historian, "was probably our salvation." [114]

The saga of reinforcements from the Army of the Potomac, although they were dispatched after and largely as a result of the near disaster to Union arms at the Battle of Chickamauga, is here related in conjunction with the prior Confederate movement.

Informed that Rosecrans had retreated to Chattanooga and was besieged there, his situation increasingly critical, Secretary Stanton called a council of war. It convened in a capital, long the cynosure but now strangely silent. "Washington was like a tiny concert hall, vacated by a great orchestra. The music could still be heard; but

it was no longer deafening." [115] Imperatively troops must be rushed
to the defense of the gateway. Sherman was hurriedly ordered east
from the Mississippi with divisions of his Army of the Tennessee
to the danger spot, but it was impossible for them to arrive in time.
Burnside was not available; he could not abandon Knoxville. The
only remaining reservoir of reinforcement was the Army of the
Potomac. Two corps, some 20,000 men, were alerted for entrainment. Yet they, also, even if the trip were made in the five days
estimated, would reach the scene too late, President Lincoln firmly
believed.

The Confederates had sent of their best: Longstreet and his corps.
As much could not be said of part of the Union reinforcement and
its commander. Choice of XI Corps could not be considered a happy
one for a vital rescue mission. Called "The German Corps" because
of its high percentage of units of Teutonic extraction, it bore the
brand of a hard-luck outfit. Routed at Chancellorsville, faring little
better on the first day at Gettysburg, it was scorned by the rest of
the Army of the Potomac. Yet the blame lay on poor leadership. The
German-American had proved his soldierly qualities elsewhere—
in the Regulars, as well as in volunteer regiments of the western
armies. Distinctly superior to XI, though smaller, was XII, termed
"the corps that never lost a color or a gun." Most questionable was
the selection to lead the westbound contingent of "Fighting Joe"
Hooker, whom defeat at Chancellorsville had relegated to semi-
retirement. Still Hooker had once earned that nickname of his, and
hope of redemption is a sharp spur.

Again the Iron Horses snorted. They and the trains they pulled
were confronted by difficulties similar to those of their Southern
counterparts, though Northern rolling stock and road equipment
were in far better condition to surmount them. Four changes of cars
must be made: in Washington, at the Ohio River near Wheeling,
in Indianapolis where no connecting link existed, again at the Ohio
River for the crossing to Louisville. Railroad lines used included
the Baltimore & Ohio, Central Ohio, Louisville & Nashville, and
finally the Nashville & Chattanooga to complete the journey through
Stevenson and to Bridgeport, Alabama.

Entrainment commenced. Infantry climbed aboard, units with 40 rounds per man, camp equipment, and hospital tents. Artillery-men loaded 200 rounds per guns and five days' forage for horses. Their animals along with the wagon train mules and horses totaled more than 3,000. The great troop movement was smoothly launched and admirably co-ordinated throughout its 1,157-mile journey. Tele-graph wires hummed, as dispatchers flashed back to the War Depart-ment bulletins on progress.

Troubles were handily overcome, delays minor. Once General Carl Schurz, of the XI Corps, tried to halt trains with his advance elements so that he could move up to a front one. To his fury he was balked by a station agent, who was promptly backed up by a blistering reprimand for Schurz from Washington. On another occa-sion a trainload's rations were exhausted, and six hours lost while more were cooked. More often the troops en route were surfeited with food by basketladen townsfolk lining the tracks. "Our mouths were crammed with cakes, pies, cookies, meat, eggs, and fruit, which the loyal Ohio people brought us without money or price," a Wis-consin infantryman remembered.[116]

General O. O. Howard briefly stopped his train to pick up several men who had tumbled out of cars. Correctly diagnosing the cause, the General observed:

For some reason the soldier's thirst for whiskey (which is perhaps greater with them than with other men) seemed to be increased by the unusual excitement of the move, and it was ordered that all liquor shops should be closed during the passage of the troops. Two or three men, while drunk, had met with fearful falls from our box cars.

The Demon Rum was anathema to "the Christian General," who was once immeasurably discomfited when an empty flask was spotted in his tent during a visit by General Grant. Hastily disclaiming it, Howard declared, "I never drink." His visitor (undoubtedly with one of the best poker faces on record) replied, "Neither do I." [117]

Breaks in the line by enemy raiders were quickly repaired. Prob-ably the most retarding factor was one encountered at the end of the trip. Equipment had not been "combat-loaded," in a latter war's phrase; that is, items that would be first required first, were not so packed that they would be reached first when baggage was removed from the cars.

All sorts of material were mixed together: tents, mess-chests, army clothing, and what not. Brigade and regimental baggage was thrown together savagely, so that for many subsequent days and weeks the lesson was impressed upon all the officers, more particularly upon the indefatigable quartermasters of the command, that unless under compulsion they would never again allow railroadmen to handle baggage of other troops.[118]

The first trains made it to Bridgeport in five days, with the movement completed in eleven and a half. General Hooker and his corps came none too soon to attempt the relief of the Army of the Cumberland, besieged in Chattanooga and facing starvation after the retreat from Chickamauga.

The transportation of troops from the East for the Chattanooga campaign was indeed an accomplishment "epoch making in military annals, for nothing on a similar scale had been attempted." [119] Not least of the difficulties were those changes of cars—at least four in the case of both armies—along with the necessity of ferrying over unbridged rivers. The detoured Army of Northern Virginia contingents—7,000 men, guns, animals, and baggage—had accomplished wonders in trips that ranged from 650 to 925 miles over frail lines. A notable record was also set by the reinforcements from the Army of the Potomac: 25,000 men, 10 batteries of artillery and their horses, and 100 cars of baggage safely transported to Tennessee over 1,200 miles in eleven and one-half days.

When all these trains had delivered their cargo, the cars and engines were returned promptly to their owners and the railroads resumed their normal operations. An incredible thing had happened. American railroads, not yet of military age and still widely referred to as "contraptions," had accomplished an unparalleled military feat.[120]

Nor did efficient railroading cease after the eastern troops had been transported to the theater of operations. Solid hospital trains, replacing makeshifts, were first regularly operated by the Union Army in Tennessee and were particularly valuable in evacuating the overcrowded hospitals around Chattanooga. Each train was in charge of a surgeon and carried nurses and cooks.

The service so impressed General Thomas that, when he took command of the Army of the Cumberland, he assigned to the hospital trains the very best locomotives available and manned them with the most efficient crews. The smokestacks, cabs and tenders of the engines were painted a brilliant scarlet, and when running at night three red lanterns hung in a row beneath the headlights. On each side of the cars the words, HOSPITAL TRAIN, were painted in large letters.[121]

Chivalrous treatment was accorded such trains by Confederate generals, who gave orders that their operation be not interfered with and that they be prevented from running into a track break.

Troop and supply trains were fair game. The 3rd Wisconsin and other regiments, detrained to march to the front, forgot they were growing footsore when they passed wrecks, locomotive and cars upside down and new-made graves close beside them.

Before the advent of those special hospital trains, the wounded had been carried to base hospitals in any available ones or by wagon. Compared to the agonizing jolting the injured suffered in wagons on rough roads, the lot of those sent by rail was easy. Yet the ordeal of the latter, packed into all sorts of cars for a long, slow journey, sometimes with little or no attention or food, was no bed of roses.

Correspondent Taylor told the poignant story of "The Night Ride of the Wounded Brigade" after Chickamauga and Chattanooga, the cars "floored with the sick and wounded," going "as cattle go."

Two platform cars were paved with them, forty on a car. Seven boxes were so packed you could not set your foot down among them as they lay. The roofs of the cars were tiled with them, and away we pounded, all day, all night, into the next morning, and then Nashville. Half of the men had not a shred of a blanket, and it rained steadily, pitilessly. [This time there was some food: coffee, two crackers apiece, and a little fruit.] Wearily wore the hours and heavily hammered the train. At intervals the guard traversed the roofs of the cars and pulled in the worn-out boys who had jarred down to the edges—pulled them in toward the middle of the cars without waking them! [122]

CHAPTER 9

Battle in the Woods

Chickamauga—Dwelling Place of the War Chief in the language of the Creek Indians. White men had rechristened it the River of Death, and on two September days of 1863 it bloodily fulfilled its name.[123]

Chickamauga Creek, about to become historic, sinuously wound its ways between the armies. Where bridges or fords gave passage, it must be crossed for delivery of assault and turning of flank. Now the character of its quiet flow through the Georgia countryside appeared to alter abruptly like the sea or a lake at the approach of a storm. Pallid moonlight on its surface and the eerie mist that rose from it at dawn cast a spell on the minds of men. Its ripples seemed to whisper the stream's second name—the River of Death. Soldiers who heard that whisper were seized by a strong presentiment that they would not survive the battle before them. Most of them, striving vainly or successfully to brush that premonition aside, never voiced it. A few confided it to a diary or a comrade.

Dark forests, covering the battleground between Chickamauga Creek and Missionary Ridge, wore a still more ominous aspect. Here and there depths were opened for a space by glades or clearings, sites of small log cabins. Elsewhere light filtered faintly through the shrouding branches of oaks and hickories and pines. At the end of the first day's conflict murky moonbeams glimmered on a stagnant pool, ringed by dead and dying men and horses. The living dragged them aside to slake frenzied thirst in those noisome waters. Through the mind of an Indiana infantryman,[124] shuddering at the brink of the polluted pond, ran lines of Poe's "Ulalume":

> It was down by the dank tarn of Auber,
> In the ghoul-haunted woodland of Weir.

Neither song of bird nor chirp of cricket sounded in those gloomy shades. They swallowed the armies. Battle lines shredded, officers would lose contact with units on their flanks, even with their own commands. The woods loomed to mask artillery fire and betray batteries, which sought to penetrate them, into the hands of the enemy. Where tree trunks and dense undergrowth afforded aisle and glimpse, billowing smoke of cannonade and musketry would be swift to drop a curtain until combatants could see scarcely twenty paces ahead. Spurts of red flame from muzzles were the only beacon. As blasts from guns ignited the dry grass and brush, and patches of the woods began to burn, moaning wounded strove to drag themselves clear.

Such was Chickamauga's stage of conflict, as sinister as the following battles around Chattanooga would be spectacular.

 It was now or an irretrievable never for General Bragg, and the former verged uncomfortably on the latter.

Rosecrans, aware of his peril at last, had hurriedly concentrated his army. Granger's Reserve Corps was ordered up in closer support. The distant McCook hastened from Alpine, some of his troops making forced marches of twenty-five miles a day. But he had chosen the longest of several routes, and it was five days before he joined Thomas, who had closed on Crittenden. Thereupon the Union line, with its left flank at Lee and Gordon's Mills, extended west and south through McLemore's Cove to Steven's Gap in Lookout Mountain.

Bragg, having let slip those four precious days without interfering with the Union concentration, now received some of the reinforcements from the East for which he had delayed. The three advance brigades of Longstreet's Corps under Hood arrived on September 18. He waited no longer for the rest. Orders went out for crossings of the Chickamauga. Envelop the Union left flank. Crush Crittenden's Corps or batter it back on the enemy center in the Cove. Block off the Army of the Cumberland from its only base of supplies, the town on the Tennessee River, and drive it into the slaughter pens of dead-end mountain valleys. It was an excellent plan, whose execution twenty-four hours earlier, when the Union corps were not yet massed, might have have made Chickamauga altogether decisive and its sequel an Armageddon. Yet it still held high promise.

When Hood's Division made its long march from detrainment at Ringgold to Chickamauga, footsore soldiers of the 3rd Arkansas Infantry spotted fifty horses of the 3rd Arkansas Cavalry tied, unguarded, to fence rails. As many doughboys promptly fell out, mounted up, and enjoyed a restful ride to the next halt. However, as a courtesy to a unit from the same state they left a poem tacked to a tree for the marooned troopers.

> Tired of long walking and needing a rest,
> Your steeds we have gratefully seized and impressed,
> Feeling it but fair you should do a little walking,
> And put yourself where you can do a lot of talking
> With the Third Arkansas Infantry, your old friends and neighbors,
> Who have come from Virginia to share in your labors,
> And the Lord being willing, the Yankees to smite
> And set them to running with all of their might.
> We'll camp, beyond doubt, after a while,
> Though you may have to foot it mile after mile;
> But come till you find us—it will give you exercise,
> As well as a heartful of gallant enterprise
> When, the Yanks on the run, we follow them close,
> And of bullets and steel, give them a dose.[125]

Hood's Texans had come into the line next to a South Carolina brigade. The newcomers, eying their neighbors, realized that picket duty hereabouts would not be quiet, once the Palmetto men were identified by the Yankees. South Carolina had been the first state to secede. She stood accused of starting the war, and the enemy had early begun to single out her citizens to make them pay for it. Until battle commenced, hostilities would be reduced to a live-and-let-live status so far as the Texans and the blue-clad troops across from them were concerned; not so for soldiers from the state whose guns had fired the first shot at Fort Sumter.

But the South Carolinans, whose picket line began at our left [wrote one of the Texans],[126] their first rifle pit being within fifty feet of the last one of the First Texans, could make no terms whatever. The Federals charge them with being the instigators and beginners of the war, and, as I am informed, always exclude them from the benefit of truces between the pickets. It is certainly an odd spectacle to see the Carolinians hiding in the rifle pits and not daring to show their heads, while, not fifty feet away, the Texans sit on the ground playing poker, in plain view and within a hundred yards of the Yankees. Worse than all, the palmetto fellows are not even permitted to visit us in daylight, except in disguise—their new uniforms of gray always betraying them wherever they go. One of them who is not only very fond of, but successful at, the game of poker, concluded the other day to risk being shot for the chance of winning the money of the First Texas and, divesting himself of his coat, slipped over to the Texas pit an hour before daylight, and by sunrise was giving his whole mind to the noble pastime.

An hour later a keen-sighted Yankee sang out, "Say, you Texas Johnnies! ain't that fellow playing cards, with his back to a sapling, one of them d——d South Carolina secessionists? Seems to me his breeches are newer'n they ought to be." This direct appeal for information placed the Texans between the horns of a dilemma; hospitality demanded the protection of their guest—prudence, the observation of good faith toward the Yankees. The delay in answering obviated the necessity for it by confirming the inquirer's suspicions, and, exclaiming, "D——m him, I just know it is!" he raised his gun quickly to his shoulder and fired. The South Carolinian was too active, though; at the very first movement of the Yankee, he sprang ten feet and disappeared into a gulch that protected him from further assault.

The Union–South Carolina feud ran its bitter course through the destructive invasion of the state. While Sherman's army was approaching Columbia, the capital, soldiers, about to suit action to the words, sang:

> Hail Columbia, happy land,
> If I don't burn you, I'll be damned.

Rifles crackled at the bridges, stoutly defended by Blue cavalry fighting dismounted. Minty's carbines and Wilder's Spencers could hold them only a few hours. So fierce was the enemy pressure that Alexander's Bridge was left dismantled but not destroyed and Reed's unburned. Troopers swung into saddles and rode before Gray columns, splashing through fords between and beyond the spans, could cut them off. That afternoon and night all of Bragg's army but three divisions crossed Chickamauga Creek and thrust into the woods of the west bank.

Both sides, groping through the darkness, drew up their battle lines for the morrow's combat. Weary, grumbling men were somehow assembled by regiment, brigade, and division before they were allowed to wrap blankets around themselves and snatch some rest. The more rank, the less sleep. "Pap" Thomas paid for his general's stars by getting not a wink. No wonder he could not keep awake at the war council of the next night.

Dawn of September 19 revealed the two armies facing each other on a six-mile front. Although the lines at points were only a few hundreds yards apart, the shrouding woods still cloaked them with uncertainty.

Neither army knew the exact position of the other; none of the Federal commanders was aware that "seven-tenths of Bragg's army was on the west bank of the Chickamauga." It is probable that division commanders on either side hardly knew where their commands were, in the thick woods, let alone the other troops of their own army, or the troops of the hostile army.[127]

But one all-important fact soon became clear. Rosecrans, fathoming Bragg's design to turn his left and fling him into the mountain valleys, now stood athwart the roads to Chattanooga. Granger's Reserve Corps was on the march to Rossville to secure them. The

Army of the Cumberland could still be beaten back, though not shunted aside. Its line of retreat lay open.

Shots shattered the stillness of the woods. Thomas had sent two brigades forward in reconnaissance, and they had struck the enemy—dismounted troopers of Forrest's cavalry. The Battle of Chickamauga had begun. A private in the 10th Tennessee glanced skyward and saw an owl, flushed by the gunfire, attacked by three crows. "What a country!" he exclaimed. "Even the birds in the air fight!"

Forrest, as usual, fought all out, coolly and calculatingly—dashingly but not rashly except for the constant risk of his own life, testified to by the twenty-nine horses shot from under him during the war. One of them was lost in this battle. When the animal was hit, Forrest plugged the hole in its neck where arterial blood was spurting and rode to a point where he could find a new mount. As soon as he withdrew his finger, the horse fell dead.

As always, Forrest's horse artillery gave him close support. "The Wizard of the Saddle" often called for his guns to gallop into action in front of his cavalry skirmish line, and young John Morton, his battery commander, was happy to oblige.

From the first Morton had been a dashing gunner with a fondness for dressing the part. Once, like Yankee Doodle (he would not have liked the comparison), he stuck a feather in his cap and preened himself on it. Then he heard a grinning infantryman call out: "Pretty bird, I'll catch him a worm in the morning." Blushing, Morton plucked out the feather and rolled it in the dirt. As ignominious was the fate of a new uniform he was carrying in his blanket roll to be donned on his twenty-first birthday. Alas, just before that occasion the uniform was chewed up by a hungry mule.

It is hard to blame the gallant Morton for quoting a highly laudatory verse in his reminiscences.

> Of Forrest's brave artillery sons,
> John Morton was the chief,
> Who in the thunder of his guns
> Oft sought his soul's relief.

As Pelham of the West, may he
  Be hailed throughout the South!
His wartime eloquence, most free,
  Came from his cannon's mouth.

In him our Wizard found a man
  On whom he could rely;
And when his service first began,
  His fame was made on high.[128]

Now at Chickamauga Morton was letting his guns speak for him. The four 6-pounders and two 12-pound howitzers he called his "Bull Pups" barked and flamed, wreathed in smoke. Over their thunder a historically minded cannoneer harked back to the Revolution in a shout to the battery commander: "All right, Captain. We'll whip this fight, or Molly Stark's a widow!"

General Hill leveled his field glasses, observing the spirited behavior of the dismounted troopers and their guns.

"What infantry are those?" he asked.

"Bedford Forrest's cavalry," came the answer, and the General's jaw dropped. In Virginia he had made himself unpopular with the mounted army by declaring that he had never seen a dead man with spurs on. "No one," he later told Forrest, "can speak disparagingly of such troops as yours."

But Blue brigades that struck the cavalry line were too strong for it. Troopers gave ground, fighting. Only one man broke and ran for the rear. Forrest, wrathfully spurring after him, was barely persuaded by an aide not to pistol the fugitive. The Federals were close now. One of the Gray guns, its team down, was about to be captured. Forrest ordered four of his escort to dismount and harness in their horses, and the gun was pulled to safety.

Across the lines a Union battery swung off the road and went into position. A boy jumped from his seat on one of the caissons, shouldered his musket, and hurried forward to fight with the infantry. Johnny Clem was no artilleryman, and he was no longer beating a drum as he had at Shiloh.

Back in 1861, when Johnny tried to enlist, no regiment would take him. Both the 3rd Ohio and the 22nd Michigan turned him down. The former's colonel snorted that he "wasn't enlisting infants." John Lincoln Clem was only ten. Although there were drummer boys as young in both the Union and Confederate armies,

National Park Service

Johnny Clem

Johnny was short and light for his age—weighing only sixty pounds. But he would not give up. On the chance that the 22nd's mind might be changed, the youngster ran away from home and joined the Michiganders after they had marched too far to send him back readily.

They let him stay with the regiment and made him Company C's drummer. If the little fellow began to stumble from fatigue during long hikes, an officer would dismount and hoist him up in the saddle. One pictures him riding along gratefully, still beating out cadence on his slung instrument—a one-boy mounted band. Officers chipped in a private's thirteen dollars a month for him until he was put regularly on the payroll in May of 1863.

Musician Clem beat his drum expertly and fervently until a shell smashed it at Pittsburgh Landing. Thereupon he became "the Drummer Boy of Shiloh" but promptly abandoned his wrecked instrument for a musket, cut down to his size. "I did not like to stand and be shot at without shooting back," he said.

Now as he joined the infantry line at Chickamauga he had his chance. A Confederate colonel galloped down on him, saber upraised, shouting, "Surrender, you damned little Yankee!" Johnny raised his gun, shot him out of the saddle, and went forward. He had taken the first of his two war wounds, a shell fragment in the hip, when an enemy attack cut him off along with a number of comrades. As the prisoners were being herded to the rear, Johnny dropped in tall grass and played dead until he was able to crawl back to his own lines. While in the hospital, he was promoted to lance sergeant— at the age of twelve. "Think of a sixty-three-pound Sergeant, fancy a handful of a hero, and then read the 'Arabian Nights' and believe them," Taylor wrote.

Admiring Chicago ladies sent him a new uniform in which he posed proudly for his photograph, and Kate Chase, the Secretary's daughter, presented him with a silver medal. Johnny, not resting on laurels, served on. He was carrying dispatches for Thomas during the Atlanta campaign when a bullet shredded one of his ears and his pony was shot from under him.

After the war he sought admission to West Point, but inadequate schooling disqualified him. However, President Grant commissioned him a lieutenant in 1871, and then five feet tall, weighing 105 pounds, he joined the 24th Infantry as one of the army's shortest and smallest officers on record. Later transferring to the Quartermaster Corps, "the Drummer Boy of Shiloh" had risen to the ranks of major general when he retired in 1916.[129]

The tide of battle ebbed and flowed in sudden, bloody freshets, as it would all day. Confederate reinforcements rushed in, whooping the Rebel yell. Absalom Baird's Union division came in to counter them, but both it and Brannan's brigades it was backing were driven back in disorder.

Confusion was compounded in the smoke-filled woods. Reports, written days later, and the final battle maps, with their arrows marking advances and retreats, would bring clarity out of the chaos, somehow resolved that day. They would show the movements and ground of stubborn encounters between regiments and batteries, battalions and brigades, divisions and corps. "In obedience to orders the battery went into action. . . ." "The regiment was placed in position. . . ." "At 10 A.M., as ordered, the division moved forward. . . ." So run the reports. And the marvel is that in the maelstrom of combat—with mounted couriers and runners the only communication, except for the signalers and telegraph line that kept in touch with Chattanooga—with no vantage points from which generals could watch and direct—the marvel is that almost always those orders were received, understood, and gallantly obeyed.

McCook's Corps was at Crawfish Springs now and ready to throw in its weight. One of its divisions, Johnston's, was summoned in hot haste by Rosecrans to help Thomas on the left, hard pressed by the Confederate onslaught. The newcomers smashed in the flank of Liddell's division, and it reeled back with heavy losses.

The tide turned blue for a time. Crittenden's troops were drawn in, and more of McCook's. That long, hard march by XX Corps to reach the battleground was a lifesaver for the Army of the Cumberland. For all Bragg's army was now over the Chickamauga and fighting with terrific *élan*. Two Union corps could never have stood before it.

Fresh divisions of both sides, threading the forest, marched to the sound of the guns. Rifle fire and the boom of cannon, rising in crescendo, guided them to points of crisis. Again and again the balance was tipped by their coming, then restored, then swung back again.

Midafternoon, and John B. Hood, one sleeve limp, was leading his brigades in headlong advance. The time since Gettysburg was none too long to recover from an arm's shattering. But Hood con-

tinued to be the same doughty fighting man he had always been.
The pride of the Army of Northern Virginia was behind the des-
perate assault he launched against the divisions of Reynolds and
Van Cleve. They were hurled back, their line pierced. For a while
Hood's men held the vital Lafayette Road, but not for long. Negley's
Division, that spearhead Bragg had meant to lop off back at Pigeon
Mountain, charged cheering into action, along with part of Brannan's. It was the turn of the Texas and the other brigades to recoil
now and be driven. Men fought hand to hand in the dark woods,
while night blotted them blacker until gray uniforms could not be
distinguished from blue.

Even then some of them still fought on. It was quite dark when
General Preston Smith began to move his Confederate brigade
forward in support of another command. Since those troops were
falling back and blocking him, the General rode ahead to clear the
way. Yonder in the obscurity he came upon a line of men at a halt
and called out to identify them. It may have been his Southern voice
that betrayed him. The crimson flashes of a volley answered, and
the General and his aide fell dead. Following, Colonel A. J. Vaughan,
Jr., 13th Tennessee, of Smith's Brigade, almost suffered the same
fate when he questioned a Union soldier. The man fired but missed,
and was killed by files at the Colonel's side. Quickly the dead blue-
coat's regiment, the 77th Pennsylvania, believing itself surrounded,
surrendered and was herded to the rear as prisoners, though numbers escaped in the darkness.[130]

Clashing of battle lines, collision of columns, attack and repulse.
They sketch the conflict only in broad outline. It is the individual
soldier and his deeds, apart from the general action, that bring it
to vivid life. Reports can seldom dwell on them, though citations
and the invaluable diaries do. Otherwise, merging into the mass,
they vanish.

Of such are stories of the outcome of some of those premonitions
that preyed on men before Chickamauga.

Bob Stout, Company H, 1st Tennessee, had so surely sensed he
was about to die that he refused rations and distributed his keep-

sakes to friends to send home to his family. Yet all next morning he went unscathed. During a lull in an enemy cannonade, a messmate called over to him: "Bob, you weren't killed, as you expected." At that very moment a gun across the lines banged, and a solid shot disemboweled the self-doomed soldier.[131]

A like warning had obsessed Johnny Green, 9th Kentucky Infantry, C.S.A., and small wonder, for Johnny had been close to death often enough to know its face. Murfreesboro had left such bloody gaps in the ranks of the 1st Kentucky Brigade that when it mustered for General John C. Breckinridge after the battle, he sadly exclaimed, "My poor orphans!" Since then it had been known as the Orphan Brigade and had worn the name proudly.

The night before Chickamauga, when his strong presentiment of death seized him, Johnny Green had "offered up a prayer that the Lord would guide me and strengthen me and that when death came to me, it would find me gallantly doing my duty, that my first desire should be not that I might escape death but that my death should help the cause of right to triumph." Then he lay down to sleep peacefully. It was the devotion of such young soldiers that so long sustained the Lost Cause.

Undismayed, Johnny marched with his brigade into action in the Chickamauga woods. He saw comrades at his side cut down by the humming "minnie" balls: John Fightmaster, who would fight no more; Benjamin F. Butler, who would no longer have to disclaim relationship to the hated Northern general of that name; Flying Cloud, a Mohawk Indian chief. Death still passed him by. At last he all but kept his rendezvous. In a furious charge against a Blue battery he was struck in the groin with such force by a canister ball that he was knocked flat on his back. Trembling with shock, he groped for the wound—found only the missile that had ripped into his pocket and been stopped by his wallet's steel clasp—struggled to his feet and limped back into the fray.[132]

It may be that Union Brigadier W. H. Lytle, with his poet's sensitivity, felt a presentiment of death. His poem, "Anthony and Cleopatra," was popular, and men recalled lines of it on Chickamauga's second day.

I am dying, Egypt, dying;
Hark! the insulting foeman's cry.
They are coming! quick, my falchion.
Let me front them ere I die. . . .

A Confederate sharpshooter spotted the mounted officer, high ranking and likely a general, since he was directing a large body of bluecoats. A man could not ask a better target, better even than a color-bearer or the cannoneers of a troublesome battery. A long shot—estimated range about 800 yards—but not too far for a picked marksman with a first-rate weapon. He rested his finely made English Whitworth rifle, squinted through its telescopic sight, squeezed the trigger. General Lytle toppled from his saddle, killed by a bullet that was swifter than and as deadly as Cleopatra's asp.

Thus death or wounds met them in the woods. Private Fletcher of the 5th Texas, a bullet through one foot, staggered and dropped out of the attacking line. He hopped back to a field hospital where they lifted him onto a table. A surgeon probed the wound with his finger, muttered something about gangrene, and prepared to amputate. Fletcher drew back his leg with the good foot, kicked the doctor away, and hobbled out of the hospital. Heroic treatment with acid prevented gangrene. Fletcher recovered, transferred to the cavalry, and served through the rest of the war.[133]

"My command behaved with great gallantry." So read the reports, with only here and there mention of a few that failed in their duty or played the coward.

On both days of that jumbled nightmare of conflict in the forest, valor had need to be conspicuous to be noted. Such was that of Bugler William J. Carson, Company E, 1st Battalion, 15th U.S. Infantry. He made the woods ring with the calls he sounded: "Forward" and "Rally" and "To the Color," and a whole brigade answered their summons. Not content to act as musician, Carson, whose conduct would win him a Medal of Honor, plunged into action with both sword and musket.[134]

Also of the 15th was Sergeant John Marrs, one of those fine old

Regular noncoms who are the backbone of an army. Steadily, rifle at right shoulder, the sergeant covered his company's rear as it fell back under enemy attack. When the captain called for a rally, Marrs saluted as smartly as on the drill field and asked, "Does the commanding officer know we are out of ammunition?" Fix bayonets then, he was ordered, and charge. He was killed in the forefront of the surging wave of steel.[135]

Again and again exhaustion of ammunition inspired deeds of heroism like that of Sergeant William G. Whitney, Company B, 11th Michigan Infantry.

As the enemy were about to charge [declares the citation], this officer went outside the temporary Union works among the dead and wounded enemy and at great exposure to himself cut off and removed their cartridge boxes, bringing the same within the Union lines, the ammunition being used with good effect in again repulsing the attack.

Sergeant Axel H. Reed, Company K, 2nd Minnesota Infantry, under arrest for some infraction of discipline, could have stayed safely in the rear. When the firing began, he broke arrest, found a rifle, and fought bravely through the two-day battle. Though as a result charges against him were dropped, he still did not consider that he had vindicated himself. At Missionary Ridge he led his company, its officers killed and wounded, and lost an arm, but declined discharge and remained on active duty to the end of the war.

More lines shine bright on the honor rolls. "Saved the regimental colors." "Single-handed, between the combatants, captured an armed and mounted Confederate major." "Seized the colors of a retreating regiment and led it into the thick of the attack." "Held out with a small force against the advance of superior numbers." "Rallied enough fugitives to hold the ground under heavy fire long enough to effect the escape of wagon trains and batteries." Many other deeds of heroism went unsung.

The night of the nineteenth again staged a frustrating game of hide-and-seek through the dark woods for men almost too exhausted to go through its motions. Lost units to be found, organizations to be regrouped. It was eleven o'clock before the last sputtering of gunfire dwindled into silence.

At last bivouacs among the trees and in the clearings. Cold rations and calling of rolls to take count of the day's grim toll. Searching stretcher-bearers in gray picked up their own wounded along with injured men in blue, many of those now lying within the Confederate lines. Utter weariness postponed burial of the dead. Not-to-be-neglected cleaning of fouled rifles and cannon. Requisition for ammunition that would be needed on the morrow. Then shivering men wrapped themselves in blankets and lay down in exhausted sleep for what remained of the night.

Late in the Union lines sounded the thud of axes where breast-works of logs and rails were being thrown up. And at General Rose-crans' headquarters in the Widow Glen's house sober voices rose in a midnight council of war.

Lines of fatigue creased the general's sensitive face. Perhaps some of them were smoothed a trifle by a sense of relief. Parts of his command had stood on the brink of catastrophe too often this past week, and only the grace of God, manifested by the enemy's delays, had saved them. His corps had been assembled in the nick of time. Today, blocking the roads to Chattanooga, they had fought off the foe's most determined assaults. Inevitably there must be another battle tomorrow. By then Bragg might have received further re-inforcements of Longstreet's Corps that were on the way, as Wash-ington had warned. Were the lines on Rosecrans' face deepened again by presentiment, not of death, but of disaster?

By his side sat his efficient Chief of Staff, General Garfield, who would ride from tomorrow's field on into the House of Representa-tives and thence into the White House. The three corps commanders faced them. Thomas, grave and stolid, nodding in his chair; Critten-den of the pensive eyes and neat mustache; bluff, ruddy McCook, of the family whose service in various wars won it the name of "the Fighting McCooks." Also present and given due deference was a civilian: Assistant Secretary of War Charles A. Dana, listening with the keen perception of a good newspaperman to every word said.

A great stone ear is carved on the wall of a room in England's Westminster Cathedral, where Parliament once met. An orifice is pierced through the ear to an adjoining chamber where the King might sit and hear the legislature's deliberations. Secretary Dana symbolized that ear whose auditory canal ran to Washington through the telegraph lines, kept humming by the Administration's observer.

As discussion of battle plans dragged on, Thomas's eyes closed, and he fell fast asleep. When Rosecrans asked him directly what course he would recommend, he would come awake, straighten up, and make an answer, always the same one: "I would strengthen the left." The commanding general's plaintive inquiry, "Where are we going to take it from?" drew no reply. That was an army not a corps commander's problem. Thomas napped again.

At last the talk ended. To liven up its somewhat gloomy tone McCook was asked to provide a finale by rendering his favorite ballad. His hearty voice almost raised the rafters of the Widow Glen's little house, as he sang "The Hebrew Maiden." [136]

Back at the small station called Catoosa Platform travel-grimed troops in gray detrained on the afternoon of the nineteenth—two more brigades of Longstreet's Corps with the General himself but no artillery. Trains bringing the batteries were still bumping along over the strap iron several days behind. Longstreet would have to go into battle without trusted Colonel Alexander and his battalion— must borrow guns from the Army of Tennessee.

The big, bearded leader glanced quickly about him. No officer from Bragg's staff was on hand to meet him, nor had guides been provided. "Old Pete" waited two hours for a following train with horses aboard. Still no guides. He and two members of his staff mounted and rode to find Bragg.

Darkness descended on the woods. Although the moon was bright, beams filtered only fitfully through the foliage. The little cavalcade lost its way. Ahead, blurred shadows moved among the trees. Longstreet reined in and called out, asking to what regiment the men belonged. A shouted number answered him. Yankee twang or not, that was enough. If the men had been Confederates, they would have given their commander's name. Southern units were usually thus designated, not numerically, as in the Union Army.

The three riders were so close to the enemy outpost that if they had wheeled to gallop away, they would have made perfect targets.

Longstreet solved the problem with ready wit, for he was never better than when peril forced him to think quickly.

"Let us ride down a little way to find a better crossing," he said aloud.

The outpost let the officers move off without disturbance, and presently Longstreet and his companions were under cover and safe. But it had been a narrow escape.[137]

Death in the dark forest, which had marked down General Smith, had passed over General Longstreet. Because a key corps commander was spared, the fortunes of tomorrow's battle would take a sudden turn, and many more men would die.

About eleven o'clock Longstreet's search ended. Bragg, asleep in an ambulance, was wakened, doubtless without much ceremony. The General from the East was given orders he had come so far to receive. He would have command of the army's left wing, whose attack would follow an assault at daybreak by the right wing under Polk. The battle plan was unchanged from that for the past day and held greater promise now that Longstreet had come. Envelop and crumple up the Union left. Roll its remnants back into the mountains to the south and destroy the rest of the weakened Army of the Cumberland before any help could come to it.

The conference concluded, Longstreet took a few hours' rest at the headquarters campfire. Then he rode back to his own command through the Chickamauga woods. Hoofbeats were muffled in confines that seemed airless and were growing damper. There would be fog tomorrow.

CHAPTER 10

"Hell Broke Loose in Georgia"

Night of September 19 merged almost imperceptibly into dawn of the twentieth, exchanging a black cloak for a gray one as fog smothered the woods. After the first stirrings of wakening, mess, and standing to arms, formations waited quietly under the hush of the heavy haze. There was still no sound of firing. The thoughts of soldiers turned inward.

With battle imminent, some may have hummed the tune of the war song about hell breaking loose in Georgia. It would suit the occasion. Through the head of a little-schooled recruit in an Alabama regiment ran a reflection he would soon scrawl in a letter to his sister: "Have all ways crave to fite a lit[tle] gust to no what it is to go in to a bat tle." That craving was about to be all too well satisfied, and he would be willing to follow his letter home.[138]

Riflemen took thought to their ammunition. They filled their cartridge boxes and stuffed extra rounds, when they could get them, into their pockets. If fighting today were as heavy as yesterday, they would need and use every bullet. When the last one was expended ... they felt for the scabbarded bayonets at their belts, a gesture that was part reassurance, part apprehension. Standing behind a tree and shooting was a lot better. An ugly weapon, cold steel, especially when it was wielded by the fellow in front of you.

Unworried about ammunition failure, Wilder's mounted infantrymen checked their Spencer repeaters and the extra seven-shot cylinders in their pouches. The volume of fire the Spencers delivered could stop an attack with rounds to spare. They gave a man con-

fidence. One Indianan felt it strongly, as he remembered vivid
moments in yesterday's combat.

The rebels advance in full view up the slope. Now they open fire
and raise the infernal rebel yell, and charge us on a sweeping run!
Our retreating men are hardly out of their way when we open fire
on them, and such slaughter as our Spencers worked would surely
delight the worst demons in Hades. A sheet of flame extends from
our works to the advancing foe. The crashing of our guns is as if
the foundations of the earth were being crushed. The enemy falls
as grain before the advancing reaping machine. In two minutes
there is not a man of those three splendid lines seen upon his feet
in our front.[139]

On the other side of the front George Cagle of the W. P. Lane
Rangers may have been longing for one of those all-week-shooting
guns of the Yankees, while he cleaned his single-shot musket. Well,
a man made do with what he had, and if he picked up and loaded
the guns of fallen comrades, he could stage a right handsome lot of
firing all by himself.

Northern woodsmen looked over the tops of log breastworks they
had built last night along Thomas's front. That had taken hard
work, but it was considerable comfort being behind them. If a whole
slew of Johnny Rebs came storming out of the woods, those stout
barricades could keep the line from bending and breaking.

A Confederate colonel woke, like many another man, with a
sick feeling in the pit of his stomach. Nerves taut, he may have
smoothed the gold braid on his uniform's sleeves and reminded
himself he must prove worthy of his rank and responsibilities—
a resolution that would not hold for him. The battle today would
see him galloping toward the rear, calling for help for his regiment.
And his ears would ring with the taunts of the gray ranks through
which he rode. "What regiment? Why ain't you with them, then,
you cowardly puppy? Take off that coat and those chicken guts.
Ain't you ashamed of yourself?" [140]

Across the lines an Indiana rifleman fondly reread his wife's latest
letter. Folding it carefully, he put it in the left breast pocket of his

blouse with the packet of eight previous missives, still treasured. In a few hours a bullet, striking him in the chest, would be stopped by the layers of letters before it reached his heart. When Correspondent Taylor heard the story, he asked the women readers of his paper: "Have you been making such a shield, dear lady, for anybody? Take care that it does not lack one letter of being bulletproof."

Chaplains in gray or blue moved among the men. Now, in prelude to battle, came the moment when they could most worthily serve their high calling. Confessions were heard; letters and keepsakes for families entrusted to them by men who knew this day might be their last. Faithful ministers, most of them, filling their difficult role: "To mingle with the men, and share in their frolics as well as their sorrows, without losing self-respect; to be with them and yet not of them; to get at their hearts without letting them know it."

Among the few not fit to wear the cross was a Union chaplain who studded all his talk with profanity for the sake of being considered a hail-fellow-well-met. The day before this battle almost all his regiment had signed a petition demanding his resignation. Before it could be acted upon, he redeemed himself nobly. During the fighting he was at the hottest parts of the front, carrying water to parched soldiers; through the nights he toiled with the surgeons. Then there was the visting Confederate dominie who deemed it his duty to go into action with the 1st Tennessee but whose nerve failed under fire. He rode forward, exhorting the men to be brave, aim low, and kill the Yankees as they would wild beasts. "Remember, boys," he shouted, "that he who is killed will sup tonight in Paradise." A soldier hallooed back, "Well, parson, you come along and take supper with us." At that instant a shell burst close. The exhorter put spurs to his steed and "limbered to the rear," followed by the Tennesseans' yell: "The parson isn't hungry, and never eats supper." [141]

Preparing for the second day of battle, artillerymen scowled as they harnessed, hitched, and limbered. Action in these woods was the very devil. You had no decent field of fire unless you were lucky enough to go into position at the edge of one of the few clearings or on a rise of ground. Driving six-horse teams and careening carriages through gaps in the close-spaced trees and the clutching underbrush was a feat that called for circus riders, but the farm boys on the backs of the near horses had to manage it. In this maze of a forest a battery suddenly found enemy riflemen on its flanks and even in its rear. Your own infantry support, if you had any, might melt away. Whistling bullets from behind the tree trunks, and cannoneers slumped beside the wheels and over the trail. Lead dropped the horses bringing up the limbers. If there were enough animals still on their feet, hook up, pull out, and save the guns. If not, try to fight off the foe with rammer staff and handspike until your own infantry could come to the rescue, or suffer the disgrace of capture of your guns.

The conflict ahead was no pleasant prospect for artillery. Yesterday's actions forecast it, and today's would prove even darker than expected, especially for gunners in blue.

Dawn, then sunrise of Sunday, September 20, 1863, and still a Sabbath quiet at Chickamauga.

Longstreet had been given his orders in person. On an earlier visit to Bragg's headquarters Polk had "received a verbal order to attack the enemy at daylight," and so acknowledged.[142] Polk directed that order be transmitted to his subordinate commanders, but "a courier sent to General Hill, after searching for the general through the night, returned about daylight, saying that he could not find him."[143] Hill, finally apprised by one of his major generals at seven-twenty-five, allowed his men to finish eating the rations they had just cooked. Bragg rode storming up, first to Hill, then to Polk. There were explanations—which should never have to be made or be accepted in any army. Hill's: No orders till now. (But knowing there must be battle today, he had not checked to find out why none had come.) Polk's: His courier had failed to reach Hill. (But no other couriers had been sent when the first one did not return promptly with acknowledgment of receipt of orders.)

The fog, still dense, hindered movement of troops into attack positions. Not until two hours later did the racket of battle rise along the lines.

Like a string of giant firecrackers igniting each other, battle exploded from the Confederate right toward the left. Cracking carbines of Forrest's dismounted cavalrymen set off flashing volleys of Breckinridge's Division. A sheet of flame spread along Cleburne's front. Behind billowing clouds of smoke edged with crimson the Gray lines rolled forward.

To General Rosecrans the direction of the din of firing was confirmation of the estimate he had made when he watched the enemy moving into position. Bragg's plan today, as yesterday, was to cave in the Union left. The words of the drowsy Thomas at the war council last night, "I would strengthen the left," must have echoed in Rosecrans' mind, along with his own query, "Where are we going to take it from?" The answer now was clear: From your right, General.

Negley's Division and other troops, ordered over from that flank, came none too soon. Cleburne's assault and part of Breckinridge's had been halted by fire from the Union defenses; those toilsome log breastworks were paying off. But the latter general's right circled the barricades and thrust on past the Lafayette Road, threatening to take Thomas's line in the rear.

"American troops cannot stand flank and rear attacks," General Hill would write.[144] But "Pap" Thomas's men could and did, then and later. With the help of reinforcements from the Union right, surging up just in time, they beat back the enemy.

Now that vital artery to Chattanooga, the Lafayette Road, was in danger. Stewart's Gray Division struck for it and drove Reynolds's and Brannan's Blue ones beyond the road. Union artillery, heavily supported by infantry, brought salvation. A storm of shells pounded the Confederate front and both flanks. The assailants fell back over their mounting dead.

With Stewart already in action, it was approaching the turn of the rest of Longstreet's wing in the progressive order of attack. Although Polk on the right had not broken through, he made it

GENERAL BRAXTON BRAGG

MAJOR GENERAL
WILLIAM STARKE ROSECRANS

LIEUTENANT GENERAL
JAMES LONGSTREET

MAJOR GENERAL JOSEPH HOOKER

LIEUTENANT GENERAL
LEONIDAS POLK

GENERAL WILLIAM TECUMSEH
SHERMAN

GENERAL PHILIP HENRY SHERIDAN

GENERAL ULYSSES SIMPSON GRANT

By A. R. Waud, from Brown, *The Mountain Campaign in Georgia*

The first gun at Chickamauga. The Confederates open fire on Union cavalry, which had begun the destruction of Reed's Bridge.

Photograph by Stanrich Studio

Diorama of Snodgrass Hill, where "the Rock of Chickamauga" made his stand

By Vizetelly, from *The London Illustrated News*

The wounding of General Hood at the Battle of Chickamauga

Thomas's men repulsing the Confederate charge at Chickamauga

Harper's Weekly

A troop train passing through a cut on the Louisville & Nashville Railroad.

Harper's Weekly

Bridging the Tennessee River under Confederate fire from Lookout Mountain

Harper's Weekly

Harper's Weekly

The destruction of Union wagons by Confederate Cavalry, October 2, 1863

Pulling into position

Edwin Forbes, *Thirty Years After*

Harper's Weekly

General view of Chattanooga and Union encampments from the Union Signal Station, Cameron Hill. The Confederate forces were beyond the belt of timber.

The charge near Orchard Knob, November 24, 1863

From *The Confederate Soldier in the Civil War*, edited by Ben La Bree

Hooker capturing Lookout Mountain

The storming of Missionary Ridge

easier for his colleague when so much strength was drawn from the Union right to meet his offensive. And the gods of battle were about to proffer General Longstreet as splendid a gift as any commander could ask.

The place of bestowal was the Brotherton House. Chickamauga redeemed that little log cabin from oblivion. It stands restored today on its clearing. One of those historic buildings on Civil War battlefields, ranging from the Henry House of Bull Run to the McLean House at Appomattox, the Brotherton cabin is a monument to stirring and memorable moments. Surely it long remained etched deep in the memories of Lieutenant General Longstreet, C.S.A., and Brigadier General Thomas J. Wood, U.S.A.

Wood, "an old regular from Kentucky, solid and dependable, with a first-rate combat record," [145] commanded a division holding the line through the field where the cabin stood. His skirmishers were actively engaged but not hard pressed. If a determined enemy attack developed from the thick woods over there, Wood must meet it with his full strength, for he was covering a stretch of the road to Chattanooga.

Disaster for the Union Army was triggered by two of those happenstances upon which the outcome of a battle may turn. One was a report by a staff officer that went unchecked; the other was the fact that General Wood was smarting from a reprimand.

Captain Sanford C. Kellogg, aide-de-camp, riding along the front, believed he saw a gap in the Union line. He galloped to General Rosecrans and reported that Reynolds's right was exposed.

Rosecrans failed to check that report. In the supposed emergency he rushed a courier to Wood with a fateful order. "The general commanding directs that you close up on Reynolds as fast as possible and support him." [146]

Wood, frowning, read the dispatch. A few days earlier his corps commander had dressed him down for failure to occupy a position at Wauhatchie, and Wood had protested that compliance would have been "blind obedience to orders" (according to a later statement by Rosecrans).

The directive that Wood was reading now was definite and immediate. All right, if blind obedience was required, he'd give it. What if the only way he could reach and support Reynolds was by marching to the rear of Brannan's Division on his, Wood's, left? That was just where Brannan was, albeit slightly withdrawn in echelon—which probably had led to Kellogg's misapprehension of a gap.

And what, Wood questioned, about leaving his own front open, though the firing had died down? Well, it was a headquarters responsibility to close up the hole he would leave with other troops.

"As fast as possible," the order said. Wood turned to his staff. To the rear, march. By the left flank. At the double-quick.

Now there really was a gap in the Union line, and a big one.

Turning a flank, shattering enemy lines with enfilading fire—working around and smashing into the rear—that was the ideal attack. Polk had been vainly striving to achieve it for the destruction of the Union left. The order of battle for Longstreet called for a less promising and more costly frontal assault.

Back under cover of the woods "Old Pete" had massed to deliver it. He launched it just as Wood's rear brigade was pulling out. Gray ranks burst through the trees into Brotherton's clearing. The gap was a vacuum sucking them in, accelerating the charge. The Rebel yell shrilled skyward as the war gods presented General Longstreet with their gift of a breakthrough ready made.

Twice at Gettysburg his troops had sought to bludgeon their way through Blue lines and been bloodily, though barely, denied. Here there was nothing to bar them. A lesser general, suspecting a ruse, might have checked and slowed his men's headlong rush through such a startlingly open avenue. James Longstreet let them go, brigade after brigade bursting out of the woods, plunging into the gap, wedging it wider.

On they came like an angry flood. They struck McCook's three remaining brigades [six brigades under Sheridan, Davis, and Wilder], the remnants of the Federal right. Under the daring personal exertions of McCook and Davis, they made a gallant but vain resistance. The massed lines of the enemy swarmed around their flanks. Pouring through the opening made by Wood's withdrawal, they struck his last brigade as it was leaving the line. It was slammed back like a door, and shattered. Brannan on Wood's left, was struck in front and flank. His right was flung back; his left stood fast. Sheridan, hastening to the left with two brigades, was called back, and rushed to the rescue. His little force stayed the storm for a time. Wave after wave of Confederates came on; resistance only increased the multitude. Brannan's artillery, attacked in the flank, rushed to the rear for clearer ground, and, with the Confederates at their heels, suddenly plunged into Van Cleve marching to the aid of Thomas. Disorder ensued; effective resistance was lost.[147]

For Longstreet had not only seized his opportunity but brilliantly exploited it. Keep to the left, his orders said. But he had smashed opposition there into chaotic turmoil. Instead, he turned right to deal destruction to the remainder of the Union army.

He was paying a tax on the gift of the gap. Hood was down, his right leg so terribly mangled that it had to be amputated on the field; none who saw him carried to the rear would have believed that indomitable man would fight through the rest of the war, one arm withered and an artificial leg in the stirrup. In the wake of the advance a deep ditch overflowed with bodies in gray, slaughtered by spurting Spencers and spreading canister. But no general could grudge the price of victory, seemingly so overwhelming by mid-afternoon.

And the toll taken of the enemy mounted high. "I have never seen the Federal dead lie so thickly on the ground, save in front of the sunken wall at Fredericksburg," D. H. Hill declared. The trophies, too, mounted toward an impressive total in battle flags and prisoners; wagons and ambulances in great numbers; large quantities of ammunition and stores; 15,000 small arms and 51 cannon.

The Union artillery had laid down three sides of what in later wars would be called a box barrage on Stewart's Division, shattering its drive for the Lafayette Road. Yesterday Captain Ambrose Bierce of the Topographical Engineers had watched Blue batteries open on another threatening Confederate attack and had chronicled their devastating fire with a pen as apt for words as maps.

After some hours of close engagement my brigade, with foul pieces and exhausted cartridge boxes, was relieved and withdrawn to the road to protect several batteries of artillery—perhaps two dozen pieces—which commanded an open field in the rear of our line. Before our weary and virtually disarmed men had actually reached the guns the line in front gave way, fell back behind the guns and went on, the Lord knows whither. A moment later the field was grey with Confederates in pursuit. Then the guns opened fire with grape and canister and for perhaps five minutes—it seemed an hour— nothing could be heard but the infernal din of their discharge and nothing seen through the smoke but a great ascension of dust from the smitten soil. When it was all over, and the dust cloud had lifted, the spectacle was too dreadful to describe. The Confederates were still there—all of them, it seemed—some almost under the muzzles of the guns. But not a man of all those brave fellows was on his feet, and so thickly were they covered with dust that they looked as if they had been clothed in yellow.

"We bury our dead," said a gunner grimly, though doubtless all were afterward dug out, for some were partly alive.[148]

It was the turn of the Federal artillery for burial when Longstreet's brigades came boiling through the gap. One battery after another was engulfed and submerged. Taken in front, flanks, and rear, for a time they blasted back Gray waves with double-shotted canister. Some, while there still was an aisle of escape, bugled up the limbers. Under a hail of bullets, toppling the teams, carriages crashed to a halt upon a heap of thrashing horses, tangled in bloody harness. Artillerymen tried again with their caisson limbers. Sometimes they managed to hook on the pieces and pull them out.

Guns were lost, regained by infantry charging back to the rescue, lost again. Battery D, 1st Michigan Light Artillery, was caught by a sudden attack as it was about to change position. Captain Josiah W. Church shouted, "Action rear!" He beat back his assailants, then switched fire to a Rebel battery and silenced it. But the Michiganders and their supports could not hold their ground against a renewed onslaught. A final volley of double canister stemmed it a few minutes. Church, wounded, helped his cannoneers manhandle four pieces off through the bushes. They succeeded in limbering three of them under a galling fusilade. With drivers whipping teams into a gallop, the battery joined a group of reserve artillery on a ridge. It found no respite there. Gray infantry stormed it. Sweeping volleys dropped gunners, slaughtered horses. Battery D had only enough animals left to pull one 12-pounder howitzer into the stream of retreat to Chattanooga.[149] What if a Rebel general later acknowledged it had cost him several hundred men to take those cannon? Nothing is full solace for a battery that loses its guns.

In a hot duel with Confederate artillery, Battery H, 4th U.S. Artillery, had one gun disabled. Expending all its ammunition, it withdrew to find its caissons and refill. Scarcely was it back in action when all the horses of the right gun team were shot down. Part of the crew of another piece were killed or wounded, the pole of its limber broken, its horses jammed in an uncontrollable mass. Lieutenant Harry C. Cushing and two of his men struggled to haul the gun from the field. Their utmost strength could not move it, and Gray riflemen were close on them. Just before the two last guns were overrun, they were limbered—drivers unhitched and dragged clear a dead wheel horse—the remnant of the battery galloped away.[150]

The 8th Indiana Battery, which had twenty-one horses killed or disabled on the first day and thirty-five on the second, was charged from the right and rear. It lost all six of its guns and limbers and most of its caissons.[151] Four of its abandoned guns were recovered by the 27th Illinois Infantry, who paid for it when a runaway caisson team dashed over its line of prone riflemen, injuring several.[152]

Captain Eli Lilly's 18th Indiana Battery, which had done that fine shooting across the Tennessee River, went into action amply gunned but underofficered. With half the battery Lilly fought a rear-guard action on the extreme right. A sergeant commanded the other half, four mountain howitzers, detached to another part of the field. Fending off a heavy attack, the little cannon boomed and recoiled in rapid fire, doing as much execution as pieces twice their size. Then their infantry support shrank away, leaving the gunners to fight alone. (How Lilly, when he heard of it, would rail against "the miserable shoulder-strapped poltroons who allowed the support to

run away from the pieces in the hour of danger!" His men with
chevrons would do honor to commissions.)

Sergeant Eli W. Anderson, commanding, reeled and fell, severely
wounded. Another sergeant, William B. Edwards, took over. In the
face of that close-pressed attack about to flood over his howitzers, he
brought off three of them and the fourth's limber.[153]

Longstreet's assault was rolling up the Union left and reinforcements from its right that had come to bolster it against Polk's prior
attack. Panic spread as the ordered Blue battle lines were struck
in flank and rear. Brave men died where they stood, threw up their
hands in surrender, or joined in headlong retreats. It was not only
the irresolute and the craven who broke and ran from that stricken
field, from a battle that seemed hopelessly lost.

The sword that had severed the Army of the Cumberland swung
right and left. General Rosecrans, with McCook and Crittenden,
in the segment south of the breakthrough point, galloped with staff
and escort along disintegrating lines, vainly trying to build them up
into a shield. A storm of musketry and canister barred him from
reaching Thomas's Corps on the left. "All became confusion. No
order could be heard above the tempest of battle. With a wild yell
the Confederates swept on far to their left. They seemed everywhere
victorious. Rosecrans was borne back in the retreat." [154]

Assistant Secretary of War Dana rode past at that heartbreaking
moment. He saw Rosecrans, a devout Roman Catholic, raise his right
hand to brow and breast and said to himself: "Hello! If the general
is crossing himself, we are in a desperate situation." [155]

To Chief of Staff Garfield, Rosecrans bore the look of a man at
the very limit of nervous endurance. There was no persuading him
to remain on the field and make further attempts to organize resistance. That, he was convinced, could now be achieved only at
Chattanooga. It was a broken spirit that quit the field. Indeed, when
the General reached the town on the Tennessee, he would have to
be helped from his horse into headquarters.

There was no stemming the rout. An officer attempted to halt
a fleeing soldier who charged him, bayonet leveled; when the officer
held his ground, the man turned back but only to find another ave-

nue of escape. Roads channeled torrents of fugitives—wounded or whole—artillery carriages, ambulances, baggage wagons. And through the jetsam of defeat rode the commander of the Army of Cumberland and two of his three corps commanders, Crittenden and McCook. The day was lost. The next stand must be made at Chattanooga.

Secretary Dana hastened to a telegraph station. The wires to Washington throbbed with his dispatch, which began:

"My report today is of deplorable importance. Chickamauga is as fatal a name in our history as Bull Run." [156]

"Come on, boys, we've got the damyankees on the run!" The shout Fighting Joe Wheeler would echo in the Spanish-American War spread through the battlefield of Chickamauga.

They kept them on the run. The battle flag of the 2nd Battalion, Alabama Legion, pierced eighty-three times, was carried on forward, its tattered folds flaunted close on the heels of the fleeing Federals.

As the pursuit pressed the enemy hard, one company of Gray foot longed for horses, a longing it had never been able to overcome. The W. P. Lane Rangers had originally been cavalry and eventually would happily return to that arm. Meanwhile, they were serving through an interval as infantry and liking it not at all. The former horsemen hated the long marches through wet pine woods, the trees so thick that they were "warranted airproof." Feet seemed to develop almost solid blisters, and shoulders were worn raw by the straps from which hung arms and equipment: rifle, cartouche box, canteen, a blanket which, when sodden, felt as if it added thirty pounds— to say nothing of a heavy sack of rations, a knapsack, and sixty rounds of ammunition "to keep her steady." Yet the Rangers refused to join the "wagon dogs"—shirkers who sneaked off to the wagon trains for rides. There were few stragglers in Hardee's Corps; that strict veteran insisted that his book on regulations and tactics be taken literally. Through the East Tennessee campaign the Texans lived up to their conception of the duty of a soldier: he fights like blue blazes when told to and runs like a wild turkey when he knows he's whipped. (Later, during the retreat from Chattanooga, the former cavalrymen decided they had had all they could take. By twos and threes they slipped off from Bragg's army and made their way back to the old outfit to climb on a horse again.) [157]

But today it was the Yankees who were doing the retreating. One of the Lane Rangers, George Cagle, saw a chance to speed the parting foe even though he lacked a horse. He picked up and loaded four or five abandoned muskets. What if one of them had belonged to a corpse in blue, a piece of hardtack gripped in rigid hand, a mouthful still between his teeth? The dead man didn't need his gun any more. Cagle lined up his armament close to hand—banged away —reloaded—loosed off one relay of rounds after another. While he shot he yelled, "Attention, Cagle's Battery. Make ready, load, take aim, fire!" [158]

General Longstreet was declaring exultantly, "They have fought their last man, and *he* is running." From where resistance was developing on his right, a distraught brigadier, Benning of Georgia, galloped up to report that his command was utterly destroyed and routed. Longstreet with that admirable calm of his faced the jittery officer and quietly asked:

"Don't you think you could find *one* man, General?"

"One man? I suppose I could."

Longstreet, straight-faced, ordered: "Go and get him and bring him here; then you and I and he will charge together. This is the sacred soil of Georgia, General, and we may as well die here as elsewhere."

Benning burst into laughter and rode off. Soon he swept by into action at the head of his rallied command.[159]

Toward their right the roar of battle still rose high. A remnant of the Army of the Cumberland was making a stand, probably a rear-guard action covering the retreat. Triumphant Gray ranks closed in.

CHAPTER 11

"Rock of Chickamauga"

General George H. Thomas, corps commander, was not far from being hemmed in on what had been the Union left and was now all the Union force remaining on the field. Indeed he was pent up much as he had been as a young lieutenant in a Monterrey street in the War with Mexico. Now, as then, the enemy closed in for the kill.

"No more dependable soldier for a moment of crisis existed on the North American continent, or ever did exist." [160] For just such an occasion seemingly had been cast the mold in which his character and career were formed. Steady, utterly unruffled except for his gray whiskers through which he kept running his fingers, he stood gauging the battle tide surging so strongly against him. No use asking again for reinforcements. Apparently he had received all he was going to get, for no more appeared. Constantly the Confederate concentration upon him increased; under what circumstances he did not yet know. He was not then aware of the disaster to the right and center of the Army of Cumberland.

Thomas and his corps stood fast and fought on. Brannan brought his battered troops up into line but so far to the right of Reynolds's that an appallingly empty space—enough for a whole division—lay between them. And Longstreet, eager as before to accept a gift from the war gods, was advancing toward that wide, inviting aperture, his men already within rifle range.

General Wood, U.S.A., had left one gap open today, and it would be long before he heard the last of it. Now he made amends by trying to plug another, potentially as perilous as the first—one through which the *coup de grâce* might have been dealt the third Union corps with the finality the other two had suffered. Wood rushed regiments toward the opening; it was too wide for them to span. August Willich's Brigade came in to fill it.

But the battle line, emerging from the trees toward the narrowing gap, wore blue. It might be reinforcements, some of McCook's men, after all. Thomas rode up and peered at the oncoming troops. "Wave all your flags," he told Wood's soldiers, "and let them see who you are, but if they open fire, let them have it; some of the Rebs are wearing blue here." [161] Then he galloped away.

That brigade in blue drew closer. Muskets leveled and crackled. A cloud of smoke rolled along the front. These were Longstreet's men in blue uniforms, spoils of some Union supply depot. Their color would have aroused the suspicions of defenders back in the Army of the Potomac who had seen the like from First Bull Run onward. Rebs in blue were strange to Wood's westerners. Even those who had heard Thomas's warning held their reply fire too long. They took another rattling volley that strewed the ground with dead and wounded. Then they staggered back blazing away, furious at seeming trickery, which was nothing more than an expedient demanded by the Confederate clothing shortage. However, the surprised Yankees recovered in time to reform in front of the Snodgrass cabin. Building a barricade of fence rails, they beat back the blue-clad enemy.

Thomas forged his lines in the shape of a horseshoe circling Snodgrass Hill. The bellows of battle blew it white-hot, and Longstreet and Polk hammered it mightily upon the anvil of the hill. They could not bend it. From left to right the divisions of Baird, Johnson, Palmer, Reynolds, Wood, and Brannan held.

A big man, George Thomas, six feet, two hundred pounds. Easy to spot on his charger through the battle smoke and riding where the rank and file could not miss seeing him—or feeling his eyes on them. Cool, completely unflurried, "a majestic presence." Soldiers, steadied and stirred, fight their best for such a general.

Jackson won his "Stonewall" at First Manassas on Barnard Bee's shout, "Look at Jackson's brigade; it stands like a stone wall!" In the desperate hours at Chickamauga no one is recorded as having acclaimed George H. Thomas as a rock. Neither the Indiana infantryman, who so aptly quoted Poe by the stagnant pool in the woods, nor any other was reminded of lines from Scott, no less apposite.

> Come one, come all!
> This rock shall fly
> From its firm place
> As soon as I.

Yet many men remembered Thomas, standing rocklike, and inevitably he would win his accolade, "the Rock of Chickamauga."

Gray regiments, flushed with earlier victory, assaulted again and again. Federal ammunition was running low.

For five long hours the shocks and carnage were as close and deadly as men could make them. Thomas often came within speaking distance of his men, and wherever the energy of the attack most endangered our line, he strengthened it with cannon and regiments drawn from points in less peril; and when the soldiers asked for more ammunition Thomas said: "Use your bayonets." [162]

Steel flashed as they used them, Ohio and Indiana and the rest. About four o'clock Longstreet drew off and asked for reinforcements —help that might well have carried the day if he had been given it. He was answered that the right wing was already so shattered that it could not aid him. Bragg unforgivably had kept no reserves at hand. Earlier, ready reserves might have maintained the momentum of Longstreet's breakthrough. Failing that, they could now have added weight enough to sweep from the field Thomas's Corps, whose ammunition had dwindled to the point where cartridge boxes of the dead must be scoured. Those rounds would last little longer.

But there were no reserves for the Confederate Army of Tennessee except for Cheatham's Division, which was not sent in until dusk— too late.

Four miles to the rear on the Chattanooga-Ringgold Road Major General Gordon Granger's Union Reserve Corps was posted that morning, with positive orders from Rosecrans to hold its position. Sunday's tolling church bells punctuated the din of conflict reverberating from the front where Polk was attacking.

Granger, a hard-bitten Regular, a man of impulsive action, turned, chafed to the core, to his Chief of Staff, General Fullerton.

"They are concentrating over there," he said. "That is where we ought to be."

Pulling at his beard, he paced up and down before his corps flag and burst out again: "Why the ——— does Rosecrans keep me here? There is nothing in front of us now. There is the battle." He pointed in the direction of Thomas's Corps.

Time ticked by. No orders. The two officers climbed a hayrick, and Granger peered through his field glasses. He jammed them back into their case and slid down, swearing.

"I am going to Thomas, orders or no orders!" he snapped.

Fullerton cautioned: "And if you go, it may bring disaster to the army and to you a court-martial."

Granger waved that aside with, "There's nothing in our front now but ragtag, bobtail cavalry. Don't you see Bragg is piling his whole army on Thomas? I am going to his assistance." [163]

The Reserve Corps marched.

The day had grown very warm, yet the troops marched rapidly over the narrow road, which was covered ankle-deep with dust that rose in suffocating clouds. Completely enveloped in it, the moving column swept along like a desert sandstorm. Two miles from the point of starting and three-quarters of a mile to the left of the road, the enemy's skirmishers and a section of artillery opened fire on us from an open wood. This force had worked around Thomas's left, and was then partly in his rear. Granger halted to feel them. Soon becoming convinced that it was only a large party of observation, he again started his column and pushed rapidly forward. [164]

Meanwhile Thomas faced the last stages of one of those classic stands so often chronicled in the history of warfare. Some have held, some been shattered, and others have ended in annihilation. One of the latter two fates appeared to be the destiny of this stand.

He was being attacked front and rear by the Gray divisions of Hindman and Bushrod Johnson. Cheatham, Preston, Breckinridge, and Buckner were driving in. Cleburne pushed forward his batteries, some of them manhandled, and blew Federal breastworks to bits. His infantry stormed them.

Still most of the Blue lines held. Musket barrels became so hot from firing they could barely be grasped for loading—when any "minnie" balls remained to ram in. Thomas rushed two cannon to a critical point with the order, "This position must be held." A colonel sent back word: "Tell General Thomas that we will hold the position or go to heaven from it!"

Then through cheering, converging Confederates ranks a courier from Forrest galloped up to Hill. General Forrest reports a strong enemy column approaching from Rossville. He is delaying it all he can, but it's still coming.

So Granger, regardless of orders, led his Reserve Corps onto the field of Chickamauga. He shook hands with Thomas, and there can never have been a heartier clasp.

Granger pointed to enemy assault lines mustering in a gorge and on the ridge. "Those men must be driven back," he said.

Thomas asked: "Can you do it?"

"Yes. My men are fresh, and they are just the fellows for that work. They are raw troops, and they don't know any better than to charge up there." [165]

A battery of 3-inch rifles barked, paving the way. While Granger watched, a shell fragment of enemy counterbattery fire ripping through his hat, his infantry charged.

With ringing cheers they advanced in two lines by double-quick— over open fields, through weeds waist-high, through a little valley, then up the ridge. The enemy opened on them first with artillery, then with a murderous musketry fire. When well up the ridge the men, almost exhausted, were halted for breath. They lay on the ground two or three minutes, then came the command, "Forward!" Brave, bluff old Steedman, with a regimental flag in his hand, led the way. On went the lines, firing as they ran and bravely receiving a deadly and continuous fire from the enemy on the summit. The

Confederates began to break and in another minute were flying down the southern slope of the ridge. In twenty minutes from the beginning of the charge the ridge had been carried.[166]

Union casualties had been heavy. A counterattack was being organized. Now the ammunition of Granger's Corps was running low, too. All its spare supply had been distributed to Thomas's men. An increasingly familiar sound ran along the lines: the rasp and click of bayonets being drawn from scabbards and fixed. Not much longer could the preponderant weight of the Army of Tennessee be withstood.

General Garfield, who had ridden back to the field, returned at a gallop to Rosecrans with the news of the gallant stand by Thomas's Corps. The commander of the Army of the Cumberland, reviving from despair, exclaimed, "This is good enough. The day isn't lost yet." He ordered stragglers halted and ammunition and rations sent to Rossville. Then he turned to the two corps commanders with him, McCook and Crittenden. "Gentlemen," he belatedly declared, "this is no place for you. Go at once to your commands at the front." [167]

The fabric of an army, rended, was long past stitches in time.

Couriers sped to Thomas with an order to fall back to Rossville. It was late afternoon before he was able to commence perilous withdrawals of his and Granger's troops. Fighting stubborn rear-guard actions, they retreated through an ever-narrowing avenue of escape.

Captain Bierce, who had marched up with Granger in the company of his brother, an officer in an Ohio battery, remembered how nearly the enemy cordon came to cutting them off.

Then away to our left and rear some of Bragg's people set up "the rebel yell." It was taken up successively and passed around to our front, along our right and in behind us again, until it seemed almost to have got to the place where it started. It was the ugliest sound that any mortal ever heard—to a mortal exhausted and unnerved by two days of hard fighting, without sleep, without rest, without food and without hope. There was, however, a space somewhere at the back of us across which that horrible yell did not long prolong itself; and through that we finally retired in profound silence and dejection, unmolested." [168]

Weary Blue columns trudged along a road lined by miles of wounded, debris of battle. Some of them hobbled or crawled along in pitiful efforts to keep up with a retreat that could not stay for them; others lay quiet by the roadside waiting for death. Darkness descended to disrupt order, mingling and mixing the various commands in what semed inextricable confusion.

At last they reached Rossville Gap in Missionary Ridge. Thomas as best he could organized and posted the remnants of his command to make another stand in the gap and behind it. Bragg's pursuit and assault must come as inevitably as tomorrow.

CHAPTER 12

Tarnished Stars

Braxton Bragg, as generals must, counted the cost of victory. Killed, 2,312; wounded, 14,674; missing, 1,468—out of a total of 66,326 troops engaged. So the casualties would stand when final reports came in.[169] They were, of course, still incomplete, but figures in hand were alarmingly high. To be balanced against them were a heavy bag of prisoners of war and considerable captures of invaluable weapons, ammunition, and supplies.

As for the Union casualties, he could only estimate them from dead on the battlefield and from the wounded and other prisoners. Losses in defensive action would normally be less than on the offensive—which was confirmed by official data. Out of a total of 53,919 engaged, the Army of Cumberland lost 1,657 killed and 9,756 wounded. It was the large number of missing, due to the break-through and encirclements, that brought the percentage of casualties on both sides to surprising equality—28 per cent.[170] So high a rate established Chickamauga as one of the bloodiest battles of the war.

Victory was undeniably Bragg's—a victory that had come very close to being a decisive one by the rout of two Union divisions and large segments of four more of McCook's and Crittenden's commands, with Thomas's Corps and Granger's Reserves finally driven from the field.

September 21 could well have been the day of decision that the twentieth had barely missed being. It was a badly battered Federal army that held Rossville Gap. At any moment an attack could be expected.

One after another his leading generals rode to Braxton Bragg—Longstreet, Forrest, Polk, and Hill—urging him to gather the fruits of victory now. Pursuit should be pressed, an assault delivered no later than this morning of the twenty-first. Bragg made the same reply to each. The army had suffered severely, he pointed out. His exhausted men needed food, water, and ammunition. Critical hours sped past, and no action was taken beyond a few cavalry demontrations.

Polk and Hill, already in Bragg's black book, went unheeded. Forrest's advice was resented as presumptuous. It would prompt an order from his angered superior to turn over his command to Wheeler, and the cavalryman would erupt in the blazing fury of that denunciation related in an earlier chapter. If Bragg finally would listen to anyone, it would be Longstreet, and that tenacious leader tried hard to persuade him before the opportunity should vanish.

Brigadier James N. Coggins happened to ride to a spot where he could overhear words of that last effort to change the course of the campaign's history.

Just at the head of our brigade we noticed a crowd collected, some of whom were on horseback. Among them we could plainly distinguish the tall form of John C. Breckinridge and our bull-dog leader, General James Longstreet, Lee's famous war-horse. Tom Wallingford, one of my company, called me, and we walked to where they (Longstreet and Breckinridge) were. I think General Buckner was also there, on horseback. General Bragg was on foot. Longstreet and Bragg were in earnest conversation—the latter calm and quiet, while the former spoke in an excited manner—his voice clear and distinct, yet very angry. We could not hear what Bragg was saying; he spoke slowly, and in low tones. Longstreet said: "General, this army should have been in motion at *dawn of day*." General Bragg made some reply, to which Longstreet said: "Yes, sir, but all *great* captains follow up a victory." Another remark from Bragg was followed by these words from Longstreet:

"Yes, sir, you *rank* me, but you cannot cashier me." [171]

Strong words, words resented like Forrest's and of no more avail. Longstreet relieved galled feelings in a letter, stringently critical of Bragg, to the Secretary of War:

Our chief has done but one thing that he ought to have done since I joined the army. That was to order the attack upon the 20th. All other things that he has done he ought not to have done. I am convinced that nothing but the hand of God can save us or help as long as we have our present commander.... Can't you send us General Lee? The army in Virginia can operate defensively, while our operations here should be offensive—until we recover Tennessee at all events. We need some great mind as General Lee's (nothing more) to accomplish this.[172]

In the gap and on the ridge the Stars and Stripes waved unassailed through the twenty-first. General Thomas kept on the alert, aware that his position might suddenly be rendered untenable. A determined Confederate advance could turn his right flank and cut him off from Chattanooga. A courier carried to headquarters his suggestion that he fall back on the main army, and Rosecrans quickly agreed. Thomas, anticipating approval, was ready when the order arrived. Reserve artillery, ambulances, and wagons began rumbling back over the roads. That night the holding force followed. By the morning of the twenty-second the Army of the Cumberland was concentrated once more and marshaled for the defense of Chattanooga.

Throughout the Confederacy jubilation over the victory of Chickamauga was quickly succeeded by bitter disappointment over the enemy's escape. Bragg was the target for many a sharp shaft.

The battle of Chickamauga did not begin until eleven, although Bragg ordered the advance at daylight [the perceptive Mrs. Chesnut wrote in her diary. The lady was bound to be fair.] Bragg and his generals quarrel [she continued]. I think a general worthless whose subalterns quarrel with him. There is something wrong about the man. Good generals are adored by their soldiers; see Napoleon, Caesar, Stonewall, Lee.

Another entry complained:

Bragg, thanks to Longstreet and Hood, had won Chickamauga; so we looked for results that would pay for our losses in battle.

Surely they would capture Rosencrantz [sic].[173] But no! There sat
Bragg like a good dog, howling on his hind legs before Chattanooga,
and some Yankee Holdfast growling at him from his impenetrable
heights. Bragg always stops to quarrel with his generals.[174]

Civilian criticism reflected long-smoldering fires in the Army of
Tennessee, embers of distrust and downright antipathy which,
officers declared, had turned the army into "a helpless machine."
Colonel Sorrel wrote: "The tone of the army among its higher officers
toward the commander was the worst conceivable. Bragg was the
subject of hatred and contempt, and it was almost openly so expressed." [175] Those fires made the presidential chair in Richmond
so hot that Jefferson Davis quit it to hasten West and settle the
direly disquieting crisis in command.

He arrived October 9 to meet a situation that rates as extraordinary in the long record of frictions and internecine dissensions in
military annals. Bragg's generals, while not quite at the point of
open revolt against him, were as close to the brink of mutiny as
they could go and still keep their oaths as commissioned officers—
and the raging Forrest would step over the line. Their animosity
spread down through their staffs to the regimental officers. In the
rank and file, inevitably infected, burning grievances had long
existed because of Bragg's strict disciplinary measures.

President Davis boldly determined upon direct confrontation.
He had been presented with a round robin, signed by most of the
leading generals, protesting against Bragg's continuance in command of the Army of Tennessee. Very well, let them step forward,
face Bragg, and back up their words. "He that is without sin among
you, let him first cast a stone. . . ." Whether Mr. Davis believed they
would actually speak out under such circumstances is a question.
He was not long left in doubt.

It is difficult, even now [Colonel Sorrel wrote in his memoirs],
to recall and realize that unprecedented scene. The President, with
the commander-in-chief, and the great officers of the army, assembled
to hear the opinion of the General's fitness for command. In the
presence of Bragg and his corps commanders he asked of each his

opinion, and his reasons if adverse. This was eye-to-eye with the President, the commander-in-chief, and the generals. There was no lack of candor in answer to such challenge with men like Longstreet, Cheatham, Hill, Cleburne, and Stewart. Some very plain language was used in answer, but it seems that one and all were agreed as to Bragg's unfitness for command of that army. These opinions were received by the President without comment, and Mr. Davis got more than he came for.[176]

No man might speak with impunity against the President's old comrade in arms of Mexico. As a result of that council generals' stars fell, or their wearers were banished. Among the stars first to fade were D. H. Hill's; he was suspected of having headed the anti-Bragg cabal. His nomination as lieutenant general, made before he came west, was not sent to the Senate by Davis and therefore went unconfirmed. Polk, under charges by Bragg of disobedience of orders, was shifted to another theater, finally to die in battle. Forrest also was transferred, glad to be shifted to service elsewhere. Longstreet's prestige was too great for summary treatment to be meted out to him. Davis called him into a private conference the following day.

Would General Longstreet be willing to assume command of the Army of Tennessee which he had once ardently sought?

Not now, Mr. President. Not after its priceless opportunity had been lost irretrievably by General Bragg's failure, despite all urgings, to follow up the victory at Chickamauga.

Jefferson Davis stiffened at the castigation of his friend. Both men's tempers flared. Longstreet offered his resignation. Davis refused it. For a while longer—until his detachment to Knoxville—Longstreet must still lead a corps under Bragg.[177]

For Jefferson Davis had adamantly avoided the only possible solution of the problem: the removal of General Bragg. So Bragg's stars remained, as fixed as heavenly constellations. Tarnished they were but not entirely by his own sins of omission and commission in command. More than once he had been ill served by some of those so eager to see those stars of his eclipsed. He would continue to wear them during the forthcoming battles around Chattanooga. Once

more, as in Mexico, the former Colonel Davis of the Mississippi
Rifles had rallied to the support of the erstwhile commander of
Bragg's Battery.

In those autumn days the firmament of high command was indeed
staging a meteoric display. Union stars were falling, too. Chickamauga caused the relief of Crittenden and McCook; the latter was
called before a court of inquiry but exonerated. Both leaders served
on in other theaters, but to all intents and purposes they were
shelved. Their depleted corps were consolidated and deservingly
given to the general who had marched without order to save the day
—Gordon Granger.

It was the downfall of Rosecrans that loomed as the most tragic
in the light of his past brilliance. Through a series of successful
campaigns he had seemed destined to rise to the very top command.
Then that unreconnoitered advance into the jaws of a trap—reprieves
from disaster—luck running out at last—a valiant spirit shattered
and sinking into the slough of despond on the stricken field of
Chickamauga. *Ave atque vale*. Rosecrans, relieved like his two corps
commanders, continued in the service, relegated to minor posts.

Command of the Army and the Department of the Cumberland
devolved upon George H. Thomas. Promotion, with its reflections
on Rosecrans, whom he relieved, was not altogether welcome. He
would learn without displeasure of a certain decision made in
Washington.

The name of the victor over Vicksburg had been impressed in
President Lincoln's mind. Assistant Secretary Dana wired he had
met U. S. Grant and would unhesitatingly recommend him. Secretary
Stanton traveled westward, conferred with the General, and con-
curred. Grant was placed in command of all the forces between the
Mississippi and the Alleghenies.

He telegraphed Thomas: "Hold Chattanooga at all hazards;
I will be there as soon as possible."

Thomas replied: "We will hold the town till we starve."

They would come close in Chattanooga to that eventuality.

CHAPTER 13

At All Hazards

Chattanooga was a stronghold under siege, its garrison the Army of the Cumberland, some 40,000 men. Nature had built circumvallations, the surrounding mountains, for the besiegers. Those commanding heights served Confederate gunners as towers and platforms had for their ancestral artillerymen, archers and catapulteers.

To the south rose the lofty wall of Lookout Mountain; to the east Missionary Ridge—both manned by the enemy. The Tennessee River, looping around the town to the north, was both moat and barrier, too broad to be crossed for either sally or storm except by boat or pontoon bridge. Rebel batteries had swept traffic from the waterway. Were it spanned, the garrison would possess a northward escape route, yet one that was little better than a forlorn hope. It led over mountain roads, few, narrow, and rough, where pursuers could fall on the rear and flanks of a retreating force and grind it to pieces.

The Federals still held the railroad running down from the north through Nashville. Potentially it was a life line for supplies, but its terminus had now become Bridgeport, some twenty-five miles downstream from Chattanooga. Thus far and no farther might the trainloads of rations and ammunition pass. Confederate divisions stood athwart the intervening tracks and dropped an iron curtain of shells and "minnie" balls that barred the way. Union quartermasters must resort to bringing provisions to the besieged by wagon trains making a long detour around the blockade over nigh-impassable roads. They could carry little more than forage enough to sustain their own animals. That little was all that could be brought to a hungry garrison and even that was menaced by raiding Gray cavalry.

On Lookout and Missionary twinkled watchful campfires, tokens of a tightening cordon so nearly closed. Surely General Bragg permitted himself a rare, grim smile of satisfaction. The enemy, all but one tenuous supply line cut, was shut up in the box where they had so recently sought to pen him.

Hold Chattanooga at all hazards were Thomas's orders. Against the hazards of battle he would hold it, but those of starvation, more formidable, had forced the capitulation of many a beleaguered town. Every day they were driving the Army of the Cumberland closer to the brink of surrender.

Full rations quickly dwindled to half, then to quarter. All the rest of the war soldiers remembered their pangs of hunger in the worst food crisis in the history of the Union Army. Gaunt men followed the commissary wagons to pick up any scraps that might fall from them. An Illinois private recorded that since Chickamauga he and his comrades had eaten "but two meals a day, and one cracker for each meal." [178] When a mess was issued five days' rations, it could not resist eating them all in three; the other two days the men starved. For a time there had been a little meat—then only hardtack and parched corn. Troops gathered acorns to roast and devour. But there was little wood for cook fires or to warm undernourished soldiers, shivering in the cold and drenched by the frequent rains.

The plight of the animals was pitiful, too. Soon a daily feed was down to three ears of corn. Even of that the poor beasts were robbed by ravenous men until a guard had to be placed over troughs. Desperate creatures gnawed each other's tails, and crunched saplings and hitching posts until nothing was left of them. They bit chunks from the sides and wheel spokes of wagons, destroying a number of them. More than ten thousand horses and mules dropped and died of starvation. Before long the artillery would be unable to muster teams to draw the guns, and ambulances and wagons would stand immobilized.

So [wrote a Kansas infantryman] to the horrors of bitter cold and scanty clothing, of hard work and almost constant showers, of danger and ever-anxious watchfulness, was added the startling terror of want and the near approach of grim and gaunt starvation. Cattle, almost dead from lack of food, were killed and their flesh doled out in stinted quantities; the hungry and tired men haunted the slaughter houses in crowds, and snatched eagerly for the hoofs, tails, heads, and entrails of the animals that were butchered, cooking and eating with avidity garbage they would before have shrunk from in disgust. The writer one day saw a commissary train which had just arrived from Stevenson, and was unloading at the depot, surrounded by several hundred half famished soldiers, who eagerly snatched and struggled for the crumbs of crackers that fell into the road from broken boxes as they were being carried into the storehouse. Behind our camp was a park of artillery horses, and over them a guard had to be stationed to keep the half starved men from taking the poor rations of corn doled out to the almost famished animals. The writer has seen soldiers during that siege picking up the few grains of corn that had been spilled by the horses from their troughs, and trampled into mud and filth underfoot. One of the regiments of our Brigade caught, killed and ate a dog which wandered into the camp.[179]

Despite all privations, morale remained amazingly high. Men still managed to joke and sing and performed sentry duty and work details with no more than normal soldier grumbling. Yet everyone from General Thomas down realized that the time was rapidly approaching when they could hold out no longer. There was still a chance of breakout and escape, but it was slimmer than ever. "If a retreat had occurred at this time, it is not probable that any of the army would have reached the railroad as an organized body, if followed by the enemy." [180]

Bragg sent his cavalry under Fighting Joe Wheeler to sever the last thin, roundabout Union supply line, sixty tough miles from Bridgeport over Walden's Ridge and down through the Sequatchie Valley. On October 1 the dashing little cavalryman crossed the river, knifed through a screen of Federal horsemen, and swooped down next day on a long column of lumbering wagon trains and their escorts. It was a field day for the yelling raiders, shooting and saber-ing the guards, while fear-crazed teams piled up vehicles in frightful confusion. For miles the road was strewn with bodies in blue, dead animals, and the wreckage of burning wagons.

Wheeler, riding off with considerable booty, struck for Murfrees-boro to cut the railroad. Just in time a division of Union cavalry headed him off, drove him back, and recaptured some of the spoils.

It was high time the Blue horse proved itself. With some excep-tions, it had neither been capably led nor its efforts co-ordinated in this campaign. However, it was composed of good regiments such as the 2nd Michigan Cavalry, which in its early career had been commanded by officers who led a corps and division at Chickamauga. The future corps leader, Gordon Granger, then a Regular Army captain, had trained the regiment sternly. A frown from "Old Granger" was reputed to kill further than a flintlock musket, but not all the 2nd stood in awe of him. Once the C. O., wearing no insignia of rank, made a surprise inspection of stables and bawled out a trooper for the way he was grooming his horse. When the man made an impudent retort, the Colonel demanded, "Do you know who I am?" "No," snapped back the answer, "and I don't give a damn." The story went that Granger picked up a board but beat nothing but a hasty retreat before a pitchfork grabbed by the trooper. "Let Old Granger put on his shoulder straps if he wants to give any orders around here," the trooper announced, and got away with it. No charges were preferred, which may well have been one of the reasons why the regimental historian wrote of its first com-mander: "Later in the war the regiment thought much of him; in fact, were proud of him." [181]

Phil Sheridan later headed the 2nd for a time, after the 3rd had refused to be saddled with that "little red-faced Irishman." And the 2nd also had cause to be proud that it had once followed the future chief of cavalry of the Army of the Potomac.

After the first division of Union cavalry had driven off Joe Wheeler, a second division galloped up and closed in on the raiding Con-federates. The Gray horse fought off the attack, taking ninety-five casualties in the rear-guard action as it successfully recrossed the

river on October 9. But Confederate losses were light compared to
the Union's in vital means of supply: 1,000 mules and more than
300 wagons—nearly fatal for the besieged in Chattanooga.

U. S. Grant's telegram had promised that he would be in Chattanooga as soon as possible. How promptly that might be was a question, for possible came close to being impossible. No railroad could
take him through, and the General, one leg damaged in an accident,
was able to ride only with difficulty and could not walk without
crutches.

That injury was one of those small cogs upon which the gears of
great events turn. About two months before he was given top command in the West, Grant was riding on a borrowed mount, returning to quarters from a review in New Orleans. A young cavalry
officer on a Kentucky thoroughbred challenged him to a race. The
General could not resist. As they galloped neck and neck along
a smooth shell road and rounded a curve, a locomotive puffed past,
whistling shrilly. Grant's horse jumped and suddenly swerved. That
was too much even for a rider who had been a superb horseman
from boyhood. He sailed over his mount's head to a fall so hard that
he was confined to bed for several weeks.[182]

But Grant, still crippled though he was, kept his promise that he
would reach Chattanooga. He and his staff traveled by train through
Nashville to Stevenson, Alabama, arriving October 21; thence on to
Bridgeport, decreed the last stop by the Confederate blockade. There
the General was helped on a horse. With heroic endurance he dared
a ride over the dreadful mountain roads where so many wagons had
come to grief. At several dangerous places he had to be lifted out
of the saddle and carried across. That agonizing journey, stretched
to sixty miles by detours, was nevertheless accomplished in two days.
A little before dark on the second day the short general with the
stubby beard swung on crutches into Thomas's headquarters, where
he conferred all evening on the situation.[183]

Grant, as he must have expected, found that Thomas was by no
means ready to give up. An idea suggested by an enterprising officer,

General W. F. Smith, Chief Engineer of the Army of the Cumberland, had been encouraged, and work was under way. "Baldy" Smith was building a steamboat, starting from scratch. He commandeered old engines to power a sawmill and the boat when she was built, while the mill also turned out planks for pontoons and supply barges.

Smith already had some pontoons on hand, built by the 1st Michigan Engineer Regiment of Pioneers and Mechanics from scrap lumber: pulled-up station platforms and torn-down houses. When their small quantity of spikes was exhausted, relays of mounted couriers, each rider carrying a ten-pound sack, had rushed more over the roundabout route from Bridgeport. These boats, with the newly constructed ones, added up to enough for the necessary bridging and transport. If the steamship could run the river gantlet with tows of provision-laden craft, the specter of hunger would be banished at last.

Meanwhile reinforcements from the East, Hooker and his two corps from the Army of the Potomac, whose train trip has previously been narrated, had reached the Bridgeport railhead. Thomas had ordered them concentrated there. For them to drive through to Chattanooga, where there was so little to eat, would be futile unless a free flow of provisions were established.

A plan was ready, and Grant ordered it executed.

During the night of October 26–27, pontoons would float troops down the river from Chattanooga. Another force was to march across Moccasin Point and support the landings of the river-borne troops. Coincidentally Hooker would advance from Bridgeport by the road along Raccoon Mountain into Lookout Valley and break through enemy opposition to Brown's Ferry. Thus a supply line would be opened to run by boat from Bridgeport upstream to Kelley's Ferry where swift currents made the stream unnavigable for available craft. Debarked rations would be carried by wagon over Raccoon to Brown's Ferry, thence across the river via pontoon bridge —across Moccasin Point—then over the river once more and into Chattanooga.

One after another, each part of the plan's mechanism meshed and clicked. Hooker crossed the Tennessee on the twenty-sixth of October and began his advance. Early next morning 1,300 picked men from the Chattanooga garrison in fifty-two pontoon boats floated noiselessly down-river with the current. They surprised the Confederate picket at Brown's Ferry and captured most of it. There against the nine-mile current a 600-foot pontoon span was thrust out into the river. As it grew, a Rebel battery opened fire from a mile downstream. A shell holed one of the center boats. Private Adrian Musty of the 1st Michigan Engineers plugged the water-spouting gap with his coat and hat; the boat stayed afloat and was taken ashore and repaired.[184] With the Gray guns silenced by counterbattery, the bridge was completed and ready for Hooker's Corps, coming up the valley from Bridgeport, to cross and clear the way beyond.

"Baldy" Smith led 5,000 men across the neck of Moccasin Point to the ferry, crossed the river in barges, and pushed on into the hills. He threw up log fortifications and planted three batteries to sweep the narrow road that was the only route by which the Confederates could march troops around Lookout Point without climbing over the mountain. Hooker's 10,000 meanwhile advanced along the railroad past Wauhatchie, brushed aside an enemy brigade, and seized all the roads into the valley.

The passage of the mountains remained to be conquered, route for the bulk of supplies into besieged Chattanooga. Whips cracked and teams strained at the traces, as the army wagoners tackled it.

How they brought the wagons over seemingly insuperable heights is forever memorable.

Nobody but a soldier can understand the difficulties of the tumbled-in and heaped-up world of mountains, nor the horrible gashes and torrent-beds called roads, over which our half-empty army-wagons have been knocking to pieces, or sinking below a wheelwright's resurrection. The mountain achievements of Hannibal and Bonaparte were trifles in comparison, and going over the ridges and through the clefts and up the craggy sides, the wonder grows, not so much how a vast army with ponderous artillery could ever have surmounted them, as how, once over, it ever could have been maintained.[185]

Teams of horses and mules were increased until ten animals might be tugging at a wagon's traces. Companies of infantrymen heaved on the wheels, helping. On the steep descents, when brakes and chains failed, wagoners were forced to rein around and throw the wheel pair of mules sharply upgrade to lock wheels under a wagon frame to keep it from crashing down the slope. Without the mule, said Taylor, "the creature to which a thistle is a treat, the battle of Mission Ridge could never have been won."

So the mighty feat was achieved. "The Cracker Line," as the Union Army triumphantly acclaimed it, was open.

From Lookout Bragg and Longstreet impotently watched the Union life line wedged open. A sudden, determined effort must close it again, or siege would be raised and near triumph vanish. Longstreet brought most of his corps down into the valley on October 28 to fling it on Hooker's rear guard, Geary's Division at Wauhatchie, in a midnight assault. But to Longstreet's rage only part of it reached position to make the attack.

Looming Lookout Mountain cast a dark shadow that blotted out most of the faint and fitful moonlight. Flash of rifle and cannon alone illuminated the battlefield, briefly distinguishing friend from foe in the dreadful confusion of nocturnal combat. Hooker heard the outburst of firing to his rear and ordered Howard to hasten back over the intervening three miles to Geary's rescue. Law's Gray brigade cut in between and blocked off the reinforcements. Howard's men pushed it back but could not break through.

The hours mounted toward four, as Geary's Division fought off hard-driving onslaughts, masked by the night. Surely, despite the press of conflict, the General must have been unable to banish from his mind worry over his son, a Pennsylvania artillery officer in his division.

A veteran unit, young Geary's, and strong in pride of its arm of the service. Battery E of Pennsylvania was called Knap's Battery after Joseph M. Knap who had organized it and given it four cannon.

To us [its members declared] the cavalry were only "turkey stickers" and the poor, looked-down-upon "doughboys" only useful to pull our mired guns out of the mud when the horses were unable to do so; in our eyes no branch of the service was equal to the artillery, and no battery equal to our own, Knap's Pennsylvania Battery.[186]

Now E Battery proved its boasted mettle. In position on a little knoll it was hotly engaged. Confederate riflemen whittled down the cannoneers and dropped the horses until only thirteen out of forty-eight animals were left. One advanced piece, on the point of capture, was dragged clear by supporting infantrymen, tailing on to the prolonge ropes, and served by them and the two surviving members of its crew.[187] In the darkness rammers and swabbers groped with their staffs for muzzles. Numbers 3 stopped scorching vents with thumbstalls while the pieces were loaded, then thrust primers through into powder charges. By touch, too, Numbers 4 fastened lanyard hooks to those friction primers—stepped clear of recoil—jerked lanyards.[188] Cannon flamed and roared. Firing over the heads of their own infantry, they flung shells into the blur of the oncoming attack.

Colonel William Rickards, 129th Pennsylvania Infantry, raced to the gun flashes on the knoll. "You're shooting short!" he shouted. "Your shells are bursting in my line." Lieutenant Geary called an order to ammunition passers to cut fuses longer. As the guns barked again, he asked, "How's that?" Rickards watched, answered "Right!" —ran back to his men.

E Battery fought on, but it was taking more losses every minute, and there were few survivors to man it now. Most of the sergeants were killed or wounded. Captain Atwell fell, a bullet ranging through a hip and lodging close to the spine. Lieutenant Geary, taking a gunner's place and aiming the piece, slumped over its breech, shot through the brain. It would be some time before the tragic news reached his father.

As the fight raged on and the enemy closed in, panicking Union teamsters jumped from wagon seats and ran. Mule teams, harnessed or tethered, wildly stampeded. Right and left the terrified animals plowed through the Confederate ranks. A cavalry charge, for which the onrushing mules were mistaken, could have wreaked no greater havoc. Longstreet's men scattered before them. By 4 A.M. the repulse was complete.

The "Charges of the Mule Brigade" could not go unheralded. An infantryman of the 29th Ohio immortalized it in verse.

> Half a mile, half a mile,
>   Half a mile onward,
> Right towards the Georgia troops,
>   Broke the two hundred.
> "Forward, the Mule brigade.
> Charge for the Rebs!" they neighed;
> Straight for the Georgia troops
>   Broke the two hundred.
>
> Mules to the right of them,
> Mules to the left of them,
> Mules behind them,
>   Pawed, brayed, and thundered.
> Breaking their own confines,
> Breaking through Longstreet's lines,
> Into the Georgia troops
>   Stormed the two hundred.
>
> When can their glory fade?
> O! the wild charge they made!
>   All the world wondered.
> Honor the charge they made,
> Honor the Mule Brigade,
>   Long-eared two hundred.[189]

The attack at Wauhatchie was the last Confederate attempt to keep the siege lines tight. "Baldy" Smith's little steamboat, *The*

Chattanooga, puffed up the Tennessee, laden barges made fast to her sides. From them were landed:

40,000 rations and 39,000 pounds of forage within five miles of General Hooker's men, who had half a breakfast ration left in haversacks; and within eight or ten miles of Chattanooga, where four cakes of hardbread and a quarter pound of pork made three days' ration. In Chattanooga there were but four boxes of hardbread left in the commissary warehouses on the morning of the 30th of October. [An] orderly . . . reported that the news went through the camps faster than his horse, and the soldiers were jubilant, and cheering, "The Cracker line open. Full rations, boys! Three cheers for the Cracker line," as if we had won another victory, and we had.[190]

The opening of the Cracker Line was indeed a triumph. "It is such beautiful operations as this that makes military history a fascinating study." [191] Grant recommended "Baldy" Smith for promotion to major general. And a tribute to the Union feat soon appeared in a Richmond newspaper: "The admirably conceived and perfectly executed *coup* at Brown's Ferry . . . has robbed the Confederacy of all its dearly earned advantages gained at Chickamauga."

Yet while the Cracker Line lay open, the gateway to the Southeast remained closed. Bragg's army still held those redoubtable heights, Lookout Mountain and Missionary Ridge, which seemed impregnable. From them Confederate cannon glared down on the town in the bend of the Tennessee.

CHAPTER 14

Sound of the Guns

Artillery fire echoed through the hills, flushing frightened deer. Down in Chattanooga, Yankees, in plain view of Rebel batteries on the heights, were tempting targets. Bragg sent a warning to evacuate noncombatants; he was about to shell the town. Escape was open by the Cracker Line, but most citizens preferred the shelter of the bank vault and cellars.

A correspondent for *The Richmond Sentinel* watched teams toil up the mountain trails, pulling the guns into position.

Colonel E. P. Alexander, General Longstreet's active and skilful Chief of Artillery, hoped he might be able to shell Chattanooga, or the enemy's camps, from this mountain, and three nights ago twenty long-ranged rifle pieces were brought up, after great difficulty. It was necessary to bring them up at night, because the mountain road is in many places commanded by the batteries on Moccasin Ridge. We used mules in getting our heaviest pieces up. They pull with more steadiness than horses. Every gun was located behind some huge rock, so as to protect the cannoneers from the cross-fire of the "Ridge." The firing was begun by some guns upon the right in General Polk's corps. Only one gun in that quarter (twenty-four-pound rifle gun) could reach the enemy lines. At one P.M. order was given to open the rifles from the mountain. Parker's battery, being highest up the mountain, opened first, and then down among the rocky soils of the mountain Jordan's, Woolfolk's and other batteries spoke out in thunder tones. The reverberations were truly grand. Old Moccasin turned loose upon us with great fury; but "munitions of rocks" secured us. All their guns being securely casemated, we could do them little or no injury; so we paid little or no attention to them. Colonel Alexander with his glass and signal flag, took position higher up in the mountain, and watched the shots. Most of our fuses (nine-tenths of them, indeed) were of no account, and hence there was great difficulty to see where our shots struck, only a few exploding. The Yankees in their rifle pits made themselves remarkably small. They swarmed before the firing began, but soon disappeared from sight. We fired slowly, every cannoneer mounting the rocks and watching the shot. After sinking the trail of the guns, so as to give an elevation of twenty-one degrees, the shots continued to fall short of the camps and the principal works of the enemy, and the order was given to cease firing. It has been reported we killed and wounded a few men in the advanced works.[192]

Inflicting a few casualties and holing roofs here and there was not good enough for Colonel Alexander. Shifting to counterbattery against Federal artillery on Moccasin Point, he ordered his gun crews to prop trails high to depress muzzles and ingeniously rigged howitzers as mortars (as described in an earlier chapter) to drop shells behind his opponents' parapets. The Gray guns on Lookout and well-entrenched Blue ones on the Point [193] snarled and snapped at each other like giant bulldogs coming to grips although a mile apart. Yet the cannonading caused no great damage on either side. Long-range bombardment proved ineffective. If artillery were to play its part, ranges must be closed.

A Confederate battery achieved just that with a gallant little exploit. Charles L. Lumsden's artillerymen were as well disciplined as might have been expected of a captain who had graduated from Virginia Military Institute and served as commandant of cadets at the University of Alabama. After the first payday, when a few good cardplayers cleaned out the rest of the outfit, Captain Lumsden forbade gambling. However, he tolerated such soldier pranks as filling the bugle with water on cold nights so that it froze and "Reveille" could not be blown. Whenever possible, the battery lived in comfort, waited on by a dozen Negro body servants belonging to officers, noncoms, and privates. Those excellent cooks managed even during hard campaigning. They baked dough on entrenching shovels and, breaking up hardtack with an ax, made a palatable dish with it. Recently the battery's foragers, sacks of corn and sheaves of hay across their saddle pommels, had galloped across the front of blazing Federal cannon on Moccasin Point. As they rode clear, unscathed, they yelled back derisively at the enemy, "You can't shoot worth shucks!"

Lumsden's men were ready for another daring feat now. By night the battery quietly moved down from the hills into position on the river, cut fuses for 200 yards, loaded and laid on an enemy camp on the opposite bank. A Yankee bugler's "Reveille" at daybreak served as the signal to fire. Eight guns roared, pouring in four devastating rounds each per minute for six to eight minutes. Then Federal artillery opened fire, and Lumsden shouted: "Limber to the rear. To the right, march. Gallop!" and the battery whirled off into the cover of the woods with only one casualty, a cannoneer with an arm shot off near the shoulder.[194]

Would other Gray guns be advanced to deal such sudden, telling strokes? Lumsden had been driven off by the counterbattery fire of Blue cannon that happened to be at hand. There might be none at other threatened points, and none could reach them. For the Union artillery was virtually immobilized, as enemy observers on the heights could have estimated from watching horses and mules die by the thousands from starvation.

Grant considered his army still besieged. So did Thomas, more eager than ever to break out and even scores with Bragg, both for Chickamauga and for a recent insult. The Virginian, loyal to the Union, had forwarded through the lines a harmless message from the North for a Confederate officer. Fuming rage broke through the renowned Thomas imperturbability when his courtesy was flung back in his face. The message was sent back under a flag of truce with Bragg's endorsement: "Respectfully returned to General Thomas. General Bragg declines to have any intercourse or dealings with a man who had betrayed his State." [195]

Sherman and his Army of the Tennessee had not yet arrived from

Mississippi to reinforce the troops in Chattanooga. They would tip the scales in favor of the Union. The time to strike was now.

It was not in Braxton Bragg to conceive or execute such a master stroke as Robert E. Lee might have delivered. Instead of attacking, he gravely weakened his forces. Whether the plan was Bragg's own, or he was following instructions left by Jefferson Davis, is an undetermined question. In any event Longstreet was ordered out of the lines to capture Knoxville from Burnside. "Old Pete" bowed to the plan, military folly or not. It offered escape from detested service under Bragg. Any army that man commanded was doomed.

It was a grave mistake and hardly excusable [Fiske declares]. Bragg must have known that the fate of Chattanooga must have to be settled by battle; and it ought to have been clear to him that if he won that battle, Knoxville would be at his mercy, while if he lost it, Knoxville would be relieved. To risk the loss of the battle at Chattanooga, in order to pick from the bough an apple that was sure to fall into his lap if he won it, would seem the height of imbecility.[196]

Longstreet's Corps with Wheeler's Cavalry (later to be recalled)—20,000 men and eighty guns—marched away November 3 with orders to return after fulfilling their mission. The contingent from the Army of Northern Virginia would assault the Knoxville fortification with their customary *élan* but suffer repulse. They would not again serve under Bragg's command. So far as the campaign in the West went, they had reached the point of no return.

Artillery fire from Missionary Ridge slackened. Alexander's guns were gone.

Although Bragg was unconcerned as to his ability to keep the Federals cooped up in Chattanooga, Washington was desperately worried by the report that Longstreet had left to assail Knoxville. Frantic telegrams poured in to Grant, urging an all-out attack on Missionary Ridge that would force Longstreet's recall and thus relieve Burnside.[197]

Thomas's answer was epitomized by a line from Ben Franklin: "For want of a horse the rider is lost." He could not attack because he lacked enough animals to pull his guns. Survivors from the ravages of starvation were too few to move cannon out of the parks into assault positions, let alone advance them in close support. Unless in the direst emergency no general could fairly ask infantry to charge those steep slopes uncovered by artillery fire. The Cracker Line was open but except for forage for such animals as remained it was not yet a Horse Line.

Grant directed Thomas "to take mules, officers' horses, or animals wherever he could get them, to move the necessary artillery. But he persisted in the declaration that he could not move a single piece of artillery, and could not see how he possibly could comply with the order." [198]

Mules, superb in draft, will seldom pull a battery into action under fire. Officers' mounts, as a rule, are too light for gun teams or unused to working in traces. In the end Grant, whose arm was infantry, heeded Thomas, the old artilleryman, and the attack order was canceled.

The commanding general wired Burnside to hold on and urged Sherman to hurry.

Without that right-hand man of his Grant would have been reluctant to launch an offensive even if his artillery had been mobile. William Tecumseh Sherman stood far higher in his confidence than Thomas. Hooker and his reinforcements had done well thus far, but XI Corps, unaccustomed to victory, could at best be considered no more than a blunted spearhead. Pending Sherman's arrival, the front relapsed into stalemate, rendered uneasy for Federal headquarters by Washington's frequently telegraphed anxiety over Burnside.

Opposing pickets crossed the river and other lines to pay friendly visits, warning each other if officers approached. Before the departure of Longstreet's Corps one of his men, wearing a blue uniform, chanced to meet Grant, who was making a tour of inspection; they enjoyed a pleasant little talk and parted in amity. Again Grant, "riding the picket lines, saw Confederate outposts a few feet from his on the opposite side of a creek come to attention and salute him as politely as if he had been one of their own generals.... On the heights Bragg's men, polishing their cannon, grew lazy, thinking their position impregnable." [199]

General Sherman, organizing his command and starting from Memphis for Corinth on October 11, was having tough going.

His instructions required him to repair the road in his rear in order to bring up supplies. The distance was about 330 miles through a hostile country. His entire command could not have maintained the road if it had been completed. The bridges had all been destroyed by the enemy and much other damage done; a hostile community lived along the road; guerrilla bands infested the country, and more or less of the cavalry of the enemy was still in the west. Often Sherman's work was destroyed as soon as completed, though he was only a short distance away. [200]

He could never make Chattanooga soon enough under such circumstances in spite of river-borne supplies that met him en route. Grant, unable to reach him by wire, sent a canoe courier down the Tennessee on over Muscle Shoals to Iuka. Drop railroad repairs, the order read. Detach the division of General Grenville M. Dodge, crack engineer and good soldier, to attend to them and new trackage for supply lines. [201]

Sherman's leading divisions arrived at Bridgeport on November 15, and he proceeded to Chattanooga to report. Standing beside his superior, he scanned the encircling heights, ringed with enemy cannon, entrenchments, and tents.

"Cump" Sherman burst out: "General Grant, you're besieged!"

"It's too true," answered Grant. [202]

He did not intend to stay besieged much longer. His plan, already prepared, placed the standard in the hands of his trusted subordinate with the bristling reddish whiskers. Sherman was to cross the Tennessee at Brown's Ferry, march behind the hills, concealed from the enemy, and marshal his men under cover of the woods opposite the mouth of Chickamauga Creek. If he had been spotted by Confederate observers, his disappearance in that direction might delude them into believing that he was on the way to relieve Burnside at Knoxville. Then he was to emerge from the woods, recross the river at the point of the creek's confluence by pontoon bridge, and advance with all speed.

Deliver a sudden, surprise assault on the enemy flank at the northern end of Missionary Ridge, General Sherman. It's lightly held; no attack appears to be expected there. Carry the railroad tunnel before the graybacks can occupy it. With the rest of the army supporting you, you will sweep the Rebels up the valley, cutting them off from their base of supplies at Chickamauga Station. Close in and smash them.

Thomas would move to the left, connect with Sherman's lines, and join the advance. So much for "the Rock of Chickamauga." If the plan worked, there would be no need for last stands.

Hooker and his corps were posted in general reserve on the north bank of the river. Bitter memories of Chancellorsville must have risen up to haunt Fighting Joe when he read those orders. Grant was taking no risk that he would lose this battle.

But across the route designated for Sherman's march lay, unsuspected, a wide gap in the hills, one not shown on inadequate Union maps. And rain clouds were gathering in cumulous masses.

The rains fell. Through drenching cloudbursts Sherman pushed the head of his column up to Brown's Ferry on November 20. He got one division across and another the next day. Then he scanned the rapidly rising Tennessee and the tossing pontoons that bridged it and shook his head. It was impossible for him to cross enough of his troops to deliver on time the attack ordered by Grant. He would not be able to advance for two days more when the weather partially cleared. Bogged down, he waited it out in his concealed camp.

Back in Chattanooga General Grant read the report from the Ferry and bowed to the inevitable. If "Clump" Sherman said he couldn't move, there was no doubt about it. But in the interim there was something to be done on his own front.

Observers had detected activity in the Confederate lines on Missionary Ridge. General Bragg was by way of making another of his mistakes, one that could prove as disastrous as the others—or more so. He had ordered two strong divisions to pull out and march to reinforce Longstreet at Knoxville and was shifting other troops along the Ridge from his extreme right to his left.

Grant told Thomas to find out what was going on. The latter, orders in hand for a reconnaissance in force, must have grinned to himself. He was scheduled for a secondary role when Sherman got into action, but now he was to attack on his own and this time he could horse his guns, having borrowed teams from other commands.

Early afternoon, November 23. Thomas marshaled 30,000 men for an assault on Orchard Knob, a low hill about halfway between the town and Missionary Ridge.

Flags were flying; the quick earnest steps of thousands beat equal time. The sharp commands of hundreds of company officers, the sound of drums, the ringing notes of the bugle, companies wheeling and countermarching and regiments getting into line, the bright sun lighting up ten thousand polished bayonets till they glistened and flashed like a flying shower of electric sparks,—all looked like preparations for a peaceful pageant, rather than for the bloody work of death.[203]

Enemy pickets climbed out of their rifle pits in front of the Knob to watch curiously. This must be a grand review the Yanks were staging, so well ordered and steady were those serried ranks. But the ranks did not wheel. They marched forward, and the artillery thundered, field and siege pieces flinging shells above them. Between the crashes of bursting projectiles the Knob's defenders, tumbling back into pits and trenches, heard the rat-tat-tat of drums beating the charge.

Smoke of musketry volleys rolled along the lines as the charge was driven home, and the mound was clothed in blue. One of Grant's fronts had been handsomely advanced, and in Orchard Knob he had been presented with a splendid observation post affording a panorama of the frowning Ridge above.

The battle redeemed Bragg's mistake before it became irretrievable. Hastily he summoned back the troops sent for reinforcing Longstreet. Pat Cleburne's Division hurried back to Missionary, and

Bragg further strengthened his right there. He spared only a cursory glance for a signal message handed him. It could be no more than a bad guess.

What his station on Lookout Mountain had warned was: The next enemy attack will be made here.

CHAPTER 15

"Battle Above the Clouds"

The theater darkened, and the footlights flashed on. The curtain was about to rise on the last stirring scenes of the campaign's drama.

They were lofty and far ranging, those lights—the torches of the signalmen. To War Correspondent Taylor, newly arrived, they resembled the jewels of the Southern Cross, miraculously transplanted in Northern skies. He gazed at one:

just over the edge of the highest lift of Raccoon Range, a crazy planet, bigger than Venus at the full, waltzing in a mad fashion about another soberer light.... The antic light describes a quadrant, makes a semi-circle, stops, rises, falls, sweeps right, sweeps left, rounds out an orbit, strikes off at a tangent. The Lieutenant of the Signal Corps is talking to somebody behind Lookout. Turning toward Mission Ridge, you would have seen lights of evil omen, for the hostile signals were working, too; blazing, disappearing, showing here and there and yonder; now on the Mountain, now along the Ridge, like wills-of-the-wisp.[204]

In this campaign of heights and distances the signalers preeminently proved themselves. They had come a long way in a comparatively short time in developing their form of communication, invaluable throughout the Civil War and following wars.

An army surgeon stood in the New Mexico one day in the 1850's and watched two parties of Comanche warriors facing each other from the tops of buttes. Feathered lances waved back and forth and were answered in patterns by those on the opposite rise. Obviously the Comanches were exchanging messages as other tribes used smoke signals. Surgeon Albert J. Myer was immediately interested, having earned his way through college by working as a telegraph operator and written a graduating thesis on sign language for deaf mutes. Here was another phase of the science of communication. By day flags could be substituted for these lances—torches or rockets at night.

Such was the genesis of the United States Army Signal Corps. With its Confederate counterpart, it would play a part of high importance at Lookout Mountain, as elsewhere in the war.

Prevailing over official indifference, Myer became the first signal officer of the United States Army in 1860. Early the next year he operated his system successfully in a Navajo campaign. By June he had organized a corps that grew to 300 officers and 2,500 enlisted men.[205]

Flag or torch messages were sent by combinations of three separate motions: a swing to right or left or a dip to the front. They represented numerals, which in turn translated into letters. The number 1, for example, was indicated by a wave of the left and return from the ground to the upright position. Two 1's equaled the letter A; 1221 (one left wave, two rights, and a left) was B, and so on. White flags with a red square in the center were most frequently used, with reversed colors more visible against varying backgrounds, and a black flag preferred against snow. Average range for messages in clear weather was from eight to fifteen miles, but they were sometimes legible with field glasses as far as twenty-five miles.

To encode messages an ingenious gadget of two concentric disks was devised. During the Atlanta campaign the Confederate code was broken. The Federals took happy advantage of intelligence on enemy moves until a war correspondent brashly printed the news. Thereupon Confederates, reading the paper, promptly changed their code. General Sherman furiously ordered the offender hanged, but Thomas commuted the sentence to banishment from the front.[206]

Besides flags and torches, rockets were used for long-distance signaling; also composition flares, red, green, or white, as cartridges for a pistol, forerunner of the Very pistol of the world wars.

Ready!   2!

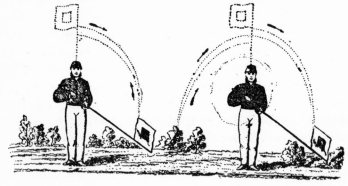

1!   14!

2343!   5!

From The Signal Corps, U.S.A., in the
War of the Rebellion *by J. Willard Brown*

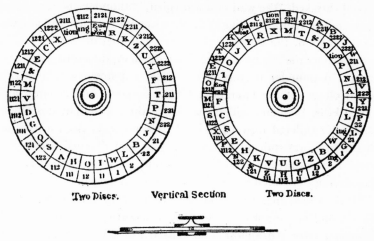

Two Discs.   Vertical Section   Two Discs.

From The Signal Corps, U.S.A., in the
War of the Rebellion *by J. Willard Brown*

The Confederacy, realizing the value of the system, quickly adopted it in a corps organized by Major E. Porter Alexander, who had been one of Myer's pupils. Although Alexander left the corps to devote his talents to the artillery, it flourished, and the South's signalers celebrated their achievements with a song.

> Hurrah for the bonnie white flag
> That bears the crimson square.[207]

They were gallant men, they of the Gray and Blue Signal Corps. Exposed on hilltops, towers, and in trees, they were not infrequently picked off, the proportion of killed to wounded being notably high. When telegraph wires were cut or could not be strung, when mounted couriers were shot down, it was the signalers who got the messages through.

In Chattanooga and on the surrounding heights signal flags seldom ceased to wave by day and torches to gleam at night. Now and again they prompted quick action when a signal station spotted a marching column or a wagon train. The message, sent by distant, fluttering cloth, was passed to a battery commander. A cannon boomed, and a shell shrieked, "the wail of a lost spirit," "thunder and a cloud at both ends of its line of flight." It burst among the men and animals on the road, or the woods or the river swallowed it.

Sometimes the flag men called down death on themselves. A round from a 10-pounder Parrott in the valley cut down a Confederate signal officer on the mountain. Union signalers on Cameron and Crane hills, Walden's Ridge, and Moccasin Point went unscathed. One, later ordered forward to send back messages from a division in the line, was quickly packed off. "Get that damned flag out of here! You're drawing fire." Colors to rally on were needed; let the flag-waving signalmen stay back where they belonged.

Dusk merged into the night of November 23–24. Signal torches on hill and mountain began to flash with unwonted brilliance like borrowed stars. An almost total eclipse was shuttering the moon. Tremors of mingled wonder and apprehension ran through the armies, as the luminous disk slid into a black slot in the sky. A Federal officer, walking through camp, listened to the hushed talk of upward-gazing soldiers. Some scholar of the rank and file was remarking that among the ancients an eclipse on the eve of battle was considered a bad omen. Comrades agreed it might be a sign of defeat, not for the Union but for old Bragg, perched up yonder on the mountaintop. Wasn't he nearest the moon? [208]

The rains still fell. They swelled the river even higher and broke the pontoon span, stalling Sherman's skin-soaked corps, ready to cross very early in the morning of November 24. By daylight barges and a ferryboat had carried over 8,000 infantrymen, but the bridge had to be repaired for the cavalry and artillery. Then the moored boats tore loose again, with Osterhaus' Division still on the other bank. Grant sent a replacement division, and Sherman pushed on, time running out. It was four o'clock in the afternoon before they reached the terminal slopes of Missionary Ridge and massed three divisions for assault.

But now this brilliant general was rudely reminded that there is many a slip betwixt the cup and the lip. Up to this moment the crest of Missionary Ridge, as viewed from below and from a distance, had appeared to be continuous, so that Sherman had expected, after ascending it, to march without hindrance southward past the tunnel of the Cleveland railroad, and thus to reach a point where he could cut off the Confederate army from Chickamauga station. . . . But now it was near sunset when Sherman, looking southward from his new vantage ground, saw before him not a continuous crest, but a yawning valley, with another frowning crest beyond.[209]

It was too late for surprise now. Two Gray divisions, Walker's and Cleburne's, under Hardee's wing command, had come down from Lookout Mountain and were strongly entrenched around the tunnel. Imminent darkness forbade the determined onslaught it would take to dislodge them. Grant ordered Sherman: Stay where you are. Attack at daybreak. Thomas will then support you by hitting the Rebel center.

Meanwhile Hooker had been ordered to demonstrate against Lookout and distract the enemy from strengthening his right to fend off Sherman's intended assault when it developed.

Now, at long last, Hooker saw a chance to make his "Fighting Joe" ring true again. He asked permission to convert a feint into a *coup de maître* by storming the very summit of Lookout if he could. All right, let him try. He had two divisions: Geary's, XII Corps, of his own command; Cruft's, IV Corps, Army of the Cumberland. Give him one of Sherman's—Osterhaus's, delayed back at Brown's Ferry. Let him see what he could do with that mélange of a force, units that had never before fought side by side. They numbered 10,000, and the Confederate garrison of the mountain had been reduced by diversion of troops to Missionary Ridge to two brigades, totaling 1,295 men. Yet the barest glance at those steep and rocky slopes, rising up to Lookout Point's sheer precipice, warned Hooker that he had taken on a tremendous task.

He tackled it on the misty morning of November 24. A water barrier, Lookout Creek, was the first hazard in that mighty obstacle course his troops must run. Geary's Division and a brigade of Cruft's forded it, swollen though it was, near Wauhatchie. Capturing a picket, they disappeared into the covering mist creeping down the mountainside to meet them. The remainder of the assault force seized one lightly guarded bridge and built another. Tardily alerted defenders rushed down from camps to man rifle pits in a vain attempt to contest the crossings. Blue columns surged over and fanned out, Osterhaus and the rest of Cruft's men linking up with Geary. Hooker's line was a long scythe, swung from the base of the mountain in an upward slash.

It was the moment for the guns. Heavy Parrotts thundered from the redoubts, paving the way for the infantry with bursting shells. Fieldpieces, channeled over the bridges, followed the foot troops. Captain Clement Landgraeber's Battery F, 2nd Missouri Artillery, repeatedly commended in reports for its fine shooting, led off. It was horse artillery and moved fast, but it had to break into a trot, then a gallop, to keep pace with the swift surge of the tide of infantry lapping the base of Lookout Mountain.

As the incline steepened, the going grew sharply tougher, worse for artillery than its comrade arm. Batteries grimly flung themselves at the grades, angling where they could, swinging around obstacles. Guns, caissons, and limbers were reduced to a slow, steady crawl. There could be no slackening or they'd stall and slide back. "Keep 'em rolling." The field artillery slogan, which years later would be immortalized in song, never meant more than it did that day on the sides of Lookout.

Over where Geary's Division was advancing, whips rose and fell as artillery drivers, bent low over pommels, flogged their struggling teams. The horses, bellies close to the ground, scrambled up rock-strewn, brush-cluttered ascents, formidable enough for a man on foot—more than could be sanely asked for animals dragging heavy loads, even with cannoneers heaving at wheels and on prolonge ropes to help them.

From the flank, westerners of the other divisions stared over at the climbing guns Hooker had brought from the Army of the Potomac. "It isn't possible the fool is taking artillery up there! The Potomac fellows have lost what little sense they had. They'll never get a gun back. Didn't I tell you they'd better have stayed at home where they were well off—kid gloves and all?" [210]

Senseless or not, the Potomac fellows drove up and on. Their horses responded nobly, haunch muscles cracking, legs trembling under the frightful strain. White-faced drivers could not banish the dread of what might happen if they struck a hidden stump or boulder. They pictured their pairs rearing and toppling backward—traces snapping—"a horrible cascade of men, metal, and horseflesh surrendered to the slope"—a grinding, shattering crash and "a writhing, lashing, kicking tangle of men and horses and harness that reddened horribly." [211]

The guns could not make it—could never climb far up Lookout. The rocky, heavily timbered western slope proved inaccessible for artillery. Batteries that had gone as far as they could took support positions and cheered the infantry passing them. If the daring assault failed and was hurled back down the mountain, the guns stood ready to cover its retreat.

Although the Union artillery was brought to a halt after the early stages of the advance, there was compensation in the fact that Confederate cannon were able to add little to the defense.

From the little plateau halfway up Lookout, site of the Craven House, Lieutenant R. T. Gibson's section of Howell's Georgia Battery prepared for action. So did other Gray guns, clinging to the mountainsides. All had trouble depressing muzzles sufficiently to sweep oncoming Blue infantry. When climbing attack waves came into range of Gibson's two 6-pound howitzers, he could not bring them to bear. Fire to the flanks was masked by his own infantry, some of Walthall's Brigade. If that support ever left him, he would likely lose his section. He had been ordered to send his limbers to the foot of the mountain, and it began to look doubtful whether they could return in time if he needed them.[212]

They who hold the righ ground. Theirs has been the advantage since war first was waged. The Gray defenders held it and held it valiantly from behind breastworks, man-made and natural. But the odds were dreadfully heavy against them—more than five to one. Many a rifleman was aiming too high, as all but the more experienced marksmen are apt to do when firing downhill. Before long the tables were being turned. Wings of the assaulting force overlapped both ends of Walthall's line and pushed on higher up. Flanking fire from above began to pour down on the Confederates. And their assailants were increasingly covered by the gathering mist. "That curtain of cloud was hung around the mountain by the GOD of battles—even our GOD," was correspondent Taylor's paean. "It was the veil of the temple that could not be rent." [213]

"The hours slowly wore away; the roar of battle increased, as it came rolling around the point of the mountain, and the anxiety grew." Grant and Thomas, watching from Orchard Knob, saw the slanted banners of red, white, and blue climbing, inching upward. Mist momentarily submerged them. Then gusts of wind blew rifts in the haze. Once more the watchers beheld the flags. Some of them fell but were caught up to flaunt their folds again. Gallantly they climbed on.

Yonder flew the color of the 40th Ohio, thrusting toward the white beacon of the Craven House. As Ohio passed through a spent front line, exhausted, panting men cheered them. "Here come fresh troops to relieve us. Go to it, boys. We've chased them up for you. Pour it into them! Give 'em hell!" The regiment charged on over ditches and walls, up onto the plateau. In the last rush its major was shot through the heart and its color-bearer, who had come all the way, reeled and fell, his number up at last. Dead hands relaxed their grip on the staff.

The brave color-bearers. Those bright banners they carried, making them such conspicuous targets, beckoned the regiments on. The flags of the 3rd Brigade, 2nd Division, XII Corps, were waving over enemy works before its commander finished shouting his order to fix bayonets and charge. "Seeing our colors so far in front, our men advanced on the run; and such was their impetuosity that abatis and felled timber were no obstacles whatever." They dashed on—60th, 149th, and 137th New York Volunteers—storming two Gray cannon. "They swept their colors over the guns." [214]

Emerging from a deep ravine, the 59th Illinois forged straight up the mountain. The regiment struggled upward, clinging to rocks and bushes to keep footholds. Volleys of musketry blazed down on it. Men who slipped or were hit tumbled backward. Rolling bodies crashed into tree trunks or were catapulted off bending saplings. Some picked themselves up and began climbing again. Many lay still against whatever barrier finally stopped them.

Cartridge pouches were emptying. Ammunition carriers, bent low under the weight of their burdens, toiled up, and none too soon, for many a rifleman had fired his last bullet. Following them came hospital corpsmen to pick up the wounded and cope with the difficult task of bringing laden stretchers down the mountain. Streams of prisoners joined the downward trek.

Clouds seemed to wreathe the peak of Lookout. They began to roll down the mountainsides, cloaking them in fleece, blotting out the battle lines.

Up and up they went into the clouds, which were settling down upon the lofty summit, until they were lost from sight, and their comrades watching anxiously in the Chattanooga valley could hear only the booming of cannon and the rattle of musketry far overhead, and catch glimpses of fire flashing from moment to moment through the dark clouds, as if the old mythmaker's notion of the thunderstorm were realized, and elemental spirits were engaged in a deadly struggle for the dominion of the upper air.[215]

The three assaulting Union divisions converged on the Craven house. Walthall's Gray brigade rallied there. No more than briefly could it hold against such odds. The Blue waves smashed it back, flooding over Gibson's howitzers. Their crews abandoned them, as their support melted away. Walthall's men, reinforced by two brigades from the mountaintop, made a stand in prepared defense works about 400 yards beyond the white house.

Muffling the din of battle, rendering invisible all but the nearest objects, the dense gray-white curtain of the mist descended on the plateau. No wind could lift it now nor gun flashes pierce it.

For the first time, perhaps, since that mountain began to burn beneath the gold and crimson sandals of the sun, it was in eclipse. The cloud of the summit and the smoke of the battle had met half-way and mingled. Here was Chattanooga, but Lookout had vanished! [216]

Cease firing. Fighting Joe Hooker gave the order at two o'clock in the afternoon. His men, their ammunition dwindling low, could fight no longer when they could not see the enemy.

"The Battle Above the Clouds" was over. It would not win that romantic name, borrowed from mist and fog, until years later. A few of its veterans would still be living when grandsons of their generation in soaring planes joined combat with an enemy, the clouds beneath them. Yet the name's shining legend lingers, for it was born of valor and glory. Let the young men of the age of flight see their visions. The old men could still dream their dreams. We, too, in our way, they could say, remembering, once fought above the clouds.

That night the remnants of Lookout's Confederate garrison were withdrawn and marched to Missionary Ridge. The smitten shield was lowered. Next morning, November 25, dawned in clear and frosty air. The mist had fled before a bright and dazzling sun. Down in the valley every eye turned eagerly toward the top of Lookout Mountain.

On the plateau a call for volunteers to scale the mountain's peak was issued. Captain John Wilson, 8th Kentucky Infantry, stepped forward. He chose five men from his color company and others. With the regiment ready in support in case the enemy were still holding the heights, the little party clambered up the precipice to the Point. [217]

Thousands below gazed upward to witness a glorious sight—such a vision as Francis Scott Key had beheld on the ramparts of Fort McHenry when he wrote an anthem.

From the summit of Lookout Mountain waved the Star-Spangled Banner.

CHAPTER 16

The Last Rampart

Siege guns in the Chattanooga redoubts saluted the flag floating over Lookout's peak. Bands jubilantly blared "Hail to the Chief." Then over at the northern end of Missionary Ridge echoes of the saluting cannonade were caught up by the rolling drumfire of field-pieces. Distant bugles sounded the urgent, staccato notes of "Charge." At the first rays of the bright sunrise of November 25 Sherman was advancing to the assault.

As his divisions marched down into the gap that had balked him yesterday, Grant and Thomas again watched from Orchard Knob. Once more that eminence justified its conquest as an ideal command post. The generals stood at the central point of a cyclorama [218] of the far-flung battle about to be fought. Theirs was a magnificent prospect of the full length of Missionary Ridge, none of it to be obscured this clear day by the mist that had veiled Lookout. An observation balloon could scarcely have bettered it.

The generals watched, field glasses sweeping the Ridge. Around them on the Knob, now a reservation of the Military Park, were grouped their staffs, escorts, and an attendant battery. Grant's calm seemed a trifle less iron than usual. The grave Thomas gave no hint that he did not care for his role of general in waiting. Granger was chafing as he had been when he climbed the hayrick and decided to march to the sound of the guns at Chickamauga.

Up on the Ridge they saw Gray troops streaming northward. Bragg, evidently with no thought of retreat,[219] seemed to be further reinforcing his right. Grant's glasses veered around. Bragg might soon regret that shifting of strength, for Hooker had been ordered to quit his triumphant perch on Lookout—follow the trail of the enemy he had driven from the mountain—cross Chattanooga Creek, and strike the Confederate left. That should force Bragg to pull back many of the men sent to hold off Sherman. If he did not do so, and do it quickly, his left flank would be rolled up, and his line of retreat to Chickamauga Station would be cut.

General Grant was turning the screw of a vise gripping Missionary Ridge; playing both ends against the middle, as it were. If both ends were crushed, the middle would cave in. Perhaps only Thomas gazed meditatively toward the Ridge's center of which the Army of the Cumberland that afternoon would have a much closer view.

Sherman's bugles blew again, and his drums rolled. Through the wooded gullies and on up the slopes he launched three divisions in a hard-driving attack on the Confederate citadel of Tunnel Hill.

One division bore the brunt of opposition, but it was a stanch one, and Cleburne commanded it. It was a bad turn of the fortunes of war for Sherman and the Union when Pat Cleburne was called back when just about to entrain to reinforce Longstreet at Knoxville. Now his line of entrenchments, rifle pits, and log barricades, with a second one higher up covering the first, barred the way. And those lines were manned by crack troops under as fighting an Irishman as ever deserved the name. Also Cleburne was able to draw on two brigades of other divisions for reinforcements at critical moments. A third brigade came in to support his left flank, fending off by heavy skirmishing the Federal attempts to turn it. Defensive works were skillfully placed and constructed and stubbornly manned. The front they protected was a narrow one. No more than three or four of Sherman's brigades were able to assault it at one time. As a result several brigades of the force at his disposal went unused; they remained in reserve and saw no action all day.

But Sherman's men of the Army of the Tennessee had helped take Vicksburg, high on its bluff, and behind them rose lofty Lookout, newly stormed. They charged, cheering, toward Tunnel Hill.

From the hill's apex guns of the Warren Light Artillery of Mississippi poured down rapid volleys. They cut wide swaths in the right of the Blue line. It faltered, wilted, and lay down, the living among the dead and wounded. But the Union left charged on through the woods and up the slopes, driving for that deadly battery. The Mississippi artillerymen were swept by a fury of cross fire. Its two officers and all the sergeants fell. Corporal F. M. Williams took command, and his depleted crews, with infantrymen filling in, stood valiantly to their guns. They shifted to canister. Blasts of balls sprayed from muzzles, but still the Blue charge came on. It forged to within fifty paces, and the battery was all but lost when a Gray countercharge struck and routed the assailants, sending them reeling back downhill.

Sherman, that dour, determined fighter, kept pounding away. Imperatively he needed his guns to breach that wall of opposition. The 6th Wisconsin and other batteries, summoned forward, struggled to reach positions to silence the enemy's cannon and shatter his infantry.

A devil-may-care outfit, the 6th, but a crack one. When it first took the field, it had turned in its sabers as encumbrances but kept a fiddle, banjo, tambourine, and clarinet. After the fall of Vicksburg it celebrated with another relaxation. "The demon of the bowl prevailed," an abstemious young cannoneer wrote in his diary, and quantities of "infernal liquid" were downed. Otherwise the 6th was attentive to its duty, maintaining the principle that good light artillery must always be mobile by special care of its horses. It regularly watered and fed them—whenever forage was to be found—swam and washed them when it camped near a river or creek, and suppled harness with oil. Resourcefully it picked up spares and replacements as opportunity offered; raids on Rebel plantations of East Tennessee provided ten fine horses and twenty mules. When foraging for feed failed, the artillerymen suffered, watching their hungry animals eat their halter ropes, so that chains from the battery wagon had to be substituted. But the 6th was always able to harness, hitch, and move out.

It had come a long, hard way with Sherman. For steep mountain climbs, at times it had used four pairs and a span of mules to haul

each gun. Dangerous descents were negotiated when helpful cavalrymen tailed on to prolonge ropes, braking the carriages that slid
down the frightening slopes. After crossing the Tennessee River on
the pontoon bridge, the first caisson had sunk so deeply in the mire
that an hour and a half was required to extricate it. The second
caisson, carrying a quantity of percussion fuses, crashed into a stump
and overturned, but the fuses had been well packed and did not
explode.[220]

Now the 6th Wisconsin and the other batteries were faced by the
formidable approaches to Tunnel Hill. Wooded grades slanted up
in front of them. With details of axemen ahead clearing a path,
batteries hitched an extra pair in front of teams and tackled the
shell-swept slope. Still they couldn't make it. They borrowed more
pairs from the caissons, leaving them behind. It was still more than
the toiling horses could manage. Unlimber came the order. Man
drag ropes and haul the guns up. Drivers to the left about. As the
guns were slowly pulled upward, the teams and limbers which had
left them began to slide downhill into oncoming infantry until the
carriages were stayed by ropes hastily fastened to axletrees, which
saved them from a crashing disaster.

Covered by the fire of accompanying and supporting artillery,
Sherman flung one spirited assault after another at Tunnel Hill.
His tiered battle lines blazed upward with concentrated fusilades
that Cleburne's men remembered as "one continuous sheet of hiss-
ing, flying lead." Now and again a fierce Yankee thrust pierced the
defenses and surged up the slopes for a bloody gain.

Every assault was met as gallantly as it was made. Lieutenant
Thomas J. Key, commanding the Helena Battery of Arkansas, de-
pressed his guns to the utmost and fired shell and canister down into
the face of the climbing enemy. Finally the down-peering cannon
could no longer be brought to bear. Yet missiles kept on smashing
into the Federal ranks. Cleburne's gunners and infantrymen were
rolling down on them the biggest boulders they could pry loose—
were hurling at them lighter rocks and round shot.[221]

Battered back repeatedly, Sherman would not give up. More regiments emerged from the woods, showered with tree limbs cut by a

cannonade that crashed down on them the instant they came in sight. They charged forward over open fields.

I had heard the roaring of heavy battle before, but never such a shrieking of cannon-balls and bursting of shells as met us on that run [Captain S. H. M. Byers declared]. We could see the rebels working their guns, while in plain view other batteries galloped up, unlimbered, and let loose upon us. Behind us our own batteries were firing at the enemy over our heads, till the storm and roar became horrible. The line officers screamed at the top of their voices, trying to repeat the orders to the men. "Steady, steady. Bear to the right! Don't fire! Steady, steady," was yelled till every one of us was hoarse, and until the fearful thunder of the cannonade made all commands unheard and useless. In ten minutes the field was crossed, the foot of the ascent was reached, and now the Confederates poured into our faces the reserved fire of their awful musketry. It helped little that we returned it from our own rifles, hidden as the enemy were in rifle-pits, behind logs and stumps, and trees. Still we charged, and climbed a fence in front of them, and charged again. The order was given to lie down and continue firing. Then someone cried, "Look to the tunnel!" There, on the right, pouring through a tunnel in the mountain, and out of the railway cut, came the gray-coats by the hundred, flanking us completely. "Stop them!" cried our colonel to those of us at the right. "Push them back." It was but the work of a few minutes to rise to our feet and run to the mouth of the tunnel, firing as we ran. Too late! They were through by the hundreds, and a fatal enfilading fire was cutting our line to pieces. No wonder the brigade temporarily faltered and gave way, when the whole army of the enemy seemed concentrated on a single point.[222]

That was the end of the war for Captain Byers and numbers of his men, captured by onrushing Mississippians. Herded up the hill, the officer was soon on his way to Libby Prison; most of his luckless men would die in Andersonville.

Again and again yelling Gray legions checked the desperate Union drive. Grant had dispatched a division to Sherman's aid, but it was recalled en route. In any event it was doubtful whether one more division would have added drive enough to pierce that unyielding defense.

Where was Hooker? The timing of his attack, to be delivered on the southern end of the ridge, was vital to the operation. Let that jaw of the vise close promptly, and Bragg must be given such grave concern for his left and his line of retreat that he might even order Cleburne back from the right.

Hooker had begun his march toward Rossville and his objective early that morning. But the Confederates he had ousted from Lookout had taken that road before him and done everything they could to obstruct it behind them. As soon as they had crossed Chickamauga Creek, they burned the bridge. Hooker's retarded columns telescoped in front of the unfordable water gap. If ever a top engineer such as "Baldy" Smith and a pontoon train were needed, it was now. Lacking them, Hooker's men commenced to construct a bridge. It edged slowly out over the stream. The splendid impetus, which had carried these troops up Lookout, seemed spent. Precious hours—one, two, then three—sped by. It was late afternoon before the Blue columns crossed and advanced on Missionary Ridge.

On the crest behind Sherman his signal flags fluttered, acknowledging a message from Chattanooga. Grant's order ran: Attack again.

Sherman read it grimly. He thought: The "old man" is daft. He sent a staffer to have the signalers ask the commander whether he had correctly received that order.

"Go signal Grant," Sherman snapped. "The orders were that I should get as many as possible in front of me, and God knows there are enough. They've been reinforcing all day.[223]

About this matter of Southern reinforcements mystery would always hang. Regarding it, witnesses either made honest mistakes or were touched by the moon. Grant, Rawlins, Sherman, Hazen, and General O. O. Howard (who had arrived from the East and been sent with his division to support Sherman) all declared emphatically that they saw column after column of Bragg's troops pouring eastward from the center along the crest to meet Sherman's attack. Hazen, who stood with Grant and Rawlins on Orchard Knob in easy view of the ridge top, was very specific in his statement. Yet General E. P. Alexander, the Confederate, said that no such regiments had been sent, and Wilson, studying the reports, concluded that Alexander was correct. The most sensible explanation seemed to be that the eclipse of the moon had made everybody a little crazy.[224]

Sherman's belief was a tribute to the magnificent opposition of Cleburne's Division. Yet, regardless, Grant's answer to his subordinate's query was: No mistake. Order stands as signaled. Keep pounding.

Back on the Knob, General Grant seemed to his staff to be showing unusual signs of worry. Apparently Sherman had been stopped; if he were to make any progress, pressure must be taken off him. It was too late now for the tardy Hooker to co-ordinate. A first-rate battle plan had been wrecked. Both ends Grant had meant to play against the middle were virtually static.

Well, there was still the middle. There lay that formidable alternative, a frontal assault on Missionary Ridge, rising toward 500 feet above the level ground at its base.

General Grant turned to "Pap" Thomas. "Don't you think it's about time to advance against the rifle pits?" he asked.

Thomas is said to have made no reply but continued to stare through his field glasses.[225] Some of Grant's staff believed him reluctant to commit his troops to so desperate an undertaking. But that was not like Thomas nor was it in accordance with the spirit of his army. It was strongly demonstrated when Grant made his question an order, which Thomas transmitted to his divisions. Excited men, burning for revenge for Chickamauga, cheered. A brigadier watched all the orderlies, clerks, and cooks of his command rush to find rifles and fall into ranks.[226]

So Grant had found out he couldn't save all the glory for Sherman and Hooker, had he? Now he was having to give the Cumberlanders a chance, even if he didn't consider them first-rate combat troops. Well, they'd show him.

Correspondent Taylor watched the blue ranks file by. There rode a general, splendidly uniformed. Taylor, good reporter though he was, failed to name him, but he had heard of his gallant behavior in earlier battles and had talked to him.

There is a glitter of buttons and stars where he is, and they were seen glancing like meteors at Stone River, Chickamauga and [now] Mission Ridge, in the thick of the fight. "I want my men to know where I am," the general said, explaining his shining insignia, "and those baubles light a man to danger and to duty wonderfully well. He cannot decently *run* by starlight!" [227]

At the head of the 100th Indiana Infantry rode another officer who believed a leader should always be conspicuous to his men. Colonel Timothy O'Meara to enter battle always donned his best uniform, sword at side, a foreign medal on his breast, and a bright scarlet sash around his waist. From a cord about his neck was slung an amulet which, he was devoutly certain, would protect him from harm. The Indianans would follow their vivid commander any-where. You could see it in their faces as they swung along after him toward the Ridge. Through the dust of the regiment's passing O'Meara's scarlet sash remained visible. It would soon stand out as plainly to a Rebel sharpshooter up there on the heights.[228]

Tread of marching feet at the quickstep, barely restrained from double time so eager for the storm were these troops in blue. Thomas's columns moved up to assault positions and fanned out front into line. Baird on the left, then Wood, Sheridan, and John-son. Four divisions and their artillery—20,000 men. Eyes swept up the steep sides of Missionary Ridge, gashed by two lines of entrench-ments, its summit crowned by cannon and flaunting flags. Every ear strained for the sound of the six guns on Orchard Knob that were to signal the attack.

Time: 3:30 P.M. The two Napoleons and four 3-inch rifles of Captain Lyman Bridge's Illinois Battery on the Knob were laid on the Confederate trenches and loaded. They belonged to Granger's Corps. That impatient general, standing on the parapet to their flank, raised his right arm, swung it downward, and shouted.

CHAPTER 17

Charge Without Orders

That brief interval between General Granger's shout and the jerk of a lanyard that gave it obedience was as suspenseful as the action following was dramatic. In War Correspondent Taylor's pen lay the power to chronicle it.

Strong and steady his voice rang out; "Number one, fire! Number two, fire! Number three, fire!"—it seemed to me the tolling of the clock of destiny—and when at "Number six, fire!" the roar throbbed out with the flash, you should have seen the dead line that had been lying behind the works all day, all night, all day again, come to resurrection in the twinkling of an eye, leap like a blade from its scabbard and sweep with a two-mile stroke toward the Ridge. From divisions to brigades, from brigades to regiments, the order ran. A minute, and the skirmishers deploy; a minute, and the first great drops begin to patter along the line; a minute, and the musketry is in full play like the crackling whips of a hemlock fire; men go down here and there, before your eyes; the wind lifts the smoke and drifts it away over the top of the Ridge; everything is too distinct; it is fairly palpable; you can touch it with your hand. The divisions of Wood and Sheridan are wading breast-deep in the valley of death.

I can never tell you what it was like. They pushed out, leaving nothing behind them. There was no reservation in that battle. On moves the line of skirmishers, like a heavy frown, and after it, at quick time, the splendid columns. At right of us and left of us and front of us, you can see the bayonets glitter in the sun. You cannot persuade yourself that Bragg was wrong, a day or two ago, when seeing Hooker moving in, he said, "Now we shall have a

Potomac review;" that this is not the parade he prophesied; that it is of a truth the harvest of death to which they go down. And so through the fringe of woods went the line. Now, out into the open ground they burst into the double-quick. Shall I call it a Sabbath day's journey, or a long half mile? To me, that watched, it seemed endless as eternity, and yet they made it in thirty minutes. The tempest that now broke upon their heads was terrible. The enemy's fire burst out of the rifle-pits from base to summit of Mission Ridge; five batteries of Parrotts and Napoleons opened along the crest. Grape and canister and shot and shell sowed the ground with rugged iron and garnished it with the wounded and the dead. But steady and strong our columns moved on.

> "By heaven! It was a splendid sight to see,
> For me who had no friend, no brother there,"

but to all loyal hearts, alas, and thank GOD, those men were friend and brother, both in one.[229]

They had not waited for the full count, those eager Blue assaulting ranks. Number Five had scarcely fired when they jumped the gun, the sixth shot. "Forward, guide center, march!" the regimental commanders called out. Along a two-and-one-half-mile front the waves beneath a glistening spume of fixed bayonets surged onward. For a time the alignment had indeed been parade-like. Then gullies, felled trees, and stumps bent and twisted it but never slackened its unleashed processional. Saving no breath for the climb ahead, soldiers raised resounding cheers, rippling from one end of the line to the other and back through the following files.

Not even the roar of the guns could drown those wild hurrahs. Heavy cannon in the Federal forts caught up and magnified a thousandfold the last report of the signal. Their shells soared over Thomas's men and burst among Missionary's defenses. The light battery on Orchard Knob chimed in along with the others. General Granger could no longer contain his impetuosity. He vaulted down from the parapet into an emplacement and sighted one of Bridges' fieldpieces. Stepping aside, he gave the word to fire.

In a moment, right in front, a great volume of smoke, like "the cloud by day," lifted off the summit from among the batteries, and hung motionless, kindling in the sun. The shot had struck a caisson and that was its dying breath. In five minutes away flared another. A shell went crashing through a building in the cluster that marked Bragg's headquarters; a second killed the skeleton horses of a battery at his elbow; a third scattered a gray mass as if it had been a wasp's nest.[230]

A crack gunner was lost when Gordon Granger became a general. He enthusiastically continued his artillery sharpshooting until Grant gruffly reminded him that he was commanding a corps, not a cannon. Let him bring his troops into action and quit frittering away time with "guerrilla operations."

Rifles of Rebel skirmishers sputtered in the face of the Union onsurge. It paid them no heed, sweeping them back. As it charged the first line of trenches, an infantryman of the 8th Kansas peered up toward the crest.

Then, through the branches of leafless trees, we saw a bright flame leap out and a dull grey smoke curl up all along the summit of the Ridge; a crash like a thousand thunder claps greeted us; solid shot went screaming through the timber, and hurtling shells exploded above and around the lines, sending their scattered fragments shrieking through the air like a legion of demons. Without an order the men broke into a double quick—brave fellows, they knew the work before them was quick success or sure destruction.... Our men did not even answer [the skirmishers'] fire by a single shot, but with arms trailing or on the right shoulder pressed onward, leaping over the fallen timber and brooks and crowding through the briars and brush that lined the way, until they burst like a thunderbolt out of the woods and into the open field. Then from the whole line there rose a loud, hearty, ringing cheer, and on they swept. In the fields the columns were caught in the fiercer fire and leaden sleet from the rebel line at the foot of the hill, and soon in the still deadlier volume of musketry from its summit. But there was not a waver or pause in the stern advance nor a straggler from it. In a few moments our men were nearly across the field. There was a break in the grey lines behind the rebel works; a few rushed to the rear, and with frantic eagerness began to climb the slope; but nearly all, throwing down their muskets, and holding up their hands in token of surrender, leaped to our side of the entrenchments and cowered behind them, for the hail of bullets raining down from the hill was as deadly to them as to us. The first line was won.[231]

The 8th's adjutant ordered the prisoners to the rear. "You have been trying to get there long enough," he told them, "and now charge on Chattanooga!"

Thomas had triumphantly stormed the first line in the Confederate center as ordered. Over on the Union left Sherman was still being fought to a standstill by Cleburne. The belated Hooker was across the bridged creek and moving against Missionary's southern slopes. His attack might finally prove effective, but now it was only a half-door swinging loosely on its hinges, with the other half firmly blocked. The wide aperture between alone offered entrance, and the wedge in it had not been driven deep.

It was the moment, and a fleeting one, for decision—Grant's decision. But he did not have to make it. It was taken out of his hands.

The crimson flash and billowing white smoke of bursting shells from the crest of the Ridge outlined that captured first line of entrenchments. Plunging rifle fire from the second line scoured its length. "The whole ridge in our front had broken out like another Aetna." Crumpled dead and wounded crowded the living. Officers told their men to start digging with shovels and bayonets to reverse the parapets—to raise some shelter against that avalanche of metal from above.

Those seized trenches were close to becoming untenable. Grant must have foreseen they would be and must as surely have counted on Sherman and Hooker closing in from left and right to redeem the situation now that Bragg was distracted by the attack on his center. There was no sign of any such realization. Now something would have to be done and done quickly. If it were not, the eventuality was not pleasant to contemplate. A victorious enemy clearing his front and battering back the isolated forces on his flanks. Sherman driven back across the Tennessee. Hooker mauled and repulsed. Thomas hurled back into Chattanooga.

The Confederate fire doubled in intensity. Even in the face of it a line of Union skirmishers, who had been pursuing the retreating foe, kept going, crouching low as they crawled on up the hill. For a time their comrades in the trenches, panting and exhausted, merely watched them. Burdened with weapons, eighty rounds of ammunition, blanket rolls, and other equipment, they had come the better part of a mile, much of it at the double, and they sorely needed a breathing spell. Yet if they stayed where they were, most of them would be killed. They could retreat, but plainly they held no thought of it. The only movement to the rear was the hurrying columns of prisoners.

No orders from headquarters. No galloping courier from the Knob.

Then it happened. A few blue-clad figures clambered out of the trenches and started up the slopes after the skirmishers. Squads, companies, joined them. Now there were orders, orders given on the spot. Colonels of regiments shouted them, rushing forward to lead their men.

Onward and upward they charged, all the brave regiments. It was then that a Rebel sharpshooter, peering through the smoke, spotted the bright scarlet sash of Colonel O'Meara, his glistening sword waving forward the 100th Indiana. Sights steady on the target, the rifle cracked. The Colonel died, drilled through the body. Around him on the slopes fell 132 of his loyal men, killed or wounded— 43 per cent of the regiment's strength. But all along the line that unordered charge forged ahead, unwavering, not to be halted.

From Orchard Knob Grant and his generals gaped at that spontaneous charge.

Grant angrily demanded: "Thomas, who ordered those men up the ridge?"

"Old Slow Trot" quietly answered: "I don't know; I did not."

Grant turned to Granger and snapped: "Did you order them up, Granger?"

He got a quick denial. "No, they started up without orders. When those fellows get started all hell can't stop them."

General Grant said something to the effect that somebody would suffer if it did not turn out well, and then, turning, stoically watched the ridge. He gave no further orders.

As soon as Granger had replied to Thomas, he turned to me, his chief-of-staff [General Joseph S. Fullerton], and said: "Ride at once to Wood, and then to Sheridan, and ask them if they ordered their men up the ridge, and tell them if they can take it, to push ahead." As I was mounting, Granger added; "It is hot over there, and you may not get through. I shall send Captain Avery to Sheridan, and other officers after both of you." As fast as my horse could carry me, I rode first to General Wood, and delivered the message. "I didn't order them up," said Wood; "they started up on their own account, and they are going up, too! Tell Granger, if we are supported, we will take and hold the ridge!" As soon as I reached General Wood, Captain Avery got to General Sheridan, and delivered his message. "I didn't order them up," said Sheridan; "but we are going to take the ridge!" [232]

Short, ruddy Phil Sheridan swiveled in his saddle and snatched a silver whisky flask from a pocket. He stared up at a Confederate artillery officer on the crest, raised the flask, toasted, "Here's to you," took a long pull.

That was Captain Robert Cobb's Kentucky Battery up on the ridge to which Phil Sheridan made his gesture. It manned four Napoleons christened for generals, reputedly at Bragg's request, "Lady Buckner," "Lady Breckinridge," "Lady Lyon," and "Lady Gracey"—polite designations that tough cannoneers probably disregarded or reduced to "Old Buck" and the like. The artillerymen in gray were in no mood to exchange amenities with the Yankee officer down below. An order was snapped, and two of the Napoleons spoke in a distinctly unladylike manner. Shells thudded into the ground near Sheridan, showering him with a geyser of dirt. Little

Phil brushed it out of his eyes and swore: "That's damned ungenerous; I'll take those guns for that!" He spurred forward.[233]

Formations lost, regiments intermingled, that supremely gallant, unordered charge struggled upward. A slow-rising flood, striving to inundate an irregular dike, it sought channels and crevices—the less steep ascents, ground that gave some scant, momentary cover. Shells tore at it, and bullets sifted it, yet it did not falter.

Gradually, distinctly, the charge assumed a design which the eyes of awed spectators on the vantage points in the rear could not miss. Out of the forefront of the ragged blue line, throughout its length, arrow points or spearheads were forged—triangular, wedges like the flight of wild geese. They thrust upward at the summit of Missionary Ridge. At the apex of each, sunlit glints of color glowed through the smoke.

Those were the battle flags and their following, faithful unto death.

CHAPTER 18

"Terrible as an Army with Banners"

Colors would gradually fade out of battle after the Civil War. Great garrison flags or the smaller storm ones would always fly at their staffs in military posts. National and regimental colors and standards would make a brave show at reviews and parades. Stands would brighten headquarters and form a vivid background for generals' and colonels' desks. But the firepower of modern warfare would ban them from action. Colors brought forward, furled and cased, would be broken out in command posts but no longer in the battle line.

Yet on the twenty-fifth day of November, 1863, the Stars and Stripes on the slopes of Missionary Ridge and the Stars and Bars along its crest were still the visible symbols of that for which soldiers lived, fought, and died. Some of the colors were proudly inscribed with battle names of which their shot-torn rents and tatters were tokens. Others bore legends such as that of the 10th Michigan: the grim promise, *Tuebor*—I Will Slay. On folds of the 9th Michigan's was proclaimed: "Presented on the 23rd of October, 1861, by the Rev. George Duffield, of Detroit, to the 9th Michigan Infantry, his son, Col. W. W. Duffield, commanding. 'Thou hast given a banner to them that fear Thee, that it may be displayed because of the truth. In the name of God will we set up our banners.' "

Never were the battle flags, cynosure of 250,000 eyes at Missionary Ridge, more clearly beheld. Nor did they and the superbly courageous, often foredoomed men who carried them ever more gloriously lead those who followed in their train.

And what do these men follow? If you look you shall see that the thirteen thousand are not a rushing herd of human creatures; that along the Gothic roof of the Ridge a row of inverted V's is slowly moving up almost in line, a mighty lettering on the hills' broad side. At the angles of those V's is something that glitters like a wing. Your heart gives a great bound when you think what it is—the regimental flag—and glancing along the front count fifteen of those colors that were borne at Pea Ridge, waved at Shiloh, glorified at Stone River, riddled at Chickamauga. Nobler than Caesar's rent mantle are they all! And up move the banners, now fluttering like a wounded bird, now faltering, now sinking out of sight. Three times the flag of the 27th Illinois goes down. And you know why. Three dead color-sergeants lie just there, but the flag is immortal— thank God!—and up it comes again, and the V's move on. At the left of Wood, three regiments of Baird—Turchin, the Russian thunderbolt, is there—hurl themselves against a bold point strong with rebel works; for a long quarter of an hour, three flags are perched and motionless on a plateau under the frown of the hill. Will they linger forever? I give a look at the sun behind me; it is not more than a hand's breadth from the edge of the mountain; its level rays bridge the valley from Chattanooga to the Ridge with beams of gold; it shines in the hostile faces; it brings out the Federal blue; it touches up the flags. Oh, for the voice that could bid that sun stand still! I turn to the battle again; those three flags have taken flight. They are upward bound!

The race of the flags is growing every moment more terrible. There at the right, in Colonel Sherman's brigade, a strange thing catches the eye; one of the inverted V's is turning right side up! The men struggling along the converging lines to overtake the flag have distanced it, and there the colors are, sinking down in the center between the rising flanks. The line wavers like a great billow, and up comes the banner again, as if it heaved on a surge's shoulder! [234]

Seven of the enlisted men and officers who bore colors up the Ridge won the Medal of Honor.[235] Its later ribbon, starred and blue, from the crest of the coat of arms of the United States, linked them and their memory forever with their proud burden.

Sergeant George L. Banks, the 15th Indiana Infantry's color-bearer, was wounded while the bright emblem whose staff he clutched beckoned his regiment on to the assault. He did not falter. As he climbed onto the enemy's works, he was hit again. Reeling, he thrust the staff's ferrule deep into the earth of the parapet. In a brigade of eight regiments his was the first flag to be planted there.

Wounded severely, Sergeant James B. Bell staggered forward in the van of the 11th Ohio. He was the first man of his regiment to reach the summit. There he kept his flag waving until he took four more wounds. Only then would that gallant bearer quit the field.

The 80th Ohio was checked and flung back. Sergeant Davis Freeman saw the national and regimental colors waver and go down. Under the plunging fire of a fierce enemy counterattack, he picked up both flags and saved them from capture. Bullet, shell fragment, or canister ball loosened grips on staffs, yet almost always other hands caught the colors before they fell. Second Lieutenant Thomas N. Graham seized the 15th Indiana's from their bloody bearer and carried them on over the Confederate breastworks. First Lieutenant Arthur MacArthur, Jr. (father of General Douglas MacArthur), was ready when the banner of the 24th Wisconsin began to sink. He seized and swept it forward to lead the charging line.

Sometimes it was a captured flag that became a rallying point. First Lieutenant Simeon T. Josselyn, leading his company of the 13th Illinois against outnumbering enemy, shot their color-bearer and wrested away the Stars and Bars, with the rest of his adversaries put to flight or taken prisoner. Private James C. Walker, Company K, 31st Ohio Infantry, carried the colors after two bearers had fallen. Following his uplifted flag, the regiment stormed a battery. Walker charged on to capture the colors of the 41st Alabama and their bearer.

That day for every carrier of the flag who won a decoration there were a dozen others who deserved its award. In the 26th Ohio alone five pairs of hands in turn grasped the staff before the colors surmounted those deadly slopes. As the color sergeant fell severely wounded, the senior corporal took his place and was killed. A third man stepped forward and struggled upward till he dropped from exhaustion. Soon his relief, stumbling up the steep ascent, commenced to totter. Lieutenant Colonel William H. Young, commanding the regiment, took the flag over the last one hundred and fifty yards to the final line of Rebel rifle pits.[236]

A staff officer,[237] riding forward with an order, saw a flag-bearer pressing onward far in advance of his regiment, which vainly strove to overtake him. The steepness of the grade up there was more than his horse could manage, the staffer knew. For the soldier was crawling up on his knees, one hand clutching at underbrush, the other holding the colors aloft. He climbed on toward an enemy flag floating above. Within a few feet of it he took shelter behind a log and waved his banner to urge his comrades on. As fast as they could, they dragged themselves up around him.

Yonder a second flag called its regiment after it. Now both groups converged and gathered around the bearers who had led them. They crouched under an overhang not twenty feet beneath the hostile breastworks. So long as they stayed pinned down there they were safe. For their repleted ranks to rise and rush that last lethal space, full in the face of point-blank volleys, meant annihilation.

Then the watching staff officer, torn by suspense, caught sight of a third flag and a third regiment joining them. Now there were enough to dare a dash. One of the flags darted up out of the dead space and thrust forward. The others were launched with it. Colors and regiments in triad swept over the parapet. Down in the trench swirled a melee of hand-to-hand combat—reports of rifles muffled by the bodies their muzzles were jammed against, stabbing bayonets and jabbing butts. Blue submerged Gray. The flags summoned on.

How the regiments clustered around their battle flags, in every case in the van—how nothing could stop their gallant advance, slow but steady—those were vivid memories years never dimmed for men who were there.

Above, the summit of the hill was one sheet of flame and smoke, and the awful explosions of artillery and musketry made the earth fairly tremble. Below, the columns of dark blue, with the old banner of beauty and of glory leading them on, were mounting up with leaning forms, each eager with desperate resolution to be first. Cannon shot tore through their ranks; musket balls were rapidly and fearfully decimating them; behind them the dead and wounded lay thick as autumn leaves; before them death was reveling in a whirlwind of carnage; but the lava-flood of battle pouring down upon them no more checked the grand advance than if it had been the softest rain of summer. . . . Their eyes were fixed on the blazing heights, and they moved forward with a courage as cool and devoted as if it was sublime.[238]

Along the length of Missionary Ridge were finally flaunted the flags of sixty Union regiments. Which one reached the crest first was argued on the spot, as it would be year after year at veterans' reunions. The weary, panting color-bearer of the 38th Indiana admitted: "A fellow of the 22nd Indiana was up here first, but he wouldn't have been if I hadn't had my overcoat on." Yet above all stood the glorious fact that the colors *were* there—that, in one grasp or passed on from dying hands, their slanted staffs had stormed the Ridge. There the flags flew. "And the Star-Spangled Banner in triumph shall wave."

"Terrible as an army with banners." The flags in battle. We shall not look upon their like again.

CHAPTER 19

Race for the Crest

Confederates in the trenches on the slopes of the Ridge and from the breastworks on its crest had watched the Union assault from the moment it was launched. They saw it forge relentlessly upward through their fiercest fire. To one observer it was a sublime spectacle, a feat of arms "worthy of admiration." Such tribute by the brave to the brave soon vanished in apprehension, a grim and growing foreboding of defeat.

They could see too much, those men in gray. All the blue array was spread out before them, coming on and on, seeming suddenly irresistible. Sight of those battle flags which would not halt, which, if they sank for an instant, quickly rose again, alone was enough to rack nerves. The first signs of demoralization began to show. Between shots Gray riflemen covertly glanced over their shoulders, seeking a line of retreat. Artillerymen, serving their guns at top speed, looked rearward through the smoke toward where the limbers were waiting; the time might be near when they would have to hook on the pieces and pull out in a hurry.

When the second line of entrenchments was overrun, and the Federals came storming on up toward the summit, the musketry and cannonade of its defenders slightly slackened. Here and there soldiers slipped out of the firing line but not many of them yet. They were valiant and stubborn, those men of the South. When their ammunition failed, like Cleburne's Division, they threw rocks.

Not canister bursts nor bullets nor stones could batter back the onrushing Yankee lines. Some of the assaulters still had breath enough

to cheer and, remembering a still-rankling defeat, to shout, "Chickamauga! Chickamauga!"

It became a race over those last yards to the breastworks, regiment
vying with regiment, soldier with soldier. An Indiana captain, out-
stripped by a private of his company, grabbed the latter's coattail,
jerked him back, passed him. The agile enlisted man put on speed
and reached the crest ahead, after all.[239] In Wood's Division the
uniform of a German-American infantryman was "pierced like the
lid of a pepperbox." He found he was not wounded and kept going,
calling to the next man in line: "A pullet hit de preech of mine
gun—a pullet in mine bocket pook—a pullet in mine goat-tail—dey
shoots me three, five dime, and by tam I gives dem h—l yet!"[240]
Another stormer counted fourteen bullet holes in his coat with never
a scratch on his skin.

Such as they were the lucky ones. Still, crumpled bodies and gasp-
ing wounded on the slopes behind testified to the price paid. General
Howard stopped beside a dying soldier to comfort him and asked
where he was hit.

"Almost up, sir!"

"TO THE COLOR"

"I mean what part of your body?"

"Oh, I was almost up and but for that"—pointing to his wound—"I'd have reached the top." [241]

Between an Ohio regiment of Hazen's Brigade, and one of ours that had their flags well ahead, there sprang up a fierce rivalry as to which should be first planted on the rebel lines [wrote a Kansas infantryman]. At last but a dozen yards separated the line of grey and the columns of blue, while the flags of the Eighth Kansas, Sixth and Forty-ninth Ohio and several other regiments were but a few yards from the red clay banks that were belching forth streams of fire and sulphurous smoke. With a wild cheer and a madder rush our men dashed forward, and for a few moments a sharp, desperate, almost hand-to-hand fight with bayonet and ball ensued. Before this resistless assault the rebel line was lifted as by a whirlwind, and borne backward, shattered, bleeding and confused. In quick succession half a dozen Union battle flags were planted upon the works, and in a moment more the foemen were hurrying down the hill on the opposite side and off into the woods beyond. [242]

The last defense line crumbled and dissolved. Many manning it raised empty hands in surrender. Almost the entire 38th Alabama Regiment was taken prisoner; its rolls showed 201 missing. [243] The Federals, flooding the crest, seized enemy cannon, swung them around, and blazed away at the Gray guns that still held out. It was the enfilading fire of one of those captured batteries that swept the position of the 5th Company, Washington Artillery of New Orleans. [244]

The 5th, which had distinguished itself at Shiloh, was a stanch and once a dandy unit—shining belt plates embossed with the Louisiana pelican, teams all matched grays. It was ragged now, metal tarnished, horses varicolored, but no less of a fighting outfit. Yet that deadly fire from the flanks was more than the 5th could take. Two of its limbers blew up with a roar, mangling drivers and teams. Although four of its six guns escaped just before they were surrounded and tore careening down the reverse slope, they were mired at the bottom. Their crews were forced to abandon them.

5th Company, Washington Artillery of New Orleans

Phil Sheridan had not forgotten that vow made at the foot of the Ridge when his toast had been so rudely responded to by a Confederate gunner. Yonder stood the Napoleons, "Lady Buckner" and "Lady Breckinridge," which had showered him with dirt in near misses. He charged them on foot, for his horse had been shot under him during the assault. With a band of cheering men he rushed the Kentucky battery, leaped upon one of the guns, and wrapped his bow legs around its barrel in triumph.[245]

"Never before this, and never afterward, did the Confederate Army of Tennessee succumb to panic." [246] That overwhelming vision of the uphill assault, implacable, unstoppable, had been more than the spirit of all but the bravest could endure. It was the slow, certain thrust of a blade at a man's heart, a thrust he despairingly realizes he will be powerless to ward off. Now it was about to be driven home. Flee or perish.

They broke and ran.

Grey clad men rushed wildly down the hill and into the woods, tossing away knapsacks, muskets, and blankets as they ran. Batteries galloped back along the narrow, winding roads with reckless speed, and officers, frantic with rage, rushed from one panic-stricken group to another, shouting and cursing as they strove to check the head-long flight. Our men pursued the fugitives with an eagerness only equaled by their own to escape; the horses of the artillery were shot as they ran; squads of rebels were headed off and brought back as prisoners, and in ten minutes all that remained of the defiant rebel army that had so long besieged Chattanooga was captured guns, disarmed prisoners, moaning wounded, ghastly dead, and scattered, demoralized fugitives. Mission Ridge was ours.[247]

Watching the rout stream away from the Ridge, one Indiana infantryman called to another, "My God, come and see 'em run!" They recalled it as "the sight of our lives—men tumbling over each other in reckless confusion, hats off, some without guns, running wildly." [248] Jubilant Unoin officers and enlisted men pounded each other's backs. General Wood told his cheering men: "Soldiers, you

ought to be court-martialed, every man of you. I ordered you to take
the rifle-pits and you scaled the mountain!" [249]

Above the ebbing Gray tide shoals of resistance emerged here and
there for a time. Knots of riflemen stood and fought. The colonel
of the 20th Tennessee ordered his band to strike up "Dixie," and
that rallied his regiment as nothing else could.[250] Sam Watkins,
Company H, 1st Tennessee, who had been on advanced picket, was
caught between the lines. Yankees swarmed all around him, but
none noticed the Johnny Reb in their midst, waiting to be taken
prisoner. He thought he must be invisible. Drifting back up the
Ridge, he was swept into the debacle.

I heard Captain Turner, who had the very four Napoleon guns
we had captured at Perryville, halloo out, "Number four, solid!"
and then a roar. The next order was "Limber to the rear." The Yankees were cutting and slashing, and the cannoneers were running in
every direction. I saw Day's brigade throw down their guns and run
like quarter horses. . . .

The whole army was routed. I ran on down the ridge, and there
was our regiment, the First Tennessee, with their guns stacked,
drawing rations as if nothing was going on. Says I, "Colonel Field,
what's the matter? The Yankees are not a hundred yards from here.
Turner's Battery has surrendered, Day's brigade has thrown down
their arms; and look yonder, that is the Stars and Stripes." He remarked very coolly, "You seem to be demoralized. We've whipped
them here. We've captured two thousand prisoners and five stands
of colors." [251]

A black-browed man with three stars on his collar galloped up on
a gray charger, as if making an entrance in a Shakespearean tragedy
on the cue, "The day is lost!" General Braxton Bragg was about to
drain the last bitter dregs of the cup forced to his lips.

He rode through the distintegrating ranks of Day's Brigade,
striving to rally them with a shout, "Here is your commander!"
Glory was gone from him. Derisive yells answered him, "Here's your
mule!"

Sam Watkins heard the General swear when he saw the stacked rifles of the 1st Tennessee.

"What's this?" he blazed at Colonel Field. "Ah, ha, have you stacked your arms for a surrender?"

"No, sir," the officer replied. "Take arms, shoulder arms, by the right flank, file right, march." He spoke as calmly and deliberately as on dress parade.

Watkins thought that Bragg looked frightened.

He put spurs to his horse, and was running like a scared dog before Colonel Field had a chance to answer him. Every word of this is fact. We at once became the rear guard of the whole army.

I felt sorry for General Bragg. The army was routed, and Bragg looked so scared. Poor fellow, he looked so hacked and whipped and mortified and chagrined at defeat. . . . Bragg was a good disciplinarian, and if he had cultivated the love and respect of his troops by feeding and clothing them better than they were, the result would have been different. More depends on a good general than the lives of many privates. The private loses his life, the general his country.[252]

Exit General Bragg, shortly to be relieved of his command at his own request. Appointed by President Davis as his military adviser, he continued in his country's service, the country whose cause, so considerably through his failings, was to be a lost one.

A stricken field tempts a victorious army to linger upon it—to celebrate and gather trophies—to bind up the wounds of comrades and satisfy thirst and hunger forgotten in the heat of combat—to rest wearily on its arms. The fiery Sheridan allowed no respite. Exchanging mounts, cannon for a new charger, he led two brigades whooping down the Ridge's reverse to strike the retreating foe. The future cavalryman could well have used swift squadrons of horse for his pursuit, but his tired infantrymen gave all he could ask. On a rise of ground a Confederate stand was made. Sheridan swung his brigades around, flanked the hill, and swept it clean, capturing prisoners and guns.

It was late now; night fallen but moon bright. At Grant's orders to press the pursuit, Sheridan thrust on to cut off as many of the enemy as possible. He caught their rear guard crossing Chickamauga Creek by pontoon bridge and harried them so hotly that they burned the span before all their men were across. Several hundred more prisoners were bagged, along with artillery, small arms, wagons, and ammunition.

Meanwhile Hooker had clamped his jaw of the vise against the Confederate left. With the center shattered and gaping, there was no massive resistance for the jaw to crush. Hooker turned it into pinchers. Two of his divisions nipped off a Rebel one, rounding up a thousand men.

The left jaw of the Union vise never closed. Night found Sherman's battered troops still clinging to the slopes of heights unstormed. Under cover of darkness Cleburne's valorous division, by no means yet fought out, was ordered withdrawn. Next morning Sherman joined the pursuit of Bragg's army. Shortly Grant diverted him to the relief of Burnside at Knoxville. His approach, which forced Longstreet to raise the siege and retreat, can be termed the first stage of the mighty march to Atlanta and the sea and northward toward Grant at Appomattox and the winning of the war.

It was the morning of November 26 when Thomas and Sherman put their armies on the enemy's trail, marked by burning supply depots. But victory gained on the Ridge was not to be crowned by the destruction of the Army of Tennessee. Once more Pat Cleburne and his men stood at bay. Covering retreat, they defended Taylor's Ridge near Ringgold, Georgia, and flung back the Union attack with infliction of heavy casualties. The checked pursuit ground to a halt, and the Confederate forces escaped to the south.

Nevertheless and notwithstanding, it was Thanksgiving Day in date and fact in Chattanooga and throughout the Union. There were no services in the Tennessee town's churches. They were full of wounded, and people must give thanks elsewhere. In the forts cannon boomed salutes whose echoes rolled back from Lookout Mountain and Missionary Ridge. The words of Secretary Dana's dispatch to Washington, as exultant as those after Chickamauga had been direful, spread rejoicing through the nation. "The storming of the ridge by our troops was one of the greatest miracles in military history," he wired. "No man who climbs the ascent by any of the roads that wind up along its front can believe that 18,000 men were moved up its broken and crumbling face unless it was his fortune to witness the deed. It seems as awful as a visible interposition of God."

They reckoned up the toll of the battles around Chattanooga, low considering the intensity of the conflicts and the stakes upon them. Union casualties, out of a total, of 56,359 engaged, were: killed, 753; wounded, 4,722; missing, 349. The Confederates, with 64,165 engaged, lost 361 killed, 2,160 wounded, and 4,146 missing.[253] Forty-two pieces of artillery, 69 gun carriages, and 7,000 stands of small arms were captured from the defeated army, which was forced to destroy additional quantities of weapons and supplies during its retreat.[254]

For the Union tremendous gains were counted. A strong Confederate army, veteran and valiant, vanquished and swept back into the South. The Confederacy's mountain defense line pierced. Chattanooga, the railways center, remaining in Federal hands, along with control of interior lines of communication from that section to Richmond by way of Knoxville. The rich granaries of East Tennessee seized, and its loyalties freed from enemy menace. Mr. Lincoln's general, U. S. Grant, found at last. The way to the southeast wedged wide. "A gateway wrenched asunder."

CHAPTER 20

Clasped Hands

They came back to Chattanooga at the end of the war, they who had worn blue and gray. Remembrance of fertile valleys, the broad, winding river, and the forested mountains drew them. Here, in peacetime as in warfare, lay opportunities for the taking. With the return of veterans, the town on the Tennessee, gage of battle and scene of siege and starvation, began to grow into a thriving, industrial city. Union General Wilder, whose artillery had fired across the river to silence Confederate guns, was among the foremost in developing Chattanooga's resources. In 1871 he was elected to serve a term as mayor. Many other Northerners came back, attracted by well-remembered charms of the countryside and materials and sites for mills and factories, marked down and kept in mind even in the heat of the campaign.

Southerners joined them—men whose home the city was, and others. They found there less bitterness against former enemies and greater willingness to allow them to resume their role as citizens. Tennessee, first seceded state readmitted to the Union, experienced little of the rigors of Reconstruction, compared to the Deep South. "With malice toward none; with charity for all." Lincoln's noble words were more closely heeded in the place of the stormed gateway. As witness, there is the moving story of a former Confederate officer who violated the city ordinance against wearing a gray uniform in public. He broke it perforce, since he possessed no other suit. When he was put in jail, a friend of his, a former Union officer, asked and received permission from the sheriff to share the cell, remaining there until opinion forced the one-time Rebel's release with repeal of the law.[255]

And the Blue and the Gray returned increasingly for reunions, recalling the battles fought over those fields, as old soldiers will, and paying tribute to comrades fallen and resting there. Now and again a veteran would recognize another who had worn a different-colored uniform. Perhaps they had met for an instant in combat before the tide of conflict tore them apart, or between the lines for a friendly trade of coffee for tobacco. One might have taken the other prisoner and bandaged his wounds. In any event, it was all over now. They smoked a pipe together and pledged a toast and talked as they stood in the woods or on the mountain slopes. "My division came into line about here. It must have been you Johnnies (or you Yanks) we were up against."

They were one nation again, "one Union, strong and indivisible." So they talked, looking into each other's eyes, and when they parted, hands clasped in a firm grip. Thus they met on those remembered fields where they had fought, met until in the fullness of time there were no more of them.

Fittingly a great national military park was established, eventually covering an area of that historic ground so extensive—8,500 acres—that it became our largest.

Established by Congress in 1890, the Chickamauga-Chattanooga National Military Park five years later was "solemnly dedicated for all the ages—to all the American people." [256] Its inception was inspired by the joint efforts of Confederate and Union supporters. In symbol thereof arose the New York monument on Lookout Point, atop its tall column statues of a Union and Confederate soldier clasping hands in friendship.

Necessarily the park lacks the compact entity of Gettysburg. It is the magnificent view from Lookout Point that draws the battlefields together. There stands an observatory, built by one of the park's major benefactors, Adolph S. Ochs, publisher of the *Chattanooga Times* and *New York Times*. Marble, granite, and limestone, the shafts and columns dot the landscape on ground where corps, divisions, and regiments stood and fought. Blacktop thoroughfares climb the mountains, supplanting the rough roads and trails that once bore the tread of marching men.

Weapons such as they carried are racked in the notable Fuller Arms Collection in Park headquarters on the Chickamauga battlefield. It contains almost every type of shoulder arms used by the military forces of North America. Cannon peer down from the Mountain and the Ridge—stare from Orchard Knob—mount guard around the Brotherton cabin at the breakthrough point and before the Craven house, still the white beacon it once was for troops assaulting through the fog. They stand, those guns so gallantly served, often in the very positions where they flamed in action.[257] Homes now surround the Napoleons and Parrotts, the Rodmans and the howitzers, on the smaller, separate reservations. Although they are emplaced beside graveled driveways on neatly kept lawns, one need only scan them through the mind's eye, and again cannoneers man them, loading and firing double canister against charging waves of infantry.

Moonlight still glimmers on Chickamauga's creek. The dark woods through which it winds are brighter for their memories of valor. Autumn mist still veils Lookout Mountain, mist that frames a shining vision.

> Fierce, fiery warriors fight upon the clouds,
> In ranks and squadrons and right form of war.[258]

Now it is only the elements, with rolling thunder and bolts of flashing lightning, that storm Missionary Ridge, as gallant men did on that November day of 1863.

Appendix A

LOADING THE RIFLE

Casey, *Infantry Tactics*, I, 42-46

LOAD IN NINE TIMES.

1. LOAD.

One time and one motion.

163. Grasp the piece with the left hand as high as the right elbow, and bring it vertically opposite the middle of the body, shift the right hand to the upper band, place the butt between the feet, the barrel to the front; seize it with the left hand near the muzzle, which should be three inches from the body; carry the right hand to the cartridge-box. If the rifle musket is used the right hand will be shifted to just below the upper band. The muzzle will be eight inches from the body.

2. *Handle*—CARTRIDGE.

One time and one motion.

164. Seize the cartridge with the thumb and next two fingers, and place it between the teeth.

3. *Tear*—CARTRIDGE.

One time and one motion.

165. Tear the paper to the powder, hold the cartridge upright between the thumb and first two fingers, near the top; in this position place it in front of and near the muzzle—the back of the hand to the front.

4. *Charge*—CARTRIDGE.

One time and one motion.

166. Empty the powder into the barrel: disengage the ball from the paper with the right hand and the thumb and first two fingers of the left, insert it into the bore, the pointed end uppermost, and press it down with the right thumb; seize the head of the rammer with the thumb and forefinger of the right hand, the other fingers closed, the elbows near the body.

Load.—No. 168. *Prime.—No.* 174.

5. *Draw*—RAMMER.

One time and three motions.

167. (*First motion.*) Half draw the rammer by extending the right arm; steady it in this position with the left thumb; grasp the rammer near the muzzle with the right hand, the little finger uppermost, the nails to the front, the thumb extended along the rammer.

168. (*Second motion.*) Clear the rammer from the pipes by again extending the arm; the rammer in the prolongation of the pipes.

169. (*Third motion.*) Turn the rammer, the little end of the rammer passing near the left shoulder; place the head of the rammer on the ball, the back of the hand to the front.

6. *Ram*—CARTRIDGE.

One time and one motion.

170. Insert the rammer as far as the right, and steady it in this position with the thumb of the left hand; seize the rammer at the small end with the thumb and fore-finger of the right hand, the back of the hand to the front; press the ball home, the elbows near the body.

7. *Return*—RAMMER.

One time and three motions.

171. (*First motion.*) Draw the rammer half-way out, and steady it in this position with the left thumb; grasp it near the muzzle with the right hand, the little finger uppermost, the nails to the front, the thumb along the

rammer; clear the rammer from the bore by extending the arm, the nails to the front, the rammer in the prolongation of the bore.

172. (*Second motion.*) Turn the rammer, the head of the rammer passing near the left shoulder, and insert it in the pipes until the right hand reaches the muzzle, the nails to the front.

173. (*Third motion.*) Force the rammer home by placing the little finger of the right hand on the head of the rammer; pass the left hand down the barrel to the extent of the arm, without depressing the shoulder.

8. PRIME.

One time and two motions.

174. (*First motion.*) With the left hand raise the piece till the hand is as high as the eye, grasp the small of the stock with the right hand; half face to the right; place, at the same time, the right foot behind and at right angles with the left; the hollow of the right foot against the left heel. Slip the left hand down to the lower band, the thumb along the stock, the left elbow against the body; bring the piece to the right side, the butt below the right fore-arm—the small of the stock against the body and two inches below the right breast, the barrel upwards, the muzzle on a level with the eye.

175. (*Second motion.*) Half cock with the thumb of the right hand, the fingers supported against the guard and the small of the stock—remove the old cap with one of the fingers of the right hand, and with the thumb and forefinger of the same hand, take the cap from the pouch, place it on the nipple, and press it down with the thumb; seize the small of the stock with the right hand.

Appendix B

THE OPPOSING FORCES AT CHICKAMAUGA, GA.

September 19th-20th, 1863.

Battles and Leaders of the Civil War, III, pp. 672-675.

For much of the information contained in this list and in similar lists to follow, the editors are indebted (in advance of the publication of the "Official Records") to Brigadier-General Richard C. Drum, Adjutant-General of the Army. K stands for killed; w for wounded; m w for mortally wounded; m for captured or missing; c for captured.

THE UNION ARMY.

ARMY OF THE CUMBERLAND—Major-General William S. Rosecrans.

General Headquarters: 1st Battalion Ohio Sharpshooters, Capt. Gershom M. Barber; 10th Ohio Infantry, Lieut.-Col. William M. Ward; 15th Pa. Cav., Col. William J. Palmer. Loss: w, 2; m, 4 = 6.

FOURTEENTH ARMY CORPS, Maj.-Gen. George H. Thomas. Staff loss: m, 1. *Escort:* L, 1st Ohio Cav., Capt. John D. Barker.

FIRST DIVISION, Brig.-Gen. Absalom Baird.

First Brigade, Col. Benjamin F. Scribner: 38th Ind., Lieut.-Col. Daniel F. Griffin; 2d Ohio, Lieut.-Col. Obadiah C. Maxwell (w), Maj. William T. Beatty (w and c), Capt. James Warnock; 33d Ohio, Col. Oscar F. Moore; 94th Ohio, Maj. Rue P. Hutchins; 10th Wis., Lieut.-Col. John H. Ely (m w and c), Capt. Jacob W. Roby. Brigade loss: k, 55; w, 254; m, 423 = 732. *Second Brigade,* Brig.-Gen. John C. Starkweather: 24th Ill., Col. Geza Mihalotzy (w), Capt. August Mauff; 79th Pa., Col. Henry A. Hambright; 1st Wis., Lieut.-Col. George B. Bingham; 21st Wis., Lieut.-Col. Harrison C. Hobart (w), Capt. Charles H. Walker. Brigade loss: k, 65; w, 285; m, 256 = 606. *Third Brigade,* Brig.-Gen. John H. King: 1st Battalion 15th U. S., Cat. Albert B. Dod; 1st Battalion 16th U. S., Maj. Sidney Coolidge (k), Capt. Robert E. A. Crofton; 1st Battalion 18th U. S., Capt. George W. Smith; 2d Battalion 18th U. S., Capt. Henry Haymond; 1st Battalion 19th U. S., Maj. Samuel K. Dawson (w), Capt. Edmund L. Smith. Brigade loss: k, 61; w, 255; m, 523 = 839. *Artillery:* 4th Ind. (Second Brigade), Lieut. David Flansburg (w and c), Lieut. Henry J. Willits; A, 1st Mich. (First

Brigade), Lieut. George W. Van Pelt (k), Lieut. Almerick W. Wilber; H, 5th U. S. (Third Brigade), Lieut. Howard M. Burnham (k), Lieut. Joshua A. Fessenden (w). Artillery loss included in that of brigades.

SECOND DIVISION, Maj.-Gen. James S. Negley. *First Brigade,* Brig.-Gen. John Beatty: 104th Ill., Lieut.-Col. Douglas Hapeman; 42d Ind., Lieut.-Col. William T. B. McIntire; 88th Ind., Col. George Humphrey; 15th Ky., Col. Marion C. Taylor. Brigade loss: k, 17; w, 189; m, 104 = 310. *Second Brigade,* Col. Timothy R. Stanley (w), Col. William L. Stoughton: 19th Ill., Lieut.-Col. Alexander W. Raffen; 11th Mich., Col. William L. Stoughton, Lieut.-Col. Melvin Mudge (w); 18th Ohio, Lieut.-Col. Charles H. Grosvenor. Brigade loss: k, 20; w, 146; m, 49 = 215. *Third Brigade,* Col. William Sirwell: 37th Ind., Lieut.-Col. William D. Ward; 21st Ohio, Lieut.-Col. Dwella M. Stoughton (m w), Maj. Arnold McMahan (w), Capt. Charles H. Vantine; 74th Ohio, Capt. Joseph Fisher; 78th Pa., Lieut.-Col. Archibald Blakely. Brigade loss: k, 29; w, 95; m, 142 = 266. *Artillery:* Bridges's Ill. Battery (First Brigade), Capt. Lyman Bridges; G, 1st Ohio (Third Brigade), Capt. Alexander Marshall; M, 1st Ohio (Second Brigade), Capt. Frederick Schultz. Artillery loss included in brigades to which attached.

THIRD DIVISION, Brig.-Gen. John M. Brannan. Staff loss: w, 1. *First Brigade,* Col. John M. Connell: 82d Ind., Col. Morton C. Hunter; 17th Ohio, Lieut.-Col. Durbin Ward (w); 31st Ohio, Lieut.-Col. Frederick W. Lister. Brigade loss: k, 49; w, 323; m, 70 = 442. *Second Brigade,* Col. John T. Croxton (w), Col. William H. Hays: 10th Ind., Col. William B. Carroll (m w), Lieut.-Col. Marsh B. Taylor; 74th Ind., Col. Charles W. Chapman, Lieut.-Col. Myron Baker; 4th Ky., Lieut.-Col. P. Burgess Hunt (w), Maj. Robert M. Kelly; 10th Ky., Col. William H. Hays, Maj. Gabriel C. Wharton; 14th Ohio, Lieut.-Col. Henry D. Kingsbury. Brigade loss: k, 131; w, 728; m, 79 = 938. *Third Brigade,* Col. Ferdinand Van Derveer: 87th Ind., Col. Newell Gleason; 2d Minn., Col. James George; 9th Ohio, Col. Gustave Kammerling; 35th Ohio, Lieut.-Col. Henry V. N. Boynton. Brigade loss: k, 144; w, 594; m, 102 = 840. *Artillery:* D, 1st Mich. (First Brigade), Capt. Josiah W. Church; C, 1st Ohio (Second Brigade), Lieut. Marco B. Gary; I, 4th U. S. (Third Brigade), Lieut. Frank G. Smith. Artillery loss included in brigades to which attached.

FOURTH DIVISION, Maj.-Gen. Joseph J. Reynolds. Staff loss: w, 1, m, 1 = 2. *First Brigade,** Col. John T. Wilder: 92d Ill., Col. Smith D. Atkins; 98th Ill., Col. John J. Funkhouser (w), Lieut.-Col. Edward Kitchell; 128th Ill., Col. James Monroe; 17th Ind., Maj. William T. Jones; 72d Ind., Col. Abram O. Miller. Brigade loss: k, 13; w, 94; m, 18 = 125. *Second Brigade,* Col. Edward A. King (k), Col. Milton S. Robinson: 68th Ind., Capt. Harvey J. Espy (w); 75th Ind., Col. Milton S. Robinson, Lieut.-Col. William

* Detached and serving as mounted infantry.

O'Brien; 101st Ind., Lieut.-Col. Thomas Doan; 105th Ohio, Maj. George T. Perkins (w). Brigade loss: k, 50; w, 363; m, 71 = 484. *Third Brigade,* Brig.-Gen. John B. Turchin: 18th Ky, Lieut.-Col. H. Kavanaugh Milward (w), Capt. John B. Heltemes; 11th Ohio, Col. Philander P. Lane; 36th Ohio, Col. William G. Jones (k), Lieut.-Col. Hiram F. Duvall; 92d Ohio, Col. Benjamin D. Fearing (w), Lieut.-Col. Douglas Putman, Jr. (w). Brigade loss: k, 30; w, 227; m, 86 = 343. *Artillery:* 18th Ind. (First Brigade), Capt. Eli Lilly; 19th Ind. (Second Brigade), Capt. Samuel J. Harris (w), Lieut. Robert G. Lackey; 21st Ind. (Third Brigade), Capt. William W. Andrew. Artillery loss included in brigades to which attached.

TWENTIETH ARMY CORPS, Maj.-Gen. Alexander McD. McCook.

Provost-Guard: H, 81st Ind., Capt. Will'm J. Richards.

Escort: I, 2d Ky. Cav., Lieut. George W. L. Batman.

FIRST DIVISION, Brig.-Gen. Jefferson C. Davis.

Second Brigade, Brig.-Gen. William P. Carlin: 21st Ill., Col. John W. S. Alexander (k), Capt. Chester K. Knight; 38th Ill., Lieut.-Col. Daniel H. Gilmer (k), Capt. Willis G. Whitehurst; 81st Ind., Capt. Nevil B. Boone, Maj. James E. Calloway; 101st Ohio, Lieut.-Col. John Messer (w), Maj. Bedan B. McDanald (w), Capt. Leonard D. Smith; 2d Minn. Batt'y,* Lieut. Albert Woodbury (m w), Lieut. Richard L. Dawley. Brigade loss: k, 54; w, 299; m, 298 = 651. *Third Brigade,* Col. Hans C. Heg (k), Col. John A. Martin: 25th Ill., Maj. Samuel D. Wall (k), Capt. Wesford Taggart; 35th Ill., Lieut.-Col. William P. Chandler; 8th Kans., Col. John A. Martin, Lieut.-Col. James L. Abernethy; 15th Wis., Lieut.-Col. Ole C. Johnson (c); 8th Wis. Batt'y, Lieut. John D. McLean. Brigade loss: k, 70; w, 519; m, 107 = 696.

SECOND DIVISION, Brig.-Gen. Richard W. Johnson. Staff loss: k, 1; m, 2 = 3.

First Brigade, Brig.-Gen. August Willich: 89th Ill., Lieut.-Col. Duncan J. Hall (k), Maj. William D. Williams; 32d Ind., Lieut.-Col. Frank Erdelmeyer; 39th Ind.,† Col. Thomas J. Harrison; 15th Ohio, Lieut.-Col. Frank Askew; 49th Ohio, Maj. Samuel F. Gray (w), Capt. Luther M. Strong; A, 1st Ohio Art'y, Capt. Wilbur F. Goodspeed. Brigade loss: k, 63; w, 355; m, 117 = 535. *Second Brigade,* Col. Joseph B. Dodge: 79th Ill., Col. Allen Buckner; 29th Ind., Lieut.-Col. David M. Dunn; 30th Ind., Lieut.-Col. Orrin D. Hurd; 77th Pa., Col. Thomas E. Rose (c), Capt. Joseph J. Lawson; 20th Ohio Battery, Capt. Edward Grosskopff. Brigade loss: k, 27; w, 200; m, 309 = 536. *Third Brigade,* Col. Philemon P. Baldwin (k), Col. William W. Berry: 6th Ind., Lieut.-Col. Hagerman Tripp (w), Maj. Calvin D. Campbell; 5th Ky., Col. William W. Berry, Capt. John M. Huston; 1st Ohio, Lieut.-Col. Bassett Langdon; 93d Ohio, Col. Hiram Strong (m w), Lieut.-Col. Wm. H. Martin; 5th Ind. Bat'y, Capt. Peter Simonson. Brigade loss: k, 57; w, 385; m, 126 = 568.

* Captain William A. Hotchkiss, chief of division artillery.

† Detached and serving as mounted infantry.

THIRD DIVISION, Maj.-Gen. Philip H. Sheridan.

First Brigade, Brig.-Gen. William H. Lytle (k), Col. Silas Miller: 36th Ill., Col. Silas Miller, Lieut.-Col. Porter C. Olson; 88th Ill., Lieut.-Col. Alexander S. Chadbourne; 21st Mich., Col. William B. McCreery (w and c), Maj. Seymour Chase; 24th Wis., Lieut.-Col. Theodore S. West (w and c), Maj. Carl von Baumbach; 11th Ind. Battery, Capt. Arnold Sutermeister. Brigade loss: k, 55; w, 321; m, 84 = 460. *Second Brigade,* Col. Bernard Laiboldt: 44th Ill., Col. Wallace W. Barrett (w); 73d Ill., Col. James F. Jacquess; 2d Mo., Lieut.-Col. Arnold Beck; 15th Mo., Col. Joseph Conrad; G (Capt. H. Hescock, chief of division artillery), 1st Mo. Art'y, Lieut. Gustavus Schueler. Brigade loss: k, 38; w, 243; m, 108 = 389. *Third Brigade,* Col. Luther P. Bradley (w), Col. Nathan H. Walworth: 22d Ill., Lieut.-Col. Francis Swanwick; 27th Ill., Col. Jonathan R. Miles; 42d Ill., Col. Nathan H. Walworth, Lieut.-Col. John A. Hottenstine; 51st Ill., Lieut.-Col. Samuel B. Raymond; C, 1st Ill. Art'y, Capt. Mark H. Prescott. Brigade loss: k, 58; w, 374; m, 64 = 496.

TWENTY-FIRST ARMY CORPS, Maj.-Gen. Thomas L. Crittenden.

Escort: K, 15th Ill. Cav., Capt. S. B. Sherer. Loss: w, 3.

FIRST DIVISION, Brig.-Gen. Thos. J. Wood. Staff loss: w, 1.

First Brigade, Col. George P. Buell: 100th Ill., Col. Frederick A. Bartleson (w and c), Maj. Charles M. Hammond; 58th Ind., Lieut.-Col. James T. Embree; 13th Mich., Col. Joshua B. Culver (w), Maj. Willard G. Eaton; 26th Ohio, Lieut.-Col. William H. Young. Brigade loss: k, 79; w, 443; m, 129 = 651. *Third Brigade,* Col. Charles G. Harker: 3d Ky., Col. Henry C. Dunlap; 64th Ohio, Col. Alexander McIlvain; 65th Ohio, Lieut.-Col. Horatio N. Whitbeck (w), Maj. Samuel C. Brown (m w), Capt. Thomas Powell; 125th Ohio, Col. Emerson Opdycke. Brigade loss: k, 51; w, 283; m, 58 = 392. *Artillery:* 8th Ind. (First Brigade), Capt. George Estep (w); 6th Ohio (Third Brigade), Capt. Cullen Bradley. Artillery loss: k, 2; w, 17; m, 7 = 26.

SECOND DIVISION, Maj.-Gen. John M. Palmer. Staff loss: k, 1; w, 2; m, 3 = 6.

First Brigade, Brig.-Gen. Charles Cruft: 31st Ind., Col. John T. Smith; 1st Ky. (5 co's), Lieut.-Col. Alva R. Hadlock; 2d Ky., Col. Thomas D. Sedgewick; 90th Ohio, Col. Charles H. Rippey. Brigade loss: k, 24; w, 213; m, 53 = 290. *Second Brigade,* Brig.-Gen. William B. Hazen: 9th Ind., Col. Isaac C. B. Suman; 6th Ky., Col. George T. Shackelford (w), Lieut.-Col. Richard Rockingham (k), Maj. Richard T. Whitaker; 41st Ohio, Col. Aquila Wiley; 124th Ohio, Col. Oliver H. Payne (w), Maj. James B. Sampson. Brigade loss: k, 46; w, 378; m, 76 = 500. *Third Brigade,* Col. William Grose: 84th Ill., Col. Louis H. Waters; 36th Ind., Lieut-Col. Oliver H. P. Carey (w), Maj. Gilbert Trusler; 23d Ky., Lieut.-Col. James C. Foy; 6th Ohio, Col. Nicholas L. Anderson (w), Maj. Samuel C. Erwin; 24th Ohio, Col. David J. Higgins. Brigade loss: k, 53; w, 399; m, 65 = 517. *Artillery,* Capt. William E. Standart: B, 1st Ohio (First Brigade), Lieut. Norman A. Baldwin; F, 1st Ohio (Second Brigade), Lieut. Giles J. Cockerill; H, 4th

U. S. (Third Brigade), Lieut. Harry C. Cushing; M, 4th U. S. (Third Brigade), Lieut. Francis D. L. Russell. Artillery loss: k, 10; w, 39; m, 6 = 55.

THIRD DIVISION, Brig.-Gen. H. P. VanCleve. Staff loss: m, 1.

First Brigade, Brig.-Gen. Samuel Beatty: 79th Ind., Col. Frederick Knefler; 9th Ky., Col. George H. Cram; 17th Ky., Col. Alexander M. Stout; 19th Ohio, Lieut.-Col. Henry G. Stratton. Brigade loss: k, 16; w, 254; m, 61 = 331. Second Brigade, Col. George F. Dick: 44th Ind., Lieut.-Col. Simeon C. Aldrich; 86th Ind., Maj. Jacob C. Dick; 13th Ohio, Lieut.-Col. Elhannon M. Mast (k), Capt. Horatio G. Cosgrove; 59th Ohio, Lieut.-Col. Granville A. Frambes. Brigade loss: k, 16; w, 180; m, 83 = 279. Third Brigade, Col. Sidney M. Barnes: 35th Ind., Maj. John P. Dufficy; 8th Ky., Lieut.-Col. James D. Mayhew (c), Maj. John S. Clark; 51st Ohio, Col. Richard W. McClain (c), Lieut.-Col. Charles H. Wood; 99th Ohio, Col. Peter T. Swaine. Brigade loss: k, 20; w, 135; m, 144 = 299. Artillery: 17th Ind., Capt. George R. Swallow; 26th Pa., Capt. Alanson J. Stevens (k), Lieut. Samuel M. McDowell; 3d Wis., Lieut. Cortland Livingston. Artillery loss: k, 4; w, 35; m, 13 = 52.

RESERVE CORPS, Maj.-Gen. Gordon Granger. Staff loss: k, 1.

FIRST DIVISION, Brig.-Gen. James B. Steedman.

First Brigade, Brig.-Gen. Walter C. Whitaker: 96th Ill., Col. Thomas E. Champion; 115th Ill., Col. Jesse H. Moore; 84th Ind., Col. Nelson Trusler; 22d Mich., Col. Heber Le Favour (c), Lieut.-Col. William Sanborn (w), Capt. Alonzo M. Keeler (c); 40th Ohio, Lieut.-Col. William Jones; 89th Ohio, Col. Caleb H. Carlton (c), Capt. Isaac C. Nelson; 18th Ohio Battery, Capt. Charles C. Aleshire. Brigade loss: k, 154; w, 654; m, 518 = 1326. Second Brigade, Col. John G. Mitchell: 78th Ill., Lieut.-Col. Carter Van Vleck (w), Lieut. Geo. Green; 98th Ohio, Capt. Moses J. Urquhart (w), Capt. Armstrong J. Thomas; 113th Ohio, Lieut.-Col. Darius B. Warner; 121st Ohio, Lieut.-Col. Henry B. Banning; M, 1st Art'y, Lieut. Thos. Burton. Brigade loss: k, 58; w, 308; m, 95 = 461.

SECOND DIVISION.

Second Brigade, Col. Daniel McCook: 85th Ill., Col. Caleb J. Dilworth; 86th Ill., Lieut.-Col. D. W. Magee; 125th Ill., Col. Oscar F. Harmon; 52d Ohio, Maj. J. T. Holmes; 69th Ohio, Lieut.-Col. J. H. Brigham; I, 2d. Ill. Art'y, Capt. C. M. Barnett. Brigade loss: k, 2; w, 14; m, 18 = 34.

CAVALRY CORPS, Brig.-Gen. Robert B. Mitchell.

FIRST DIVISION, Col. Edward M. McCook.

First Brigade, Col. Archibald P. Campbell: 2d Mich., Maj. Leonidas S. Scranton; 9th Pa., Lieut.-Col. Roswell M. Russell; 1st Tenn., Lieut.-Col. James P. Brownlow. Brigade loss: k, 2; w, 6; m, 7 = 15. Second Brigade, Col. Daniel M. Ray: 2d Ind., Maj. Joseph B. Presdee; 4th Ind., Lieut.-Col. John T. Deweese; 2d Tenn., Lieut.-Col. William R. Cook; 1st Wis., Col. Oscar H. La Grange; D, 1st Ohio Art'y (section), Lieut. Nathaniel M. Newell. Brigade loss: k, 2; w, 10; m, 11 = 23. Third Brigade, Col. Louis D. Watkins: 4th Ky., Col. Wickliffe Cooper; 5th Ky., Lieut.-Col. William T. Hoblitzell; 6th Ky., Maj. Louis A. Gratz. Brigade loss: k, 2; w, 8; m, 236 = 246.

SECOND DIVISION, Brig.-Gen. George Crook.
First Brigade, Col. Robert H. G. Minty: 3d Ind. (detachment), Lieut.-Col. Robert Klein; 4th Mich., Maj. Horace Gray; 7th Pa., Lieut.-Col. James J. Seibert; 4th U. S., Capt. James B. McIntyre. Brigade loss: k, 7; w, 33; m, 8 = 48. *Second Brigade,* Col. Eli Long: 2d Ky., Col. Thomas P. Nicholas; 1st Ohio, Lieut.-Col. Valentine Cupp (m w), Maj. Thomas J. Patten; 3d Ohio, Lieut.-Col. Charles B. Seidel; 4th Ohio, Lieut.-Col. Oliver P. Robie. Brigade loss: k, 19; w, 79; m, 38 = 136. *Artillery:* Chicago Board of Trade Battery, Capt. James H. Stokes.

Total Union loss: killed 1656, wounded 9749, captured or missing 4774 = 16,179.

Effective strength (partly from official reports and partly estimated):

Fourteenth Army Corps (estimated)	20,000
Twentieth Army Corps (estimated)	11,000
Twenty-first Army Corps (report)	12,052
Reserve Corps (report)	3,913
Cavalry Corps (estimated)	10,000
Total	56,965

THE CONFEDERATE ARMY.

ARMY OF TENNESSEE—General Braxton Bragg.

RIGHT WING, Lieut.-Gen. Leonidas Polk.

CHEATHAM'S DIVISION [Polk's Corps], Maj.-Gen. B. F. Cheatham.
Escort: G, 2d Ga. Cav., Capt. T. M. Merritt.
Jackson's Brigade, Brig.-Gen. John K. Jackson: 1st Ga. (Confed.) and 2d Ga. Battalion, Maj. J. C. Gordon; 5th Ga., Col. C. P. Daniel; 2d Ga. Battalion Sharpshooters, Maj. R. H. Whiteley; 5th Miss., Lieut.-Col. W. L. Sykes (k), Maj. J. B. Herring; 8th Miss., Col. J. C. Wilkinson. Brigade loss: k, 55; w, 430; m, 5 = 490. *Maney's Brigade,* Brig.-Gen. George Maney: 1st and 27th Tenn., Col. H. R. Feild; 4th Tenn. (Prov. Army), Col. J. A. McMurry (k), Lieut.-Col. R. N. Lewis (w), Maj. O. A. Bradshaw (w), Capt. J. Bostick; 6th and 9th Tenn., Col. George C. Porter; 24th Tenn. Battalion Sharp-shooters, Maj. Frank Maney. Brigade loss: k, 54; w, 317; m, 15 = 386. *Smith's Brigade,* Brig.-Gen. Preston Smith (k), Col. A. J. Vaughan, Jr.: 11th Tenn., Col. G. W. Gordon; 12th and 47th Tenn., Col. W. M. Watkins; 13th and 154th Tenn., Col. A. J. Vaughan, Jr., Lieut.-Col. R. W. Pitman; 29th Tenn., Col. Horace Rice; Dawson's Battalion * Sharp-shooters, Maj. J. W. Dawson (w), Maj. William Green. Brigade loss: k, 42; w, 284; m, 36 = 362. *Wright's Brigade,* Brig.-Gen. Marcus J. Wright: 8th Tenn.,

* Composed of two companies from the 11th Tenn., two from the 12th and 47th Tenn. (consolidated), and one from the 154th Senior Tenn.

Col. John H. Anderson; 16th Tenn., Col. D. M. Donnell; 28th Tenn., Col. S. S. Stanton; 38th Tenn. and Murray's (Tenn.) Battalion, Col. J. C. Carter; 51st and 52d Tenn., Lieut.-Col. John G. Hall. Brigade loss: k, 44; w, 400; m, 43 = 487. *Strahl's Brigade,* Brig.-Gen. O. F. Strahl: 4th and 5th Tenn., Col. J. J. Lamb; 19th Tenn., Col. F. M. Walker; 24th Tenn., Col. J. A. Wilson; 31st Tenn., Col. E. E. Tansil; 33d Tenn., ——. Brigade loss: k, 19; w, 203; m, 28 = 250. *Artillery,* Maj. Melancthon Smith: Tenn. Battery, Capt. W. W. Carnes; Ga. Battery, Capt. John Scogin; Tenn. Battery (Scott's), Lieut. J. H. Marsh (w), Lieut. A. T. Watson; Miss. Battery (Smith's), Lieut. W. B. Turner; Miss. Bat'y, Capt. T. J. Stanford.

HILL'S CORPS, Lieut.-Gen. Daniel H. Hill.

CLEBURNE'S DIVISION, Maj.-Gen. P. R. Cleburne.

Wood's Brigade, Brig.-Gen. S. A. M. Wood: 16th Ala., Maj. J. H. McGaughy (k), Capt. F. A. Ashford; 33d Ala., Col. Samuel Adams; 45th Ala., Col. E. B. Breedlove; 18th Ala. Battalion, Maj. J. H. Gibson (k), Col. Samuel Adams; 32d and 45th Miss., Col. M. P. Lowrey; Sharp-shooters, Maj. A. T. Hawkins (k), Capt. Daniel Coleman. Brigade loss: k, 96; w, 680 = 776. *Polk's Brigade,* Brig.-Gen. Lucius E. Polk: 1st Ark., Col. J. W. Colquitt; 3d and 5th Confederate, Col. J. A. Smith; 2d Tenn., Col. W. B. Robertson; 35th Tenn., Col. B. J. Hill; 48th Tenn., Col. G. H. Nixon. Brigade loss: k, 58; w, 541; m, 6 = 605. *Deshler's Brigade,* Brig.-Gen. James Deshler (k), Col. R. Q. Mills: 19th and 24th Ark., Lieut.-Col. A. S. Hutchinson; 6th, 10th, and 15th Tex., Col. R. Q. Mills, Lieut.-Col. T. Scott Anderson; 17th, 18th, 24th, and 25th Tex., Col. F. C. Wilkes (w), Lieut.-Col. John T. Coit, Maj. W. A. Taylor. Brigade loss: k, 52; w, 366 = 418. *Artillery,* Maj. T. R. Hotchkiss (w), Capt. Henry C. Semple: Ark. Battery (Calvert's), Lieut. Thomas J. Key; Tex. Battery, Capt. J. P. Douglas; Ala. Battery, Capt. Henry C. Semple, Lieut. R. W. Goldthwaite.

BRECKINRIDGE'S DIVISION, Maj. Gen. J. C. Breckinridge.

Helm's Brigade, Brig.-Gen. Benjamin H. Helm (k), Col. J. H. Lewis: 41st Ala., Col. M. L. Stansel; 2d Ky., Col. J. W. Hewitt (k), Lieut.-Col. J. W. Moss; 4th Ky., Col. Joseph P. Nuckols, Jr. (w), Maj. T. W. Thompson; 6th Ky., Col. J. H. Lewis, Lieut.-Col. M. H. Cofer; 9th Ky., Col. J. W. Caldwell (w), Lieut.-Col. J. C. Wickliffe. Brigade loss: k, 63; w, 408 = 471. *Adams's Brigade,* Brig.-Gen. Daniel W. Adams (w and c), Col. R. L. Gibson: 32d Ala., Maj. J. C. Kimbell; 13th and 20th La., Col. R. L. Gibson, Col. Leon von Zinken, Capt. E. M. Dubroca; 16th and 25th La., Col. D. Gober; 19th La., Lieut.-Col. R. W. Turner (w), Maj. L. Butler (k), Capt. H. A. Kennedy; 14th La. Battalion, Maj. J. E. Austin. Brigade loss: k, w and m = 429. *Stovall's Brigade,* Brig.-Gen. M. A. Stovall: 1st and 3d Fla., Col. W. S. Dilworth; 4th Fla., Col. W. L. L. Bowen; 47th Ga., Capt. William S. Phillips (w), Capt. Joseph S. Cone; 60th N. C., Lieut.-Col. J. M. Ray (w), Capt. J. T. Weaver. Brigade loss: k, 37; w, 232; m, 46 = 315. *Artillery,* Maj. R. E. Graves (k): Ky. Battery, Capt. Robert Cobb; Tenn. Battery, Capt. John W. Mebane; La. Battery, Capt. C. H. Slocomb.

RESERVE CORPS, Maj.-Gen. W. H. T. Walker.

WALKER'S DIVISION, Brig.-Gen. S. R. Gist.

Gist's Brigade, Brig.-Gen. S. R. Gist, Col. P. H. Colquitt (k), Lieut.-Col. L. Napier: 46th Ga., Col. P. H. Colquitt, Maj. A. M. Speer; 8th Ga. Battalion, Lieut.-Col. L. Napier; 24th S. C., Col. C. H. Stevens (w), Lieut.-Col. Ellison Capers (w). Brigade loss: k, 49; w, 251; m, 36 = 336. *Ector's Brigade,* Brig.-Gen. M. D. Ector: Stone's Ala. Battalion, ——; Pound's Miss. Battalion, ——; 29th N. C., ——; 9th Texas, ——; 10th, 14th, and 32d Tex. Cav. (dismounted), ——. Brigade loss: k, 59; w, 239; m, 138 = 436. *Wilson's Brigade,* Col. C. C. Wilson: 25th Ga., Lieut.-Col. A. J. Williams (k) ; 29th Ga., Lieut. G. R. McRae; 30th Ga., Lieut.-Col. James S. Boynton; 1st Ga. Battalion Sharp-shooters, ——; 4th La. Battalion, ——. Brigade loss: k, 99; w, 426; m, 80 = 605. *Artillery:* Martin's Battery, ——.

LIDDELL'S DIVISION, Brig.-Gen. St. John R. Liddell.

Liddell's Brigade, Col. Daniel C. Govan: 2d and 15th Ark., Lieut.-Col. R. T. Harvey; 5th and 13th Ark., Col. L. Featherston (k), Lieut.-Col. John E. Murray; 6th and 7th Ark., Col. D. A. Gillespie (w), Lieut.-Col. Peter Snyder; 8th Ark. and 1st La., Lieut.-Col. George F. Baucum (w), Maj. A. Watkins. Brigade loss: k, 73; w, 502; m, 283 = 858. *Walthall's Brigade,* Brig.-Gen. E. C. Walthall: 24th Miss., Lieut.-Col. R. P. McKelvaine (w), Maj. W. C. Staples (w), Capt. B. F. Toomer, Capt. J. D. Smith (w), 27th Miss., Col. James A. Campbell; 29th Miss., Col. William F. Brantly; 30th Miss., Col. Junius I. Scales (c), Lieut.-Col. Hugh A. Reynolds (k), Maj. J. M. Johnson (w); 34th Miss., Maj. W. G. Pegram (w), Capt. H. J. Bowen, Lieut.-Col. H. A. Reynolds (k). Brigade loss: k, 61; w, 531; m, 196 = 788. *Artillery,* Capt. Charles Swett: Ala. Battery, Capt. W. H. Fowler (w); Miss. Battery (Warren Light Art'y), Lieut. H. Shannon. Artillery loss included in loss of brigades.

LEFT WING, Lieut.-Gen. James Longstreet.

HINDMAN'S DIVISION [Polk's Corps], Maj.-Gen. T. C. Hindman (w), Brig.-Gen. J. Patton Anderson. Staff loss: w, 1.

Anderson's Brigade, Brig.-Gen. J. Patton Anderson, Col. J. H. Sharp: 7th Miss., Col. W. H. Bishop; 9th Miss., Maj. T. H. Lynam; 10th Miss., Lieut.-Col. James Barr; 41st Miss., Col. W. F. Tucker; 44th Miss., Col. J. H. Sharp, Lieut.-Col. R. G. Kelsey; 9th Miss. Batt. Sharp-shooters, Maj. W. C. Richards; Ala. Battery, Capt. J. Garrity. Brigade loss: k, 80; w, 464; m, 24 = 568. *Deas's Brigade,* Brig.-Gen. Z. C. Deas: 19th Ala., Col. Samuel K. McSpadden; 22d Ala., Lieut.-Col. John Weedon (k), Capt. H. T. Toulmin; 25th Ala., Col. George D. Johnston; 39th Ala., Col. W. Clark; 50th Ala., Col. J. G. Coltart; 17th Ala. Batt. Sharp-shooters, Capt. Jas. F. Nabers; Robertson's Battery, Lieut. S. H. Dent. Brigade loss: k, 123; w, 578; m, 28 = 729. *Manigault's Brigade,* Brig.-Gen. A. M. Manigault: 24th Ala., Col. N. N. Davis; 28th Ala., Col. John C. Reid; 34th Ala., Maj. John N. Slaughter; 10th and 19th S. C., Col. James F. Pressley; Ala. Battery (Waters's), Lieut. Charles W. Watkins. Brigade loss: k, 66; w, 426; m, 47 = 539.

BUCKNER'S CORPS, Maj.-Gen. Simon B. Buckner.

STEWART'S DIVISION, Maj.-Gen. Alexander P. Stewart. Staff loss: w, 1; m, 1 = 2.

Johnson's Brigade (attached to Johnson's Provisional Division), Brig.-Gen. Bushrod R. Johnson, Col. J. S. Fulton. 17th Tenn., Lieut.-Col. Watt W. Floyd; 23d Tenn., Col. R. H. Keeble; 25th Tenn., Lieut.-Col. R. B. Snowden; 44th Tenn., Lieut.-Col. J. L. McEwen, Jr. (w), Maj. G. M. Crawford; Ga. Battery, Lieut. W. S. Everett. Brigade loss: k, 28; w, 271; m, 74 = 373. *Brown's Brigade*, Brig.-Gen. John C. Brown (w), Col. Edmund C. Cook: 18th Tenn., Col. J. B. Palmer (w), Lieut.-Col. W. R. Butler (w), Capt. Gideon H. Lowe; 26th Tenn., Col. J. M. Lillard (k), Maj. R. M. Saffell; 32d Tenn., Col. Edmund C. Cook, Capt. C. G. Tucker; 45th Tenn., Col. A. Searcy; 23d Tenn. Batt., Maj. T. W. Newman (w), Capt. W. P. Simpson. Brigade loss: k, 50; w, 426; m, 4 = 480. *Bate's Brigade*, Brig.-Gen. William B. Bate: 58th Ala., Col. Bushrod Jones; 37th Ga., Col. A. F. Rudler (w), Lieut.-Col. Joseph T. Smith; 4th Ga. Battalion Sharp-shooters, Maj. T. D. Caswell (w), Capt. B. M. Turner (w), Lieut. Joel Towers; 15th and 37th Tenn., Col. R. C. Tyler (w), Lieut.-Col. R. D. Frayser (w), Capt. R. M. Tankesley; 20th Tenn., Col. T. B. Smith (w), Maj. W. M. Shy. Brigade loss: k, 63; w, 530; m, 11 = 604. *Clayton's Brigade*, Brig.-Gen. H. D. Clayton (w): 18th Ala., Col. J. T. Holtzclaw (w), Lieut.-Col. R. F. Inge (m w), Maj. P. F. Hunley; 36th Ala., Col. L. T. Woodruff; 38th Ala., Lieut.-Col. A. R. Lankford. Brigade loss: k, 86; w, 518; m, 15 = 619. *Artillery*, Maj. J. W. Eldridge: 1st Ark. Battery, Capt. J. T. Humphreys; Ga. Battery (Dawson's), Lieut. R. W. Anderson; Eufaula Art'y, Capt. McD. Oliver. Artillery loss: k, 4; w, 23 = 27.

PRESTON'S DIVISION, Brig.-Gen. William Preston.

Gracie's Brigade, Brig.-Gen. Archibald Gracie, Jr.: 43d Ala., Col. Y. M. Moody; 1st Ala. Battalion,* Lieut.-Col. J. H. Holt (w), Capt. G. W. Huguley; 2d Ala. Battalion,* Lieut.-Col. Bolling Hall, Jr. (w), Capt. W. D. Walden (w); 3d Ala. Battalion,* Maj. Joseph W. A. Sanford; 4th Ala.,* Maj. J. D. McLennan; 63d Tenn., Lieut.-Col. A. Fulkerson (w), Maj. John A. Aiken. Brigade loss: k, 90; w, 576; m, 2 = 668. *Trigg's Brigade*, Col. Robert C. Trigg: 1st Fla. Cav. (dismounted), Col. G. T. Maxwell; 6th Fla., Col. J. J. Finley; 7th Fla., Col. R. Bullock; 54th Va., Lieut.-Col. John J. Wade. Brigade loss: k, 46; w, 231; m, 4 = 281. *Kelly's Brigade*, Col. J. H. Kelly: 65th Ga., Col. R. H. Moore; 5th Ky., Col. H. Hawkins; 58th N. C., Col. John B. Palmer (w); 63d Va., Maj. J. M. French. Brigade loss: k, 66; w, 241; m, 3 = 310. *Artillery Battalion*, Maj. A. Leyden: Ga. Battery, Capt. A. M. Wolihin; Ga. Battery, Capt. T. M. Peeples; Va. Battery, Capt. W. C. Jeffress; Ga. Battery (York's). Artillery loss: w, 6.

RESERVE ARTILLERY, Maj. S. C. Williams: Baxter's (Tenn.) Battery; Darden's (Miss.) Battery; Kolb's (Ala.) Battery; McCant's (Fla.) Battery. Artillery loss: k, 2; w, 2 = 4.

* Hilliard's Legion.

JOHNSON'S DIVISION,* Brig.-Gen. Bushrod R. Johnson.
Gregg's Brigade, Brig.-Gen. John Gregg (w), Col. C. A. Sugg: 3d Tenn.,
Col. C. H. Walker; 10th Tenn., Col. William Grace; 30th Tenn., ——; 41st
Tenn., Lieut.-Col. James D. Tillman (w); 50th Tenn., Col. C. A. Sugg,
Lieut.-Col. T. W. Beaumont (k), Maj. C. W. Robertson (w), Col. C. H.
Walker; 1st Tenn. Battalion, Maj. S. H. Colms (w), Maj. C. W. Robertson;
7th Texas, Col. H. B. Granbury (w), Maj. K. M. Vanzandt; Mo. Battery
(Bledsoe's), Lieut. R. L. Wood. Brigade loss: k, 109; w, 474; m, 18 = 601.
McNair's Brigade, Brig.-Gen. E. McNair (w), Col. D. Coleman: 1st Ark.
Mounted Rifles, Col. Robert W. Harper (m w); 2d Ark. Mounted Rifles,
Col. James A. Williamson; 25th Ark., Lieut.-Col. Eli Hufstedler (w); 4th
and 31st Ark. and 4th Ark. Battalion, Maj. J. A. Ross; 39th N. C., Col. D.
Coleman; S. C. Battery, Capt. J. F. Culpeper. Brigade loss: k, 51; w, 336;
m, 64 = 451.

LONGSTREET'S CORPS,† Maj.-Gen. John B. Hood (w). Staff loss: w, 1.

MCLAW'S DIVISION, Brig.-Gen. Joseph B. Kershaw, Maj.-Gen. Lafayette Mc-
Laws.
Kershaw's Brigade, Brig.-Gen. Joseph B. Kershaw: 2d S. C., Lieut.-Col.
F. Gaillard; 3d S. C., Col. James D. Nance; 7th S. C., Lieut.-Col. Elbert
Bland (k), Maj. John S. Hard (k), Capt. E. J. Goggans; 8th S. C., Col. John
W. Henagan; 15th S. C., Lieut.-Col. Joseph F. Gist; 3d S. C. Battalion, Capt.
J. M. Townsend (k). Brigade loss: k, 68; w, 419; m, 1 = 488. *Wofford's
Brigade,*** Brig.-Gen. W. T. Wofford: 16th Ga., ——; 18th Ga., ——; 24th
Ga., ——; 3d Ga. Battalion Sharp-Shooters, ——; Cobb's (Ga.) Legion,
——; Phillips's (Ga.) Legion, ——. *Humphreys's Brigade,* Brig.-Gen. Ben-
jamin G. Humphreys: 13th Miss., ——; 17th Miss., ——; 18th Miss., ——;
21st Miss., ——. Brigade loss: k, 20; w, 132 = 152. *Bryan's Brigade,*** Brig.-
Gen. Goode Bryan: 10th Ga., ——; 50th Ga., ——; 51st Ga., ——; 53d Ga.,
——.

HOOD'S DIVISION, Maj.-Gen. John B. Hood, Brig.-Gen. E. McIver Law.
Jenkins's Brigade,†† Brig.-Gen. Micah Jenkins; 1st, S. C., ——; 2d S. C.
Rifles, ——; 5th S. C., ——; 6th S. C., ——; Hampton Legion, ——; Palmetto (S. C.) Sharp-shooters, ——. *Law's Brigade,* Brig.-Gen. E. McIver
Law, Col. James L. Sheffield: 4th Ala., ——; 15th Ala., Col. W. C. Oates;
44th Ala., ——; 47th Ala., ——; 48th Ala., ——. Brigade loss: k, 61; w, 329
= 390. *Robertson's Brigade,* Brig.-Gen. J. B. Robertson, Col. Van. H.
Manning: 3rd Ark., Col. Van. H. Manning; 1st Texas, Capt. R. J. Harding;
4th Texas, Col. John P. Bane (w), Capt. R. H. Bassett (w); 5th Texas, J. C.

* Provisional, embracing Johnson's and, part of the time, Robertson's brigades,
as well as Gregg's and McNair's. Sept. 19 attached to Longstreet's corps under Hood.
† Organization taken from return of Lee's army for Aug. 31, 1863. Pickett's
division was left in Virginia.
** Longstreet's report indicates that these brigades did not arrive in time to
take part in the battle.
†† Did not arrive in time to take part in the battle.

Rogers (w), Capt. J. S. Cleveland (w), Capt. T. T. Clay. Brigade loss: k, 78; w, 457; m, 35 = 570. *Anderson's Brigade,** Brig.-Gen. George T. Anderson; 7th Ga., ——; 8th Ga., ——; 9th Ga., ——; 11th Ga., ——; 59th Ga., ——. *Benning's Brigade,* Brig.-Gen. Henry L. Benning; 2d Ga., Lieut.-Col. William S. Shepherd (w). Maj. W. W. Charlton; 15th Ga., Col. D. M. Du Bose (w), Maj. P. J. Shannon; 17th Ga., Lieut.-Col. Charles W. Matthews (m. w); 20th Ga., Col. J. D. Waddell. Brigade loss: k, 46; w, 436; m, 6 = 488.

CORPS ARTILLERY, ‖ Col. E. Porter Alexander: S. C. Battery (Fickling's); Va. Battery (Jordan's); La. Battery (Moody's); Va. Battery (Parker's); Va. Battery (Taylor's); Va. Battery (Woolfolk's).

RESERVE ARTILLERY, ARMY OF TENNESSEE, Maj. Felix H. Robertson: Barret's (Mo.) Battery; Le Gardeur's (La.) Battery; Havis's (Ala.) Battery; Lumsden's (Ala.) Battery; Massenburg's (Ga.) Battery. Artillery loss: k, 2; w, 6 = 8.

CAVALRY, Maj.-Gen. Joseph Wheeler.

WHARTON'S DIVISION, Brig.-Gen. John A. Wharton.
First Brigade, Col. C. C. Crews: 7th Ala., ——; 2d Ga., ——; 3d Ga., ——; 4th Ga., Col. Isaac W. Avery. *Second Brigade,* Col. Thomas Harrison: 3d Confederate, Col. W. N. Estes; 1st Ky., Lieut.-Col. J. W. Griffith; 4th Tenn., Col. Paul F. Anderson; 8th Texas, ——; 11th Texas, ——; Ga. Battery (White's).

MARTIN'S DIVISION, Brig.-Gen. William T. Martin.
First Brigade, Col. J. T. Morgan; 1st Ala., ——; 3d Ala., Lieut.-Col. T. H. Mauldin; 51st Ala., ——; 8th Confederate, ——. *Second Brigade,* Col. A. A. Russell: 4th Ala.,† ——; 1st Confederate, Col. W. B. Wade; Ark. Battery (Wiggins's). *Roddey's Brigade,* Brig.-Gen. P. D. Roddey; 4th Ala.,† Lieut.-Col. William A. Johnson; 5th Ala., ——; 53d Ala., ——; Tenn. Reg't (Forrest's); Ga. Battery (Newell's). Loss of Wheeler's cavalry (estimated), 375 killed, wounded, and missing.

FORREST'S CORPS, Brig.-Gen. N. B. Forrest.

ARMSTRONG'S DIVISION, Brig.-Gen. Frank C. Armstrong.
Armstrong's Brigade, Col. J. T. Wheeler: 3d Ark., ——; 1st Tenn., ——; 18th Tenn. Battalion, Maj. Charles McDonald. *Forrest's Brigade,* Col. G. G. Dibrell: 4th Tenn., Col. W. S. McLemore; 8th Tenn., Capt. Hamilton McGinnis; 9th Tenn., Col. J. B. Biffle; 10th Tenn., Col. N. N. Cox; 11th Tenn., Col. D. W. Holman; Shaw's Battalion, Maj. J. Shaw; Tenn. Battery, Capt. A. L. Huggins; Tenn. Battery, Capt. John W. Morton.

* Served part of time in Johnson's Provisional Division.
† Two regiments of the same designation. Lieut.-Col. Johnson commanded that in Roddey's brigade.

PEGRAM'S DIVISION (composition of division uncertain). Brig.-Gen. John Pegram.

Davidson's Brigade, Brig.-Gen. H. B. Davidson: 1st Ga., ——; 6th Ga., Col. John R. Hart; 6th N. C., ——; Rucker's Legion, ——; Tenn. Battery (Huwald's). *Scott's Brigade,* Col. J. S. Scott: 10th Confederate, Col. C. T. Goode; Detachment of Morgan's command, Lieut.-Col. R. M. Martin; 1st La., ——; 2d Tenn., ——; 5th Tenn., ——; 12th Tenn. Battalion, ——; 16th Tenn. Battalion, Capt. J. Q. Arnold (w); La. Battery (section), ——. Brigade loss: k, 10; w, 39 = 49.

Total Confederate loss: killed, 2389; wounded, 13,412; captured or missing, 2003 = 17,804.

Appendix C

THE OPPOSING FORCES IN THE CHATTANOOGA CAMPAIGN

November 23–27, 1863

(Including General Bragg's comments on Missionary Ridge)

Battles and Leaders of the Civil War, III, pp. 727-730.

For much of the information contained in this list and in similar lists to follow, the editors are indebted (in advance of the publication of the "Official Records") to Brigadier-General Richard C. Drum, Adjutant-General of the Army. K stands for killed; w for wounded; m w for mortally wounded; m for captured or missing; c for captured.

THE UNION ARMY: Maj.-Gen. Ulysses S. Grant.

ARMY OF THE CUMBERLAND.—Maj.-Gen. George H. Thomas.
General Headquarters: 1st Ohio Sharp-shooters, Capt. G. M. Barber; 10th Ohio, Lieut.-Col. W. M. Ward.

FOURTH ARMY CORPS, Maj.-Gen. Gordon Granger.

FIRST DIVISION, Brig.-Gen. Charles Cruft.
Escort: E, 92d Ill., Capt. Matthew Van Buskirk.
Second Brigade, Brig.-Gen. Walter C. Whitaker: 96th Ill., Col. Thomas E. Champion, Maj. George Hicks; 35th Ind., Col. Bernard F. Mullen; 8th Ky., Col. Sidney M. Barnes; 40th Ohio, Col. Jacob E. Taylor; 51st Ohio, Lieut-Col. Charles H. Wood; 99th Ohio, Lieut.-Col. John E. Cummins. Brigade loss: k, 17; w, 63; m, 2 = 82. *Third Brigade,* Col. William Grose: 59th Ill., Maj. Clayton Hale; 75th Ill., Col. John E. Bennett; 84th Ill., Col. Louis H. Waters; 9th Ind., Col. Isaac C. B. Suman; 36th Ind., Maj. Gilbert Trusler; 24th Ohio, Capt. George M. Macon. Brigade loss: k, 4; w, 60 = 64.

SECOND DIVISION, Maj.-Gen. Philip H. Sheridan.
First Brigade, Col. Francis T. Sherman: 36th Ill., Col. Silas Miller,* Lieut.-Col. Porter C. Olson; 44th Ill., Col. Wallace W. Barrett; 73d Ill.,

* Temporarily in command of a demi-brigade.

Col. James F. Jacques; 74th Ill., Col. Jason Marsh; 88th Ill., Lieut.-Col. George W. Chandler; 22d Ind., Col. Michael Gooding; 2d Mo., Col. Bernard Laiboldt,* Lieut.-Col. Arnold Beck; 15th Mo., Col. Joseph Conrad (w), Capt. Samuel Rexinger; 24th Wis., Maj. Carl von Baumbach. Brigade loss: k, 30; w, 268; m, 3 = 301. *Second Brigade,* Brig.-Gen. George D. Wagner: 100th Ill., Maj. Chas. M. Hammond; 15th Ind., Col. Gustavus A. Wood,* Maj. Frank White (w), Capt. Benjamin F. Hegler; 40th Ind., Lieut.-Col. Elias Neff; 57th Ind., Lieut.-Col. George W. Lennard; 58th Ind., Lieut.-Col. Joseph Moore; 26th Ohio, Lieut.-Col. William H. Young; 97th Ohio, Lieut.-Col. Milton Barnes. Brigade loss: k, 70; w, 660 = 730. *Third Brigade,* Col. Charles G. Harker: 22d Ill., Lieut.-Col. Francis Swanwick; 27th Ill., Col. Jonathan R. Miles; 42d Ill., Col. Nathan H. Walworth,* Capt. Edgar D. Swain; 51st Ill., Maj. Charles W. Davis (w), Capt. Albert M. Tilton; 79th Ill., Col. Allen Buckner; 3d Ky., Col. Henry C. Dunlap; 64th Ohio, Col. Alexander McIllvain; 65th Ohio, Lieut.-Col. William A. Bullitt; 125th Ohio, Col. Emerson Opdycke,* Capt. Edward P. Bates. Brigade loss: k, 28; w, 269 = 297. *Artillery,* Capt. Warren P. Edgarton: M, 1st Ill., Capt. George W. Spencer; 10th Ind., Capt. William A. Naylor; G, 1st Mo., Lieut. G. Schueler; I, 1st Ohio, Capt. H. Dilger; G, 4th U. S., Lieut. C. F. Merkle; H, 5th U. S., Capt. F. L. Guenther.

THIRD DIVISION, Brig.-Gen. Thomas J. Wood.

First Brigade, Brig.-Gen. August Willich: 25th Ill., Col. Richard H. Nodine; 35th Ill., Lieut.-Col. William P. Chandler; Lieut.-Col. William D. Williams; 32d Ind., Lieut.-Col. Frank Erdelmeyer; 68th Ind., Lieut.-Col. Harvey J. Espy; 8th Kans., Col. John A. Martin; 15th Ohio, Lieut.-Col. Frank Askew; 49th Ohio, Maj. Samuel F. Gray; 15th Wis., Capt. John A. Gordon. Brigade loss: k, 46; w, 291; m, 1 = 338. *Second Brigade,* Brig.-Gen. William B. Hazen: 6th Ind., Maj. Calvin D. Campbell; 5th Ky., Col. William W. Berry (w), Lieut.-Col. John L. Treanor; 6th Ky., Maj. Richard T. Whitaker; 23d Ky., Lieut.-Col. James C. Foy; 1st Ohio, Lieut.-Col. Bassett Langdon (w), Maj. Joab A. Stafford; 6th Ohio, Lieut.-Col. Alex C. Christopher; 41st Ohio, Col. Aquilla Wiley (w), Lieut.-Col. Robert L. Kimberly; 93d Ohio, Maj. William Birch (k), Capt. Daniel Bowman (w), Capt. Samuel B. Smith; 124th Ohio, Lieut.-Col. James Pickands. Brigade loss: k, 92; w, 430; m, 7 = 529. *Third Brigade,* Brig.-Gen. Samuel Beatty: 79th Ind., Col. Frederick Knefler; 86th Ind., Col. George F. Dick; 9th Ky., Col. George H. Cram; 17th Ky., Col. Alexander M. Stout; 13th Ohio, Col. Dwight Jarvis, Jr.; 19th Ohio, Col. Charles F. Manderson; 59th Ohio, Maj. Robert J. Vanosdol. Brigade loss: k, 14; w, 160; m, 1 = 175. *Artillery,* Capt. Cullen Bradley: Ill., Battery, Capt. Lyman Bridges; 6th Ohio, Lieut. Oliver H. P. Ayres; 20th Ohio, Capt. Edward Grosskopff; B, Pa., Lieut. Samuel M. McDowell.

* Temporarily in command of a demi-brigade.

ELEVENTH CORPS,* Maj.-Gen. O. O. Howard.
General Headquarters, Independent Co., 8th N. Y. Infantry, Capt. Anton Bruhn.

SECOND DIVISION, Brig.-Gen. Adolph von Steinwehr.
First Brigade, Col. Adolphus Buschbeck: 33d N. J., Col. George W. Mindil; 134th N. Y., Col. Allen H. Jackson; 154th N. Y., Col. Patrick H. Jones; 27th Pa., Maj. Peter A. McAloon (m w), Capt. August Reidt; 73d Pa., Lieut.-Col. Joseph B. Taft (k), Capt. Daniel F. Kelly (c), Lieut. Samuel D. Miller. Brigade loss: k, 28; w, 148; m, 108 = 284. *Second Brigade,* Col. Orland Smith: 33d Mass., Lieut.-Col. Godfrey Rider, Jr.; 136th N.Y., Col. James Wood, Jr.; 55th Ohio, Col. C. B. Gambee; 73d Ohio, Maj. S. H. Hurst. Brigade loss: k, 4; w, 21; m, 4 = 29.

THIRD DIVISION, Maj.-Gen. Carl Schurz.
First Brigade, Brig.-Gen. Hector Tyndale: 101st Ill., Col. Charles H. Fox; 45th N. Y., Maj. Charles Koch; 143d N. Y., Col. Horace Boughton; 61st Ohio, Col. Stephen J. McGroarty; 82d Ohio, Lieut.-Col. David Thomson. Brigade loss: k, 1; w, 4 = 5. *Second Brigade,* Col. Wladimir Krzyzanowski: 58th N. Y., Capt. Michael Esembaux; 119th N. Y., Col. John T. Lockman; 141st N. Y., Col. William K. Logie; 26th Wis., Capt. Frederick C. Winkler. Brigade loss: w, 3. *Third Brigade,* Col. Frederick Hecker: 80th Ill., Capt. James Neville; 82d Ill., Lieut.-Col. Edward S. Salomon; 68th N. Y., Maj. Albert von Steinhausen; 75th Pa., Maj. August Ledig. Brigade loss: k, 1; w, 9 = 10. *Artillery,* Maj. Thomas W. Osborn: I, 1st N. Y., Capt. Michael Wiedrich; 13th N. Y., Capt. W. Wheeler; K, 1st Ohio, Lieut. Nicholas Sahm.

TWELFTH ARMY CORPS.

SECOND DIVISION, Brig.-Gen. John W. Geary.
First Brigade, Col. Charles Candy, Col. William R. Creighton (k), Col. Thomas J. Ahl: 5th Ohio, Col. John H. Patrick; 7th Ohio, Col. William R. Creighton, Lieut.-Col. Orrin J. Crane (k), Capt. Ernest J. Kreiger; 29th Ohio, Col. William F. Fitch; 66th Ohio, Lieut.-Col. Eugene Powell, Capt. Thomas McConnell; 28th Pa., Col. Thomas J. Ahl, Capt. John Flynn; 147th Pa., Lieut.-Col. Ario Pardee, Jr. Brigade loss: k, 25; w, 117 = 142. *Second Brigade,* Col. George A. Cobham, Jr.: 29th Pa., Col. William Rickards, Jr.; 109th Pa., Capt. Frederick L. Gimber; 111th Pa., Col. Thomas M. Walker. Brigade loss: k, 4; w, 18 = 22. *Third Brigade,* Col. David Ireland: 60th N. Y., Col. Abel Godard; 78th N. Y., Col. Herbert von Hammerstein; 102d N. Y., Col. James C. Lane; 137th N. Y., Capt. Milo B. Eldridge; 149th N. Y., Lieut.-Col. Charles B. Randall. Brigade loss: k, 26; w, 151 = 177. *Artillery,* Maj. J. A. Reynolds: E, Pa., Lieut. J. D. McGill; K, 5th U. S., Capt. E. C. Bainbridge.

* Maj.-Gen. Joseph Hooker, commanding Eleventh and Twelfth Army Corps, had under his immediate command the First Division, Fourth Corps; the Second Division, Twelfth Corps; portions of the Fourteenth Corps, and the First Division,

FOURTEENTH CORPS, Maj.-Gen. J. M. Palmer.
Escort: L, 1st Ohio Cav., Capt. John D. Barker.

FIRST DIVISION, Brig.-Gen. Richard W. Johnson.
First Brigade, Brig.-Gen. William P. Carlin: 104th Ill., Lieut.-Col. Douglas Hapeman; 38th Ind., Lieut.-Col. Daniel F. Griffin; 42d Ind., Lieut.-Col. William T. B. McIntire; 88th Ind., Col. Cyrus E. Briant; 2d Ohio, Col. Anson G. McCook; 33d Ohio, Capt. James H. M. Montgomery; 94th Ohio, Maj. Rue P. Hutchins; 10th Wis., Capt. Jacob W. Roby. Brigade loss: k, 25; w, 134 = 159. *Second Brigade,* Col. Marshall F. Moore, Col. William L. Stoughton: 19th Ill., Lieut.-Col. Alexander W. Raffen; 11th Mich., Capt. Patrick H. Keegan; 69th Ohio, Maj. James J. Hanna; 1st Battalion, 15th U. S., Capt. Henry Keteltas; 2d Battalion, 15th U. S., Capt. William S. McManus; 1st Battalion, 16th U. S., Maj. Robert E. A. Crofton; 1st Battalion, 18th U. S., Capt. George W. Smith; 2d Battalion, 18th U. S., Capt. Henry Haymond; 1st Battalion, 19th U. S., Capt. Henry S. Welton. Brigade loss: k, 23; w, 149; m, 2 = 174. *Third Brigade,* Brig.-Gen. John C. Starkweather: 24th Ill., Col. Geza Mihalotzy; 37th Ind., Col. James S. Hull; 21st Ohio, Capt. Charles H. Vantine; 74th Ohio, Maj. Joseph Fisher; 78th Pa., Maj. Augustus B. Bonnaffon; 79th Pa., Maj. Michael H. Locher; 1st Wis., Lieut.-Col. George B. Bingham; 21st Wis., Capt. Charles H. Walker. *Artillery:* C, 1st Ill., Capt. Mark H. Prescott; A, 1st Mich., Francis E. Hale.

SECOND DIVISION, Brig.-Gen. J. C. Davis. Staff loss: w, 1.
First Brigade, Brig.-Gen. James D. Morgan: 10th Ill., Col. John Tillson: 16th Ill., Lieut.-Col. James B. Cahill; 60th Ill., Col. William B. Anderson; 21st Ky., Col. Samuel W. Price; 10th Mich., Lieut.-Col. Christopher J. Dickerson. Brigade loss: w, 9. *Second Brigade,* Brig.-Gen. John Beatty: 34th Ill., Lieut.-Col. Oscar Van Tassell; 78th Ill., Lieut.-Col. Carter Van Vleck; 98th Ohio, Maj. James M. Shane; 108th Ohio, Lieut.-Col. Carlo Piepho; 113th Ohio, Maj. L. Starling Sullivant; 121st Ohio, Maj. John Yager. Brigade loss: k, 3; w, 17; m, 1 = 21. *Third Brigade,* Col. Daniel McCook: 85th Ill., Col. Caleb J. Dilworth; 86th Ill., Lieut.-Col. David W. Magee; 110th Ill., Lieut.-Col. E. Hibbard Topping; 125th Ill., Col. Oscar F. Harmon; 52d Ohio, Maj. James T. Holmes. Brigade loss: k, 2; w, 4; m, 5 = 11. *Artillery,* Capt. William A. Hotchkiss: I, 2d Ill., Lieut. Henry B. Plant; 2d Minn., Lieut. Richard L. Dawley; 5th Wis., Capt. George Q. Gardner.

THIRD DIVISION, Brig.-Gen. Absalom Baird.
First Brigade, Brig.-Gen. John B. Turchin: 82d Ind., Col. Morton C. Hunter; 11th Ohio, Lieut.-Col. Ogden Street; 17th Ohio, Maj. Daniel Butterfield (w), Capt. Benjamin H. Showers; 31st Ohio, Lieut.-Col. Frederick W. Lister; 36th Ohio, Lieut.-Col. Hiram F. Duval; 89th Ohio, Capt. John H. Jolly; 92d Ohio, Lieut.-Col. Douglas Putman, Jr. (w), Capt. Edward Grosvenor. Brigade loss: k, 50; w, 231; m, 3 = 284. *Second Brigade,* Col. Ferdinand Van Derveer: 75th Ind., Col. Milton S. Robinson; 87th Ind.,

Fifteenth Corps. Co. K, 15th Ill. Cav., Capt. Samuel B. Sherer, served as escort to Gen. Hooker.

Col. Newell Gleason; 101st Ind., Lieut.-Col. Thomas Doan; 2d Minn., Lieut.-Col. Judson W. Bishop; 9th Ohio, Col. Gustave Kammerling; 35th Ohio, Lieut.-Col. Henry V. N. Boynton (w), Maj. Joseph L. Budd; 105th Ohio, Lieut.-Col. William R. Tolles. Brigade loss: k, 19; w, 142; m, 2 = 163. *Third Brigade,* Col. Edward H. Phelps (k), Col. William H. Hays: 10th Ind., Lieut.-Col. Marsh B. Taylor; 74th Ind., Lieut.-Col. Myron Baker; 4th Ky., Maj. Robert M. Kelly; 10th Ky., Col. William H. Hays, Lieut.-Col. Gabriel C. Wharton; 14th Ohio, Lieut.-Col. Henry D. Kingsbury; 38th Ohio, Maj. Charles Greenwood. Brigade loss: k, 18; w, 100; m, 1 = 119. *Artillery,* Capt. George R. Swallow: 7th Ind., Lieut. Otho H. Morgan; 19th Ind., Lieut. Robert G. Lackey; I, 4th U. S., Lieut. Frank G. Smith.

ENGINEER TROOPS, Brig.-Gen. William F. Smith.

Engineers: 1st Mich. Engineers (detachment), Capt. Perrin V. Fox; 13th Mich., Maj. Willard G. Eaton; 21st Mich., Capt. Loomis K. Bishop; 22d Mich. Inf., Maj. Henry S. Dean; 18th Ohio, Col. Timothy R. Stanley. *Pioneer Brigade,* Col. George P. Buell: 1st Battalion, Capt. Charles J. Stewart; 2d Battalion, Capt. Cornelius Smith; 3d Battalion, Capt. William Clark.

ARTILLERY RESERVE, Brig.-Gen. J. M. Brannan.

FIRST DIVISION, Col. James Barnett.

First Brigade, Maj. Charles S. Cotter: B, 1st Ohio, Lieut. Norman A. Baldwin; C, 1st Ohio, Capt. Marco B. Gary; E, 1st Ohio, Lieut. Albert G. Ransom; F, 1st Ohio, Lieut. Giles J. Cockerill. *Second Brigade,* G, 1st Ohio, Capt. Alexander Marshall; M, 1st Ohio, Capt. Frederick Schultz; 18th Ohio, Lieut. Joseph McCafferty.

SECOND DIVISION.

First Brigade, Capt. Josiah W. Church: D, 1st Mich., Capt. Josiah W. Church; A, 1st Tenn., Lieut. Albert F. Beach; 3d Wis., Lieut. Hiram F. Hubbard; 8th Wis., Lieut. Obadiah German; 10th Wis., Capt. Yates V. Beebe. *Second Brigade,* Capt. Arnold Sutermeister: 4th Ind., Lieut. Henry J. Willits; 8th Ind., Lieut. George Estep; 11th Ind., Capt. Arnold Sutermeister; 21st Ind., Lieut. W. E. Chess; C, 1st Wis. Heavy, Capt. John R. Davies.

CAVALRY.*

Second Brigade (Second Division), Col. Eli Long: 98th Ill., Lieut.-Col. Edward Kitchell; 17th Ind., Lieut.-Col. Henry Jordan; 2d Ky., Col. Thomas P. Nicholas; 4th Mich., Maj. Horace Gray; 1st Ohio, Maj. Thomas J. Patten; 3d Ohio, Lieut.-Col. C. B. Seidel; 4th Ohio (battalion), Maj. G. W. Dobb; 10th Ohio, Col. C. C. Smith.

* Corps headquarters and the First and Second Brigades and 18th Ind. Battery, of the First Division at and about Alexandria, Tenn.; Third Brigade at Caperton's Ferry, Tennessee River. First and Third Brigades and Chicago Board of Trade Battery, of the Second Division, at Maysville, Ala.

POST OF CHATTANOOGA, Col. John G. Parkhurst: 44th Ind., Lieut.-Col. Simeon C. Aldrich; 15th Ky., Maj. William G. Halpin; 9th Mich., Lieut.-Col. William Wilkinson.

ARMY OF THE TENNESSEE, Maj.-Gen. William T. Sherman.*
FIFTEENTH CORPS, Maj.-Gen. Frank P. Blair, Jr.

FIRST DIVISION, Brig.-Gen. Peter J. Osterhaus.

First Brigade, Brig.-Gen. Charles R. Woods: 13th Ill., Lieut.-Col. Frederick W. Partridge (w), Capt. Geo. P. Brown; 3d Mo., Lieut.-Col. Theodore Meumann; 12th Mo., Col. Hugo Wangelin (w), Lieut.-Col. Jacob Kaercher; 17th Mo., Lieut.-Col. John F. Cramer; 27th Mo., Col. Thomas Curly; 29th Mo., Col. James Peckham (w), Maj. Philip H. Murphy; 31st Mo., Lieut.-Col. Samuel P. Simpson; 32d Mo., Lieut.-Col. Henry C. Warmoth; 76th Ohio, Maj. Willard Warner. Brigade loss: k, 33; w, 203; m, 41 = 277. *Second Brigade,* Col. James A. Williamson: 4th Iowa, Lieut.-Col. George Burton; 9th Iowa, Col. David Carskaddon; 25th Iowa, Col. George A. Stone; 26th Iowa, Col. Milo Smith; 30th Iowa, Lieut.-Col. Aurelius Roberts; 31st Iowa, Lieut.-Col. Jeremiah W. Jenkins. Brigade loss: k, 19; w, 134; m, 2 = 155. *Artillery,* Capt. Henry H. Griffiths: 1st Iowa, Lieut. James M. Williams; F, 2d Mo., Capt. Clemens Landgraeber; 4th Ohio, Capt. George Froehlich.

SECOND DIVISION, Brig.-Gen. Morgan L. Smith.

First Brigade, Brig.-Gen. Giles A. Smith (w), Col. Nathan W. Tupper: 55th Ill., Col. Oscar Malinborg; 116th Ill., Col. Nathan W. Tupper, Lieut.-Col. James P. Boyd; 127th Ill., Lieut.-Col. Frank S. Curtiss; 6th Mo., Lieut.-Col. Ira Boutell; 8th Mo., Lieut.-Col. David C. Coleman; 57th Ohio, Lieut.-Col. Samuel R. Mott; 1st Battalion, 13th U. S., Capt. Charles C. Smith. Brigade loss: w, 14; m, 2 = 16. *Second Brigade,* Brig.-Gen. Joseph A. J. Lightburn: 82d Ind., Col. Benjamin J. Spooner; 30th Ohio, Col. Theodore Jones; 37th Ohio, Lieut.-Col. Louis Von Blessingh; 47th Ohio, Col. Augustus C. Parry; 54th Ohio, Maj. Robert Williams, Jr.; 4th W. Va., Col. James H. Dayton. Brigade loss: k, 10; w, 76 = 86. *Artillery:* A, 1st Ill., Capt. Peter P. Wood; B, 1st Ill., Capt. Israel P. Rumsey; H, 1st Ill., Lieut. Francis DeGress. Artillery loss: w, 1.

FOURTH DIVISION, Brig.-Gen. Hugh Ewing.

First Brigade, Col. John Mason Loomis: 26th Ill., Lieut.-Col. Robert A. Gillmore; 90th Ill., Col. Timothy O'Meara (k), Lieut.-Col. Owen Stuart; 12th Ind., Col. Reuben Williams; 100th Ind., Lieut.-Col. Albert Heath. Brigade loss: k, 37; w, 331; m, 18 = 386. *Second Brigade,* Brig.-Gen. John M. Corse (w), Col. Charles C. Walcutt: 4th Ill., Maj. Hiram W. Hall; 103d Ill., Col. William A. Dickerman; 6th Iowa, Lieut.-Col. Alexander J. Miller; 46th Ohio, Col. Charles C. Walcutt, Capt. Isaac N. Alexander. Brigade loss:

* General Sherman had under his immediate command the Eleventh Corps, and the Second Division, Fourteenth Corps of the Army of the Cumberland; the Second and Fourth Divisions, Fifteenth Corps, and the Second Division, Seventeenth Corps.

k, 34; w, 201; m, 2 = 237. *Third Brigade,* Col. Joseph R. Cockerill: 48th Ill., Lieut.-Col. Lucien Greathouse; 97th Ind., Col. Robert F. Catterson; 99th Ind., Col. Alexander Fowler; 53d Ohio, Col. Wells S. Jones; 70th Ohio, Maj. William B. Brown. Brigade loss: w, 3. *Artillery,* Capt. Henry Richardson: F, 1st Ill., Capt. John T. Cheney; I, 1st Ill., Lieut. Josiah H. Burton; D, 1st Mo., Lieut. Byron M. Callender. Artillery loss: w, 2.

Seventeenth Army Corps.

second division, Brig.-Gen. John E. Smith.
First Brigade, Col. Jesse I. Alexander: 63d Ill., Col. Joseph B. McCown; 48th Ind., Lieut.-Col. Edward J. Wood; 59th Ind., Capt. Wilford H. Welman; 4th Minn., Lieut.-Col. John E. Tourtellotte; 18th Wis., Col. Gabriel Bouck. Brigade loss: w, 4. *Second Brigade,* Col. Green B. Raum (w), Col. Francis C. Deimling, Col. Clark R. Wever: 56th Ill., Maj. Pinckney J. Welsh (w); 17th Iowa, Col. Clark R. Wever, Maj. John F. Walden; 10th Mo., Col. Francis C. Deimling, Lieut.-Col. Christian Hoppee, Col. Francis C. Deimling; E, 24th Mo., Capt. William W. McCammon; 80th Ohio, Lieut.-Col. Pren Metham. Brigade loss: k, 40; w, 140; m, 24 = 204. *Third Brigade,* Brig.-Gen. Charles L. Matthies (w), Col. Benjamin D. Dean, Col. Jabez Banbury: 93d Ill., Col. Holden Putnam (k), Lieut.-Col. Nicholas C. Buswell; 5th Iowa, Col. Jabez Banbury, Lieut.-Col. Ezekiel S. Sampson; 10th Iowa, Lieut.-Col. Paris P. Henderson; 26th Mo., Col. Benjamin D. Dean. Brigade loss: k, 49; w, 145; m, 121 = 315. *Artillery,* Capt. Henry Dillon: Ill. Battery, Capt. William Cogswell; 6th Wis., Lieut. Samuel F. Clark; 12th Wis., Capt. William Zickerick.

Total Union loss: killed, 752; wounded, 4713; captured or missing, 350 = 5815. Effective strength (est.), 60,000.

THE CONFEDERATE ARMY: General Braxton Bragg.

Hardee's Corps, Lieut.-Gen. William J. Hardee.

cheatham's division, Brig.-Gen. John K. Jackson.
Jackson's Brigade, Col. C. J. Wilkinson: 1st Ga. (Confederate), Maj. J. C. Gordon; 2d Battalion Ga. Sharpshooters, Lieut.-Col. R. H. Whiteley; 5th Ga., Col. C. P. Daniel; 47th Ga., Lieut.-Col. A. C. Edwards; 65th Ga., Lieut.-Col. J. W. Pearcy; 5th Miss., Maj. J. B. Herring; 8th Miss., Maj. J. F. Smith. Brigade loss not reported. *Walthall's Brigade,* Brig.-Gen. E. C. Walthall: 24th Miss., Col. William F. Dowd; 27th Miss., Col. J. A. Campbell; 29th Miss., Col. W. F. Brantley; 30th Miss., Maj. J. M. Johnson; 34th Miss., Capt. H. J. Bowen. Brigade loss: k, 8; w, 111; m, 853 = 972. *Moore's Brigade,* Brig.-Gen. John C. Moore: 37th Ala., Lieut.-Col. A. A. Green: 40th Ala., Col. J. H. Higley; 42d Ala., Lieut.-Col. Thomas C. Lanier. Brigade loss: k, 9; w, 39; m, 206 = 254. *Wright's Brigade,* Brig.-Gen. Marcus J. Wright, Col. John H. Anderson: 8th Tenn., Col. John H. Anderson, Lieut.-Col. Chris C. McKinney; 16th Tenn., Col. D. M. Donnell; 28th Tenn., Col. S. S. Stanton; 38th Tenn. (at Charleston, Tenn.), Col. John C.

Carter; 51st and 52d Tenn., Lieut.-Col. John G. Hall. Brigade loss: k, 1; w, 11 = 12. *Artillery Battalion*, Maj. M. Smith: Ala. Battery, Capt. W. H. Fowler; Fla. Battery, Capt. Robert P. McCants; Ga. Battery, Capt. John Scogin; Miss. Battery, Capt. W. B. Turner. Battalion loss: m, 7.

STEVENSON'S DIVISION, Maj.-Gen. Carter L. Stevenson, Brig.-Gen. John C. Brown (temporarily).

Brown's Brigade, Brig.-Gen. John C. Brown: 3d Tenn., Col. C. H. Walker; 18th and 26th Tenn., Lieut.-Col. W. R. Butler; 32d Tenn., Maj. J. P. McGuire; 45th Tenn. and 23d Tenn. Battalion, Col. A. Searcy. Brigade loss: k, 2; w, 35; m, 13 = 50. *Pettus's Brigade*, Brig.-Gen. E. W. Pettus: 20th Ala., Capt. John W. Davis; 23d Ala., Lieut.-Col. J. B. Bibb; 30th Ala., Col. C. M. Shelley; 31st Ala., Col. D. R. Hundley; 46th Ala., Capt. George E. Brewer. Brigade loss: k, 17; w, 93; m, 17 = 127. *Cumming's Brigade*, Brig.-Gen. Alfred Cumming: 34th Ga., Col. J. A. W. Johnson (w), Lieut.-Col. J. W. Bradley; 36th Ga., Lieut.-Col. Alexander M. Wallace (w), Capt. J. A. Grice; 39th Ga., Col. J. T. McConnell (k); 56th Ga., Lieut.-Col. J. T. Slaughter, Capt. J. L. Morgan. Brigade loss: k, 17; w, 156; m, 30 = 203. *Reynolds's Brigade* (of Buckner's division), Brig.-Gen. Alexander W. Reynolds: 58th N. C., Col. J. B. Palmer; 60th N. C., Maj. James T. Weaver; 54th Va., Lieut.-Col. J. J. Wade; 63d Va., Maj. J. M. French. *Artillery:* Ga. Battery, Capt. Max Van Den Corput; Md. Battery, Capt. John B. Rowan; Tenn. Battery, Capt. W. W. Carnes; Tenn. Battery, Capt. Edward Baxter.

CLEBURNE'S DIVISION, Maj.-Gen. P. R. Cleburne.

Lowrey's Brigade, Brig.-Gen. Mark P. Lowery: 16th Ala., Maj. F. A. Ashford; 33d Ala., Col. Samuel Adams; 45th Ala., Lieut.-Col. H. D. Lampley; 32d and 45th Miss., Col. A. B. Hardcastle; 15th Battalion Sharpshooters, Capt. T. M. Steger. *Polk's Brigade*, Brig.-Gen. Lucius E. Polk: 2d Tenn., Col. W. D. Robison (w); 35th and 48th Tenn., Col. B. J. Hill; 1st Ark., Col. J. W. Colquitt; 3d and 5th Confederate, Lieut.-Col. J. C. Cole (m w), apt. W. A. Brown, Capt. M. H. Dixon. *Liddell's Brigade*, Col. D. C. Govan: 2d, 15th, and 24th Ark., Lieut.-Col. E. Warfield; 5th and 13th Ark., Col. John E. Murray; 6th and 7th Ark., Lieut.-Col. Peter Snyder; 8th and 19th Ark., Lieut.-Col. A. S. Hutchinson. *Smith's Brigade*, Col. Hiram A. Granburry: 7th Tex., Capt. C. E. Talley; 6th, 10th, and 15th Tex., Capt. John R. Kennard; 17th, 18th, 24th, and 25th Tex. (dismounted cavalry), Maj. W. A. Taylor. *Artillery Battalion*, Capt. J. P. Douglas: Ala. Battery (Semple's), Lieut. R. W. Goldthwaite; Ark. Battery (Calvert's), Lieut. T. J. Key; Miss. Battery (Sweet's), Lieut. H. Shannon. Battalion loss: k, 6; w, 16 = 22. Division loss: k, 62; w, 367; m, 12 = 441.

WALKER'S DIVISION, Brig.-Gen. States R. Gist.

Gist's Brigade, 8th Ga. Battalion, Lieut.-Col. Z. L. Walters; 46th Ga., Lieut-Col. W. A. Daniel; 16th S. C., Col. James McCullough; 24th S. C., Col. C. H. Stevens, *Wilson's Brigade*, Brig.-Gen. Claudius C. Wilson: 1st Ga. Battalion Sharp-shooters and 25th Ga., Maj. A. Shaaff; 26th Ga. Battalion, Maj. J. W. Nisbet; 29th and 30th Ga., Maj. Thomas W. Mangham; 66th Ga., Col. J. C. Nisbet. *Maney's Brigade,* Brig.-Gen. George E. Maney (w): 4th Confederate, Capt. Joseph Bostick; 1st and 27th Tenn., Col. H. R. Field; 6th and 9th Tenn., Col. George C. Porter; 41st Tenn., Col. R. Farquharson; 50th Tenn., Col. C. A. Sugg; 24th Tenn. Battalion Sharp-shooters, Maj. Frank Maney. *Artillery Battalion,* Maj. Robert Martin: Ga. Battery, Capt. E. P. Howell; Mo. Battery, Capt. H. M. Bledsoe; Ferguson's Battery, Capt. T. B. Ferguson. Division loss: k, 14; w, 118; m, 190 = 322.

BRECKINRIDGE'S CORPS, Maj.-Gen. John C. Breckinridge.

HINDMAN'S DIVISION, Brig.-Gen. J. Patton Anderson.

Anderson's Brigade, Col. W. F. Tucker: 7th and 9th Miss., Col. W. H. Bishop; 10th and 44th Miss., Col. James Barr; 41st Miss., ——; 9th Battalion Miss. Sharp-shooters, Maj. W. C. Richards. *Manigault's Brigade,* Brig.-Gen. Arthur M. Manigault: 24th Ala., Col. N. N. Davis; 28th Ala., Lieut-Col. W. L. Butler; 34th Ala., Capt. R. G. Welch; 10th and 19th S. C., Col. James F. Pressley. *Deas's Brigade,* Brig.-Gen. Z. C. Deas: 19th Ala., Col. S. K. McSpadden; 22d Ala.; Lieut.-Col. B. R. Hart; 25th Ala., Col. G. D. Johnston; 39th Ala., Lieut.-Col. W. C. Clifton; 50th Ala., Col. J. G. Coltart; 17th Ala. Battalion Sharp-shooters, Capt. J. F. Nabers. *Vaughan's Brigade,* Brig.-Gen. A. J. Vaughan: 11th Tenn., Lieut.-Col. William Thedford; 12th and 47th Tenn., Col. W. M. Watkins; 13th and 154th Tenn., Lieut.-Col. R. W. Pitman; 29th Tenn., Col. Horace Rice. *Artillery Battalion,* Maj. A. R. Courtney: Ala. Battery, Capt. James Garrity; Dent's Battery, Capt. S. H. Dent; Tex. Battery, Capt. J. P. Douglas. Division loss: k, 76; w, 476; m, 1124 = 1676.

BRECKINRIDGE'S DIVISION, Brig.-Gen. William B. Bate.

Bate's Brigade, Col. R. C. Tyler (w), Col. A. F. Rudler (w), Lieut.-Col. James J. Turner: 37th Ga., Col. A. F. Rudler, Lieut.-Col. J. T. Smith; 10th Tenn., Maj. John O'Neill; 15th and 37th Tenn., Lieut.-Col. R. D. Frayser; 20th Tenn., Capt. John F. Guthrie; 30th Tenn., Lieut.-Col. James J. Turner; Caswell's Battalion, Lieut. Joel Towers. *Lewis's Brigade,* Brig.-Gen. Joseph H. Lewis: 2d Ky., Col. James W. Moss; 4th Ky., Lieut.-Col. T. W. Thompson; 5th Ky., Col. H. Hawkins; 6th Ky., Lieut.-Col. W. L. Clarke; 9th Ky., Lieut.-Col. John C. Wickliffe. *Finley's Brigade,* Brig.-Gen. Jesse J. Finley: 1st and 3d Fla., Lieut.-Col. E. Mashburn; 4th Fla., Lieut.-Col. E. Badger; 6th Fla., Lieut.-Col. A. D. McLean; 7th Fla., Lieut.-Col. T. Ingram; 1st Fla. Cav. (dismounted), Col. G. T. Maxwell. *Artillery Battalion,* Capt. Robert Cobb: Ky. Battery (Cobb's), Lieut. F. J. Gracie; La. Battery, Capt. C. H. Slocomb; Tenn. Battery, Capt. J. W. Mebane. Division loss: k, 44; w, 244; m, 591 = 859.

STEWART'S DIVISION, Maj.-Gen. Ambrose P. Stewart.

Stovall's Brigade, Brig.-Gen. Marcellus A. Stovall: 40th Ga., Lieut.-Col. R. M. Young; 41st Ga., Col. W. E. Curtis; 42d Ga., Maj. W. H. Hulsey; 43d Ga., Lieut.-Col. H. C. Kellogg; 52d Ga., Maj. John J. Moore. Brigade

loss: k, 5; w, 32; m, 47 = 84. *Strahl's Brigade,* Brig.-Gen. Oscar F. Strahl:
4th Tenn., Lieut.-Col. L. W. Finley; 5th Tenn., Col. J. J. Lamb; 19th
Tenn., Col. F. M. Walker; 24th Tenn., Col. John A. Wilson; 31st Tenn.,
Lieut.-Col. F. E. P. Stafford; 33d Tenn., Lieut.-Col. H. C. McNeill. Brigade
loss: k, 16; w, 93; m, 150 = 259. *Clayton's Brigade,* Col. J. T. Holtzclaw:
18th Ala., Maj. Shep. Ruffin; 32d and 58th Ala., Col. Bush. Jones; 36th and
38th Ala., Col. L. T. Woodruff. Brigade loss: k, 21; w, 100; m, 706 = 827.
Adams's Brigade, Col. R. L. Gibson: 13th and 20th La., Maj. F. L. Campbell; 19th La., Maj. H. A. Kennedy; 16th and 25th La., Col. D. Gober;
14th La. Battalion Sharp-shooters, Maj. J. E. Austin; 4th La. Battalion,
Maj. S. L. Bishop. Brigade loss: k, 28; w, 96; m, 233 = 357. *Artillery Battalion,* Eufaula Battery (Oliver's), Lieut. William J. McKenzie; La. Battery,
Capt. Charles E. Fenner, Miss. Battery, Capt. T. J. Stanford. Battalion
loss: k, 1; w, 6; m, 5 = 12. *Escort company,* loss: w, 1; m, 1 = 2.

RESERVE ARTILLERY.

Robertson's Battalion, Capt. Felix H. Robertson: Ala. Battery (Lums-
den's), Lieut. H. H. Cribbs; Ga. Battery (Havis's), Lieut. J. R. Duncan;
Ga. Battery, Capt. R. W. Anderson; Mo. Battery, Capt. Oberton W. Barret.
Battalion loss: k, 1; w, 4; m, 6 = 11. *Williams's Battalion,* Maj. S. C. Wil-
liams: Ala. Battery, Capt. R. Kolb; Jeffress's Battery, Capt. W. C. Jeffress;
Miss. Battery (Darden's), Lieut. H. W. Bullen. Battalion loss: w, 2.

CAVALRY: Parts of the 3d, 8th, and 10th Confederate, and 1st, 2d, 4th,
and 5th Tenn.

Total Confederate loss: killed, 361; wounded, 2180; captured or missing,
4146 = 6687.

GENERAL BRAGG'S COMMENTS
ON MISSIONARY RIDGE

GENERAL BRAGG made a brief report on the Chattanooga campaign on
November 30th, 1863, and on the 2d of December was relieved of command. Of the battle of Missionary Ridge, the report says:

"About 11 A.M. the enemy's forces were being moved in heavy masses
from Lookout and beyond to our front, while those in front extended to
our right. They formed their lines with great deliberation just beyond the
range of our guns and in plain view of our position. Though greatly outnumbered, such was the strength of our position that no doubt was enter-
tained of our ability to hold it, and every disposition was made for that
purpose. During this time they [the enemy] had made several attempts on
our extreme right, and had been handsomely repulsed with very heavy loss
by Major-General Cleburne's command, under the immediate directions of
Lieutenant-General Hardee. . . . About 8:30 P.M. the immense force in the
front of our left and center advanced in three lines, preceded by heavy
skirmishers. Our batteries opened with fine effect, and much confusion was
produced before they reached musket-range. In a short time the roar of
musketry became very heavy, and it was soon apparent the enemy had been
repulsed in my immediate front. While riding along the crest congratulat-

ing the troops, intelligence reached me that our line was broken on my right, and the enemy had crowned the ridge. Assistance was promptly dispatched to that point under Brigadier-General Bate, who had so successfully maintained the ground in my front, and I proceeded to the rear of the broken line to rally our retiring troops and return them to the crest to drive the enemy back. General Bate found the disaster so great that his small force could not repair it. About this time I learned that our extreme left had also given way, and that my position was almost surrounded. Bate was immediately directed to form a second line in the rear, where, by the efforts of my staff, a nucleus of stragglers had been formed upon which to rally. Lieutenant-General Hardee, leaving Major-General Cleburne in command on the extreme right, moved toward the left when he heard the heavy firing in that direction. He reached the right of Anderson's division just in time to find it had nearly all fallen back, commencing on its left, where the enemy had first crowned the ridge. By a prompt and judicious movement, he threw a portion of Cheatham's division directly across the ridge facing the enemy, who was now moving a strong force immediately on his left flank. By a decided stand here the enemy was entirely checked, and that portion of our force to the right remained intact. All to the left, however, except a portion of Bate's division, was entirely routed and in rapid flight. . . . A panic which I had never before witnessed seemed to have seized upon officers and men, and each seemed to be struggling for his personal safety, regardless of his duty or his character. In this distressing and alarming state of affairs General Bate was ordered to hold his position covering the road for the retreat of Breckinridge's command, and orders were immediately sent to Generals Hardee and Breckinridge to retire their forces upon the depot at Chickamauga. . . . No satisfactory excuse can possibly be given for the shameful conduct of our troops on the left in allowing their line to be penetrated. The position was one which ought to have been held by a line of skirmishers against any assaulting column, and wherever resistance was made the enemy fled in disorder after suffering heavy loss. Those who reached the ridge did so in a condition of exhaustion from the great physical exertion in climbing which rendered them powerless, and the slightest effort would have destroyed them. Having secured much of our artillery, they soon availed themselves of our panic, and turning our guns upon us enfiladed the lines, both right and left, rendering them entirely untenable. Had all parts of the line been maintained with equal gallantry and persistence, no enemy could ever have dislodged us, and but one possible reason presents itself to my mind in explanation of this bad conduct in veteran troops who never before failed in any duty assigned them, however difficult and hazardous: They had for two days confronted the enemy, marshaling his immense forces in plain view, and exhibiting to their sight such a superiority in numbers as may have intimidated weak-minded and untried soldiers. But our veterans had so often encountered similar hosts when the strength of position was against us, and with perfect success, that not a doubt crossed my mind."

Appendix D

HONOR CITATIONS IN THE CAMPAIGN

Union

United States Department of the Army, Public Information Division. *The Medal of Honor of the United States Army*, pp. 144-149.

Chickamauga

CARSON, WILLIAM J.
Rank and Organization: Musician, Company E, 1st Battalion, 15th United States Infantry. *Place and Date:* At Chickamauga, Ga., 19 Sept. 1863. *Entered Service at:* ———. *Birth:* Washington County, Pa. *Date of Issue:* 27 Jan. 1894. *Citation:* Most distinguished gallantry in battle.

MYERS, GEORGE S.
Rank and Organization: Private, Company F, 101st Ohio Infantry. *Place and Date:* At Chickamauga, Ga., 19 Sept. 1863. *Entered Service at:* ———. *Birth:* Fairfield, Ohio. *Date of Issue:* 9 Apr. 1894. *Citation:* Saved the regimental colors by greatest personal devotion and bravery.

REED, AXEL H.
Rank and Organization: Sergeant, Company K, 2d Minnesota Infantry. *Place and Date:* At Chickamauga, Ga., 19 Sept. 1863. At Missionary Ridge, Tenn., 25 Nov. 1863. *Entered Service at:* ———. *Birth:* Maine. *Date of Issue:* 2 Apr. 1898. *Citation:* While in arrest at Chickamauga, Ga., left his place in the rear and voluntarily went to the line of battle, secured a rifle, and fought gallantly during the 2-day battle; was released from arrest in recognition of his bravery. At Missionary Ridge commanded his company and gallantly led it, being among the first to enter the enemy's works; was severely wounded, losing an arm, but declined a discharge and remained in active service to the end of the war.

RICHEY, WILLIAM E.
Rank and Organization: Corporal, Company A, 15th Ohio Infantry. *Place and Date:* At Chickamauga, Ga., 19 Sept. 1863. *Entered Service at:* ———. *Birth:* Athens County, Ohio. *Date of Issue:* 9 Nov. 1893. *Citation:* While on the extreme front between the lines of the combatants single-handed he captured a Confederate major who was armed and mounted.

CHAMBERLAIN, ORVILLE T.

Rank and Organization: Second Lieutenant, Company G, 74th Indiana Infantry. *Place and Date:* At Chickamauga, Ga., 20 Sept. 1863. *Entered Service at:* ————. *Birth:* Kosciusko County, Ind. *Date of Issue:* 11 Mar. 1896. *Citation:* While exposed to a galling fire, went in search of another regiment, found its location, procured ammunition from the men thereof, and returned with the ammunition to his own company.

CILLEY, CLINTON A.

Rank and Organization: Captain, Company C, 2d Minnesota Infantry. *Place and Date:* At Chickamauga, Ga., 20 Sept. 1863. *Entered Service at:* Farmington, N. H. *Birth:* Rockingham County, N. H. *Date of Issue:* 12 June 1895. *Citation:* Seized the colors of a retreating regiment and led it into the thick of the attack.

PORTER, HORACE

Rank and Organization: Captain, Ordnance Department, United States Army. *Place and Date:* At Chickamauga, Ga., 20 Sept. 1863. *Entered Service at:* Pennsylvania. *Birth:* Pennsylvania. *Date of Issue:* 8 July 1902. *Citation:* While acting as a volunteer aide, at a critical moment when the lines were broken, rallied enough fugitives to hold the ground under heavy fire long enough to effect the escape of wagon trains and batteries.

TAYLOR, ANTHONY

Rank and Organization: First Lieutenant, Company A, 15th Pennsylvania Cavalry. *Place and Date:* At Chickamauga, Ga., 20 Sept. 1863. *Entered Service at:* ————. *Birth:* Burlington, N. J. *Date of Issue:* 4 Dec. 1893. *Citation:* Held out to the last with a small force against the advance of superior numbers of the enemy.

WHITNEY, WILLIAM G.

Rank and Organization: Sergeant, Company B, 11th Michigan Infantry. *Place and Date:* At Chickamauga, Ga., 20 Sept. 1863. *Entered Service at:* ————. *Birth:* Allen, Mich. *Date of Issue:* 21 Oct. 1895. *Citation:* As the enemy were about to charge, this officer went outside the temporary Union works among the dead and wounded enemy and at great exposure to himself cut off and removed their cartridge boxes, bringing the same within the Union lines, the ammunition being used with good effect in again repulsing the attack.

VEALE, MOSES

Rank and Organization: Captain, Company F, 109th Pennsylvania Infantry. *Place and Date:* At Wauhatchie, Tenn., 28 Oct. 1863. *Entered Service at:* Philadelphia, Pa. *Birth:* ————. *Date of Issue:* 17 Jan. 1894. *Citation:* Gallantry in action; manifesting throughout the engagement coolness, zeal, judgment, and courage.

GOETTEL, PHILIP
Rank and Organization: Private, Company B, 149th New York Infantry. *Place and Date:* At Ringgold, Ga., 27 Nov. 1863. *Entered Service at:* Syracuse, N. Y. *Birth:* Syracuse, N. Y. *Date of Issue:* 28 June 1865. *Citation:* Capture of flag and a battery guidon.

PACKARD, LORON F.
Rank and Organization: Private, Company E, 5th New York Cavalry. *Place and Date:* At Raccoon Ford, Va., 27 Nov. 1863. *Entered Service at:* Cuba, N. Y. *Birth:* Cattaraugus County, N. Y. *Date of Issue:* 20 Aug. 1894. *Citation:* After his command had retreated, this soldier, voluntarily and alone, returned to the assistance of a comrade and rescued him from the hands of three armed Confederates.

BRANDLE, JOSEPH E.
Rank and Organization: Private, Company C, 17th Michigan Infantry. *Place and Date:* At Lenoire, Tenn., 16 Nov. 1863. *Entered Service at:* ———. *Birth:* Seneca County, Ohio. *Date of Issue:* 20 July 1897. *Citation:* While color bearer of his regiment, having been twice wounded and the sight of one eye destroyed, still held to the colors until ordered to the rear by his regimental commander.

STARKINS, JOHN H.
Rank and Organization: Sergeant, 34th New York Battery. *Place and Date:* At Campbell Station, Tenn., 16 Nov. 1863. *Entered Service at:* ———. *Birth:* ———. *Date of Issue:* 30 July 1896. *Citation:* Brought off his piece without losing a man.

SWIFT, FREDERIC W.
Rank and Organization: Lieutenant Colonel, 17th Michigan Infantry. *Place and Date:* At Lenoire Station, Tenn., 16 Nov. 1863. *Entered Service at:* Michigan. *Birth:* ———. *Date of Issue:* 15 Feb. 1897. *Citation:* Gallantly seized the colors and rallied the regiment after three color bearers had been shot and the regiment, having become demoralized, was in imminent danger of capture.

FALCONER, JOHN A.
Rank and Organization: Corporal, Company A, 17th Michigan Infantry. *Place and Date:* At Fort Sanders, Knoxville, Tenn., 20 Nov. 1863. *Entered Service at:* ———. *Birth:* Wachtenaw, Mich. *Date of Issue:* 27 July 1896. *Citation:* Conducted the "burning party" of his regiment at the time a charge was made on the enemy's picket line, and burned the house which had sheltered the enemy's sharpshooters, thus insuring success to a hazardous enterprise.

HADLEY, CORNELIUS M.
Rank and Organization: Sergeant, Company F, 9th Michigan Cavalry. *Place and Date:* At siege of Knoxville, Tenn., 20 Nov. 1863. *Entered Serv-*

ice at: ———. *Birth:* Oswego, N. Y. *Date of Issue:* 5 Apr. 1898. *Citation:* With one companion, voluntarily carried through the enemy's lines important dispatches from General Grant to General Burnside, then besieged within Knoxville, and brought back replies, his comrade's horse being killed and the man taken prisoner.

KELLEY, ANDREW J.
  Rank and Organization: Private, Company E, 17th Michigan Infantry. *Place and Date:* At Knoxville, Tenn., 20 Nov. 1863. *Entered Service at:* ———. *Birth:* La Grange County, Ind. *Date of Issue:* 17 Apr. 1900. *Citation:* Having voluntarily accompanied a small party to destroy buildings within the enemy's lines whence sharpshooters had been firing, disregarded an order to retire, remained and completed the firing of the buildings, thus insuring their total destruction; this at the imminent risk of his life from the fire of the advancing enemy.

SHEPARD, IRWIN
  Rank and Organization: Corporal, Company E, 17th Michigan Infantry. *Place and Date:* At Knoxville, Tenn., 20 Nov. 1863. *Entered Service at:* Chelsea, Mich. *Birth:* Skaneateles, N. Y. *Date of Issue:* 3 Aug. 1897. *Citation:* Having voluntarily accompanied a small party to destroy buildings within the enemy's lines, whence sharpshooters had been firing, disregarded an order to retire, remained and completed the firing of the buildings, thus insuring their total destruction; this at the imminent risk of his life from the fire of the advancing enemy.

BARNUM, HENRY A.
  Rank and Organization: Colonel, 149th New York Infantry. *Place and Date:* At Chattanooga, Tenn., 23 Nov. 1863. *Entered Service at:* ———. *Birth:* ———. *Date of Issue:* July 1889. *Citation:* Although suffering severely from wounds, he led his regiment, inciting the men to greater action by word and example until again severely wounded.

TOFFEY, JOHN J.
  Rank and Organization: First Lieutenant, Company G, 33d New Jersey Infantry. *Place and Date:* At Chattanooga, Tenn., 23 Nov. 1863. *Entered Service at:* Hudson, N. J. *Birth:* Dutchess, N. Y. *Date of Issue:* 10 Sept. 1897. *Citation:* Although excused from duty on account of sickness, went to the front in command of a storming party, and with conspicuous gallantry participated in the assault of Missionary Ridge; was here wounded and permanently disabled.

KAPPESSER, PETER
  Rank and Organization: Private, Company B, 149th New York Infantry. *Place and Date:* At Lookout Mountain, Tenn., 24 Nov. 1863. *Entered Service at:* ———. *Birth:* Germany. *Date of Issue:* 28 June 1865. *Citation:* Capture of Confederate flag (Bragg's army).

KIGGINS, JOHN

Rank and Organization: Sergeant, Company D, 149th New York Infantry. *Place and Date:* At Lookout Mountain, Tenn., 24 Nov. 1863. *Entered Service at:* ———. *Birth:* Syracuse, N. Y. *Date of Issue:* 12 Jan. 1892. *Citation:* Waved the colors to save the lives of the men who were being fired upon by their own batteries, and thereby drew upon himself a concentrated fire from the enemy.

POTTER, NORMAN F.

Rank and Organization: First Sergeant, Company E, 149th New York Infantry. *Place and Date:* At Lookout Mountain, Tenn., 24 Nov. 1863. *Entered Service at:* Pompey, N. Y. *Birth:* Pompey, N. Y. *Date of issue:* 24 June 1865. *Citation:* Capture of flag (Bragg's army).

BANKS, GEORGE L.

Rank and Organization: Sergeant, Company C, 15th Indiana Infantry. *Place and Date:* At Missionary Ridge, Tenn., 25 Nov. 1863. *Entered Service at:* ———. *Birth:* ———. *Date of Issue:* 28 Sept. 1897. *Citation:* As color bearer, led his regiment in the assault, and, though wounded, carried the flag forward to the enemy's works, where he was again wounded. In a brigade of eight regiments this flag was the first planted on the parapet.

BELL, JAMES B.

Rank and Organization: Sergeant, Company H, 11th Ohio Infantry. *Place and Date:* At Missionary Ridge, Tenn., 25 Nov. 1863. *Entered Service at:* ———. *Birth:* ———. *Date of Issue:* Unknown. *Citation:* Though severely wounded, was first of his regiment on the summit of the ridge, planted his colors inside the enemy's works, and did not leave the field until after he had been wounded five times.

BOYNTON, HENRY V.

Rank and Organization: Lieutenant Colonel, 35th Ohio Infantry. *Place and Date:* At Missionary Ridge, Tenn., 25 Nov. 1863. *Entered Service at:* ———. *Birth:* ———. *Date of Issue:* 15 Nov. 1893. *Citation:* Led his regiment in the face of a severe fire of the enemy; was severely wounded.

BROUSE, CHARLES W.

Rank and Organization: Captain, Company K, 100th Indiana Infantry. *Place and Date:* At Missionary Ridge, Tenn., 25 Nov. 1863. *Entered Service at:* ———. *Birth:* ———. *Date of Issue:* 16 May 1899. *Citation:* To encourage his men whom he had ordered to lie down while under severe fire, and who were partially protected by slight earthworks, himself refused to lie down, but walked along the top of the works until he fell severely wounded.

BROWN, ROBERT B.

Rank and Organization: Private, Company A, 15th Ohio Infantry. *Place and Date:* At Missionary Ridge, Tenn., 25 Nov. 1863. *Entered Service at:*

———. *Birth:* Muskingum County, Ohio. *Date of Issue:* 27 Mar. 1890. *Citation:* Capture of flag.

DAVIS, FREEMAN
   Rank and Organization: Sergeant, Company B, 80th Ohio Infantry. *Place and Date:* At Missionary Ridge, Tenn., 25 Nov. 1863. *Entered Service at:* ———. *Birth:* Newcomerstown, Ohio. *Date of Issue:* 30 Mar. 1898. *Citation:* This soldier, while his regiment was falling back, seeing the two color bearers shot down, under a severe fire and at imminent peril recovered both the flags and saved them from capture.

GRAHAM, THOMAS N.
   Rank and Organization: Second Lieutenant, Company G, 15th Indiana Infantry. *Place and Date:* At Missionary Ridge, Tenn., 25 Nov. 1863. *Entered Service at:* ———. *Birth:* ——— *Date of Issue:* 15 Feb. 1897. *Citation:* Seized the colors from the color bearer, who had been wounded, and, exposed to a terrible fire, carried them forward, planting them on the enemy's breastworks.

GREEN, GEORGE
   Rank and Organization: Corporal, Company H, 11th Ohio Infantry. *Place and Date:* At Missionary Ridge, Tenn., 25 Nov. 1863. *Entered Service at:* ———. *Birth:* ———. *Date of Issue:* 12 Jan. 1892. *Citation:* Scaled the enemy's works and in a hand-to-hand fight captured a flag.

HOWARD, HIRAM R.
   Rank and Organization: Private, Company H, 11th Ohio Infantry. *Place and Date:* At Missionary Ridge, Tenn., 25 Nov. 1863. *Entered Service at:* ———. *Birth:* ———. *Date of Issue:* 29 July 1892. *Citation:* Scaled the enemy's works and in a hand-to-hand fight captured a flag.

JOHNSON, RUEL M.
   Rank and Organization: Major, 100th Indiana Infantry. *Place and Date:* At Chattanooga, Tenn., 25 Nov. 1863. *Entered Service at:* ———. *Birth:* ———. *Date of Issue:* 24 Aug. 1896. *Citation:* While in command of the regiment bravely exposed himself to the fire of the enemy, encouraging and cheering his men.

JOSSELYN, SIMEON T.
   Rank and Organization: First Lieutenant, Company C, 13th Illinois Infantry. *Place and Date:* At Missionary Ridge, Tenn., 25 Nov. 1863. *Entered Service at:* ———. *Birth:* ———. *Date of Issue:* 4 Apr. 1898. *Citation:* While commanding his company, deployed as skirmishers, came upon a large body of the enemy, taking a number of them prisoner. Lieutenant Josselyn himself shot their color bearer, seized the colors and brought them back to his regiment.

KELLEY, LEVERETT M.

Rank and Organization: Sergeant, Company A, 36th Illinois Infantry. *Place and Date:* At Missionary Ridge, Tenn., 25 Nov. 1863. *Entered Service at:* Rutland, Ill. *Birth:* Schenectady, N. Y. *Date of Issue:* 4 Apr. 1900. *Citation:* Sprang over the works just captured from the enemy, and calling upon his comrades to follow, rushed forward in the face of a deadly fire and was among the first over the works on the summit, where he compelled the surrender of a Confederate officer and received his sword.

KOUNTZ, JOHN S.

Rank and Organization: Musician, Company G, 37th Ohio Infantry. *Place and Date:* At Missionary Ridge, Tenn., 25 Nov. 1863. *Entered Service at:* Maumee, Ohio. *Birth:* Maumee, Ohio. *Date of Issue:* 13 Aug. 1895. *Citation:* Seized a musket and joined in the charge in which he was severely wounded.

MACARTHUR, ARTHUR, JR.

Rank and Organization: First Lieutenant, and Adjutant, 24th Wisconsin Infantry. *Place and Date:* At Missionary Ridge, Tenn., 25 Nov. 1863. *Entered Service at:* ———. *Birth:* Springfield, Mass. *Date of Issue:* 30 June 1890. *Citation:* Seized the colors of his regiment at a critical moment and planted them on the captured works on the crest of Missionary Ridge.

SCHMIDT, WILLIAM

Rank and Organization: Private, Company G, 37th Ohio Infantry. *Place and Date:* At Missionary Ridge, Tenn., 25 Nov. 1863. *Entered Service at:* Maumee, Ohio. *Birth:* Tiffin, Ohio. *Date of Issue:* 9 Nov. 1895. *Citation:* Rescued a wounded comrade under terrific fire.

WALKER, JAMES C.

Rank and Organization: Private, Company K, 31st Ohio Infantry. *Place and Date:* At Missionary Ridge, Tenn., 25 Nov. 1863. *Entered Service at:* Springfield, Ohio. *Birth:* Clark County, Ohio. *Date of Issue:* 25 Nov. 1895. *Citation:* After two color bearers had fallen, seized the flag and carried it forward, assisting in the capture of a battery. Shortly thereafter he captured the flag of the 41st Alabama and the color bearer.

JUDGE, FRANCIS W.

Rank and Organization: First Sergeant, Company K, 79th New York Infantry. *Place and Date:* At Fort Sanders, Knoxville, Tenn., 29 Nov. 1863. *Entered Service at:* ———. *Birth:* England. *Date of Issue:* 2 Nov. 1870. *Citation:* The color bearer of the 51st Georgia Infantry (C.S.A.), having planted his flag upon the side of the work, Sergeant Judge leaped from his position of safety, sprang upon the parapet, and in the face of a concentrated fire seized the flag and returned with it in safety to the fort.

MAHONEY, JEREMIAH
  Rank and Organization: Sergeant, Company A, 29th Massachusetts Infantry. *Place and Date:* At Fort Sanders, Knoxville, Tenn., 29 Nov. 1863. *Entered Service at:* ———. *Birth:* ——— *Date of Issue:* 1 Dec. 1864. *Citation:* Capture of flag of 17th Mississippi Infantry (C.S.A.).

MANNING, JOSEPH S.
  Rank and Organization: Private, Company K, 29th Massachusetts Infantry. *Place and Date:* At Fort Sanders, Knoxville, Tenn., 29 Nov. 1863. *Entered Service at:* ———. *Birth:* Ipswich, Mass. *Date of Issue:* 1 Dec. 1864. *Citation:* Capture of flag of 16th or 18th Georgia Infantry (C.S.A.).

Confederate

O.R., Ser. I, Pt. 2, XXX, 532-543
  A Confederate Roll of Honor was established by Act of Congress, October 13, 1862. It authorized bestowal of medals upon officers conspicuous for courage and good conduct upon the field of battle; also a badge of distinction to be conferred on one private or noncommissioned officer of each company "after every signal victory it shall have assisted to achieve." Recipients in the latter case were to be chosen by a majority of their units' votes. Should more than one soldier be selected, the award was to be determined by lot.
  For the Battle of Chickamauga a Roll of Honor was published in General Orders, No. 64, Adjt. and Insp. General's Office, August 10, 1864. It contained from one to a dozen or more nominations per unit. Such choices as may eventually have been made are not indicated. Since the list consists of names and units only, without citations, it is not here reprinted.
  There is no such roll in *O.R.* for the following battles, which were not Confederate victories, and therefore not covered by the Act.

Appendix E

SAGA OF THE CAMPAIGN

The Chattanooga campaign inspired a remarkable number of poems, verses, and songs. They range from the products of skilled pens to homely scribblings by men fresh from battle—from grave to gay. Soldiers in all wars and the bards who celebrated their deeds have written the like, but perhaps no other single campaign ever prompted so much and such varied minstrelsy. Together they form a saga of the conflict in the West where the gateway to final victory for the Union was stormed and wrenched asunder.

AN EPICK

E. S. Buck, Company B, 3rd Battalion, Pioneer Brigade

(From the Ezra R. Rickett Collection, Ohio State Museum)

On Newyear's day we had a fight
    And one the day before,
And then we fought right strait along
    For three or four days more
Near Murfreesboro; there we found
    The Rebels by the score.
Old Bragg, Hardee, and Breckinridge,
    Each with a heavy corps.

Old Bragg he. . . .
    And told them they must hold
Stone river and the country round
    Or else they were all sold.
Hardee was in a cedar swamp
    Which lay just on our right.
Our General had his men in line,
    Was ready for a fight.

The Rebels made a desperate charge
    On Johnson and his men.
They stood the fire untill they drove
    The Rebels from there den.

233

When General Johnson saw them fire,
   He told his men to run.
He said it was no use to fight
   The rebels ten to one.

The secesh villains gave a cheer
   Because they had broke our line.
Old Hardee and his staff came up.
   Said he, your doing fine.
Our General saw it would not do
   . . . .
When General Wood said he would hold
   That bloody ground or die.

He called upon the twentieth Brigade
   To take a bloody stand.
The boys went in with a steady nerve,
   Colonel Parker in command.
The Pioneers went to the front.
   General Wood was on the right,
With Captain Stokes Battery
   Gave them another fight.

It was then the shot and shell fell thick.
   The Rebels would not yield,
Untill there dead and wounded men
   Lay piled up in the field.
And when our boys had gained the day,
   All they saw there friends around,
All mangled up with shot and shell,
   Lie dead on the cold ground.

The Rebels they fell back again,
   There hearts in sad despair,
Though Bragg soon led them to believe
   There prospects yet was fair.
Says he, my boys, we'll try there left
   . . . .
We'll skip around and I'll be bound
   We'll whip General Van Cleve.

But, oh, Rosecrans saw there a chance
   And understood their plot
And reinforced General Van Cleve,
   So made the Rebels hop.

The Pioneers again went in,
  Our General in command.
He rode in front his gallant steed,
  With glitering sword in hand.

Said he, my boys, press forward
  And the Rebels three cheers.
Hip; Hip; Huzza, just see them run.
  Come on, brave Pioneers.
I never shall forget that hour,
  The ground all stained with blood,
While hundreds of our dying men
  Lie weltering in the mud.

Again we drove the Butternuts
  And took a Rebel flag,
The Banner of that tory band,
  The god of General Bragg.
But yet the traitors would not yield,
  Although . . . .
They swore they would not leave the field,
  So Breckinridge went in.

He took advantage of the night
  While everything was still
And boldly rushed into the fight,
  And there fell General Sill.
They soon found out there sad mistake.
  There fighting was in vain.
They faced about, their heels did take
  To save there treacherous brain.

In wild confusion left the ground.
  Stone river they plunged through
And never stopped to look around
  For Yankees as they flew.
Oh, now the day is ours, my boys,
  The loss of friends we'll mourn.
Yet we're the boys that fear no noise,
  Although we are far from home.

Our noble leader Rosencrans—
  We'll give him three cheers.
He keeps the Rebels in advance
  Of us, the Pioneers.

And if they ever stop again,
  We'll give them a furlough
And send them down to see there friends
  They left at Murfreesboro.

BATTLE OF STONE RIVER

By a Private of Company F, 27th Regiment Illinois Volunteers

Fitch: *Annals of the Army of the Cumberland*

Come, freemen all, both great and small,
  And listen to my story,
And, while our country is our theme,
  We'll sing about her glory.
I guess you've heard how Braxton Bragg
  Into Kentucky paddled,
And how at Perryville he fought,
  And then he quick "skedaddled."

And how he thought, in Tennessee,
  At Murfreesboro seated,
The rout of all the Union hosts
  Would quickly be completed.
But Rosecrans, the conqueror,
  Had Buell superseded,
And justly thought this boasting Bragg
  A whipping sorely needed.

And so he thought the holidays
  The proper time for action,
To try this boasting rebel's strength
  And drive him from this section.
On Christmas day our orders came,
  And to the general handed.
McCook, a hero known to fame,
  Our gallant corps commanded.

Near Nolensville we met the foe,—
  They thought, securely seated.
Our batteries let a few shell go,
  And fast the rebs retreated.
So on we went, on victory bent,
  To view old Bragg's position:
We brought some pills to cure his ills,
  With Rosey for physician.

At break of day on the next morn,
　　While the old year was dying,
The rebel force advanced their hosts
　　To where our right was lying.
And now the news is quickly borne,—
　　The foe our right is turning!
In countless numbers, on they come,
　　All efforts swiftly spurning!

But as the foe appears so soon,
　　In full and open view, sirs,
Brave Houghtaling plays them a tune
　　Called Yankee-doodle-do, sirs.
And as the enemy bore down
　　On Sheridan's division,
We fed them with the best we had,
　　Gave bullets for provision.

Now on three sides the foe he rides
　　Triumphant, to our grief;
Brave Negley then, with gallant men,
　　Quick flies to our relief.
Firm as a rock brave Palmer stands,
　　Our centre firm securing,
While Rousseau's men, with steady aim,
　　A deadly fire are pouring.

Upon our left bold Crittenden—
　　The Union hosts reviving,
As we can hear by cheer on cheer—
　　The foe is swiftly driving.
On every hand we make a stand,
　　All steady, firm, and true, sirs;
At close of eve rings out the shout!
　　This day shall rebels rue, sirs.

But, while that shout is ringing out,
　　'Tis mingled with our pain,
To think of our brave gallant men
　　Now lying with the slain.
Brave Sill lies there, all cold and bare,
　　With Garesché so brave,
And Roberts, Schaeffer,—honored names:
　　They fill a hero's grave.

Sad duty this, to mention one
 We intimately knew,—
Our Harrington, beloved by all,
 So gallant, brave, and true.
He fell where brave men wish to fall,
 Where loudest sounds the battle,
Where stoutest hearts might stand appalled,
 Mid thundering cannon's rattle.

And, though his voice is still'd in death,
 We seem to hear his cry,
As cheering on his brave command,—
 "My boys, that flag stand by."
On New-Year's day, as people say,
 Bragg show'd his full intention
To drive us off,—make us the scoff
 Of all this mighty nation.

But Rosey knew a thing or two,
 And made him quick knock under,—
Gave him to feel the true-edged steel,
 Mid storms of Yankee thunder.
Says Bragg, "I'm sad: my cause is bad,
 And so, to save my bacon,
I will retreat, and save defeat;
 For Rosey can't be taken."

So, while our men were strengthening
 Where we were situated,
To make secure, and victory sure,
 Old Bragg evacuated.
Now let our songs ascend on high
 To the All-Wise as giver,
And Rosey's name we'll crown with fame,
 As hero of Stone River.

When those we love request a sign
 For words as yet unspoken,
That sign shall be, Remember me,
 A Rosey wreath for token.
And, now, may *roses* crown our land,
 May blissful peace soon come, sirs,
May Bragg-ing traitors soon be damn'd,
 And we in peace at home, sirs.

Then, boys, fill up the brimming cup.
We'll toast the Union ever:—
Our health, the man that can Bragg tan,
The hero of Stone River.

CHICKAMAUGA, "THE STREAM OF DEATH!"

Moore, *The Civil War in Song and Story*, p. 342.

Chickamauga! Chickamauga!
O'er thy dark and turbid wave
Rolls the death-cry of the daring,
Rings the war-shout of the brave;
Round thy shore the red fires flashing,
Startling shot and screaming shell—
Chickamauga, stream of battle,
Who thy fearful tale shall tell?

Olden memories of horror,
Sown by scourge of deadly plague,
Long had clothed thy circling forests
With a terror vast and vague;
Now to gather fiercer vigor
From the phantoms grim with gore,
Hurried by war's wilder carnage
To their graves on thy lone shore.

Long, with hearts subdued and saddened,
As th' oppressor's hosts moved on,
Fell the arms of Freedom backward,
Till our hopes had almost flown;
Till outspoke stern Valor's fiat—
"Here th' invading wave shall stay;
Here shall cease the foe's proud progress;
Here be crushed his grand array!"

Then, their eager hearts all throbbing
Backward flashed each battle-flag
Of the veteran corps of Longstreet,
And the sturdy troops of Bragg;
Fierce upon the foeman turning,
All their pent-up wrath breaks out
In the furious battle-clangor,
And the frenzied battle-shout.

Roll thy dark waves, Chickamauga;
    Trembles all thy ghastly shore,
With the rude shock of the onset,
    And the tumult's horrid roar:
As the Southern battle-giants
    Hurl their bolts of death along,
Breckinridge, the iron-hearted,
    Cheatham, chivalric and strong;—

Polk and Preston, gallant Buckner,
    Hill and Hindman, strong in might;
Cleburne, flower of manly valor;
    Hood, the Ajax of the fight;
Benning, bold and hardy warrior;
    Fearless, resolute Kershaw,
Mingle battle-yell and death-bolt,
    Volley fierce and wild hurrah!

At the volleys bleed their bodies,
    At the fierce shout shrink their souls,
While their fiery wave of vengeance
    On their quailing column rolls;
And the parched throats of the stricken
    Breathe for air the roaring flame;
Horrors of that hell foretasted,
    Who shall ever dare to name?

Borne by those who, stiff and mangled,
    Paid, upon that bloody field,
Direful, cringing, awe-struck homage
    To the sword our heroes wield;
And who felt, by fiery trial,
    That the men who will be free,
Though in conflict baffled often,
    Ever will unconquered be!

Learned, though long unchecked they spoil as,
    Dealing desolation round,
Marking with the tracks of ruin
    Many a rod of Southern ground.
Yet, whatever course they follow,
    Somewhere in their pathway flows,
Dark and deep, a Chickamauga,
    Stream of death to vandal foes!

They have found it darkly flowing
   By Manassas' famous plain,
And by rushing Shenandoah
   Met the tide of woe again:
Chickahominy! immortal,
   By the long, ensanguined flight,
Rappahannock, glorious river,
   Twice renowned for matchless fight.

Heed the story, dastard spoilers,
   Mark the tale these waters tell,
Ponder well your fearful lesson,
   And the doom that there befell:
Learn to shun the Southern vengeance,
   Sworn upon the votive sword,
"Every stream a Chickamauga
   To the vile, invading horde!"

CHICKAMAUGA, SEPT. 19 & 20, 1863

(From the Ezra R. Rickett Collection, Ohio State Museum)

1. Way down at Chickamauga not very long ago
We met a force of Rebels but could not make them go.
    CHORUS: And I'll bet ten dollars down and count it one by one.
       For the next time that we fight them, Rebels are sure to run.
2. Old Bragg he got discouraged and was on the retreat
Until he got reinforced by Johnson and Longstreet.
3. Our General came riding by. Said he you need not fear,
For Thomas is on the right wing and Granger is in the rear.
4. We fought them in the woods, boys. It was on Saturday eve.
We piled them up right sharply among the scrub oak trees.
5. It really looked right scaly, and I will tell you why.
The Second could not stand it, and it was no use to try.
6. Johnny Wright he came running. Says he it cannot be
That this is the Ninetieth running. Oh face about, said he.
7. The Ninetieth and Eleventh Ohio they charged them with a yell.
They ran them back a quarter, and many brave men fell.
8. Old Charlie he then led us back to rest us for the night.
Says he you've done well, my boys, in this the first day's fight.
9. We took a Rebel prisoner. He looked so very bold.
He said he join our army, if he was not too old.

THE BALLAD OF CHICKAMAUGA

(September 19–20, 1863)

By Chickamauga's crooked stream the martial trumpets blew;
The North and South stood face to face, with War's dread work to do.
O lion-strong, unselfish, brave, twin athletes battle-wise,
Brothers yet enemies, the fire of conflict in their eyes,
All banner-led and bugle-stirred, they set them to the fight,
Hearing the god of slaughter laugh from mountain height to height.

The ruddy, fair-haired, giant North breathed loud and strove amain;
The swarthy shoulders of the South did heave them to the strain;
An earthquake shuddered underfoot, a cloud rolled overhead:
And serpent-tongues of flame cut through and lapped and twinkled red,
Where back and forth a bullet-stream went singing like a breeze,
What time the snarling cannon-balls to splinters tore the trees.

"Make way, make way!" a voice boomed out, "I'm marching to the sea!"
The answer was a rebel yell and Bragg's artillery.
Where Negley struck, the cohorts gray like storm tossed clouds were rent;
Where Buckner charged, a cyclone fell, the blue to tatters went;
The noble Brannan cheered his men, Pat Cleburne answered back,
And Lytle stormed, and life was naught in Walthall's bloody track.

Old Taylor's Ridge rocked to its base, and Pigeon Mountain shook;
And Helm went down, and Lytle died, and broken was McCook.
Van Cleve moved like a hurricane, a tempest blew with Hood,
Awful the sweep of Breckinridge across the flaming wood.
Never before did battle-roar such chords of thunder make,
Never again shall tides of men over such barriers break.

"Stand fast, stand fast!" cried Rosecrans; and Thomas said, "I will!"
And, crash on crash, his batteries dashed their broadsides down the hill.
Brave Longstreet's splendid rush tore through whatever barred its track,
Till the Rock of Chickamauga hurled the roaring columns back,
And gave the tide of victory a red tinge of defeat,
Adding a noble dignity to that hard word, retreat.

Two days they fought, and evermore those days shall stand apart,
Keynotes of epic chivalry within the nation's heart.
Come, come, and set the craven rocks to mark this glorious spot;
Here let the deeds of heroes live, their hatreds be forgot.
Build, build, but never monument of stone shall last as long
As one old soldier's ballad borne on breath of battle-song.

MAURICE THOMPSON

GARFIELD'S RIDE AT CHICKAMAUGA

(*September 20, 1863*)

Again the summer-fevered skies,
  The breath of autumn calms;
Again the golden moons arise
  On harvest-happy farms,
The locusts pipe, the crickets sing
  Among the falling leaves,
And wandering breezes sigh, and bring
  The harp-notes of the sheaves.

Peace smiles upon the hills and dells;
  Peace smiles upon the seas;
And drop the notes of happy bells
  Upon the fruited trees.
The broad Missouri stretches far
  Her commerce-gathering arms,
And multiply on Arkansas
  The grain-encumbered farms.

Old Chattanooga, crowned with green,
  Sleeps 'neath her walls in peace;
The Argo has returned again,
  And brings the Golden Fleece.
O nation! free from sea to sea,
  In union blessed forever,
Fair be their fame who fought for thee
  By Chickamauga River.

The autumn winds were piping low,
  Beneath the vine-clad eaves;
We heard the hollow bugle blow
  Among the ripened sheaves.
And fast the mustering squadrons passed
  Through mountain portals wide,
And swift the blue brigades were massed
  By Chickamauga's tide.

It was the Sabbath; and in awe
  We heard the dark hills shake,
And o'er the mountain turrets saw
  The smoke of battle break.
And 'neath the war-cloud gray and grand,
  The hills o'erchanging low,
The Army of the Cumberland,
  Unequal, met the foe!

Again, O fair September night!
  Beneath the moon and stars,
I see, through memories dark and bright,
  The altar-fires of Mars.
The morning breaks with screaming guns
  From batteries dark and dire,
And where the Chickamauga runs
  Red runs the muskets' fire.

I see bold Longstreet's darkening host
  Sweep through our lines of flame,
And hear again, "The right is lost!"
  Swart Rosecrans exclaim.
"But not the left!" young Garfield cries;
  "From that we must not sever,
While Thomas holds the field that lies
  On Chickamauga River!"

Oh! on that day of clouded gold,
  How, half of hope bereft,
The cannoneers, like Titans, rolled
  Their thunders on the left!
I see the battle-clouds again,
  With glowing autumn splendors blending:
It seemed as if the gods with men
  Were on Olympian heights contending.

Through tongues of flame, through meadows brown,
  Dry valley roads concealed,
Ohio's hero dashes down
  Upon the rebel field.
And swift, on reeling charger borne,
  He threads the wooded plain,
By twice a hundred cannon mown,
  And reddened with the slain.

But past swathes of carnage dire,
  The Union guns he hears,
And gains the left, begirt with fire,
  And thus the heroes cheers—
"While stands the left, yon flag o'erhead,
  Shall Chattanooga stand!"
"Let the Napoleons rain their lead!"
  Was Thomas's command.

Back swept the gray brigades of Bragg;
 The air with victory rung;
And Wurzel's "Rally round the flag!"
 'Mid Union cheers was sung.
The flag on Chattanooga's height
 In twilight's crimson waved,
And all the clustered stars of white
 Were to the Union saved.

O chief of staff! the nation's fate
 That red field crossed with thee,
The triumph of the camp and state,
 The hope of liberty!
O nation! free from sea to sea,
 With union blessed forever,
Not vainly heroes fought for thee
 By Chickamauga River.

In dreams I stand beside the tide
 Where those old heroes fell:
Above the valleys long and wide
 Sweet rings the Sabbath bell.
I hear no more the bugle blow,
 As on that fateful day!
I hear the ringdove fluting low,
 Where shaded waters stray.

On Mission Ridge the sunlight streams
 Above the fields of fall,
And Chattanooga calmly dreams
 Beneath her mountain-wall.
Old Lookout Mountain towers on high,
 As in heroic days,
When 'neath the battle in the sky
 Were seen its summits blaze.

'T was ours to lay no garlands fair
 Upon the graves "unknown":
Kind Nature sets her gentians there,
 And fall the sear leaves lone.
Those heroes' graves no shaft of Mars
 May mark with beauty ever;
But floats the flag of forty stars
 By Chickamauga River.

HEZEKIAH BUTTERWORTH

(Ohio)

THOMAS AT CHICKAMAUGA

It was that fierce contested field when Chickamauga lay
Beneath the wild tornado that swept her pride away;
Her dimpling dales and circling hills dyed crimson with the flood
That had its sources in the springs that throb with human blood.

"Go say to General Hooker to reinforce his right!"
Said Thomas to his aide-de-camp, when wildly went the fight;
In front the battle thundered, it roared both right and left,
But like a rock "Pap" Thomas stood upon the crested cleft.

"Where will I find you, General, when I return?" The aide
Leaned on his bridle-rein to wait the answer Thomas made;
The old chief like a lion turned, his pale lips set and sere,
And shook his mane, and stamped his foot, and fiercely answered, "Here!"

The floodtide of fraternal strife rolled upward to his feet,
And like the breakers on the shore the thunderous clamors beat;
The sad earth rocked and reeled with woe, the woodland shrieked in pain,
And hill and vale were groaning with the burden of the slain.

Who does not mind that sturdy form, that steady heart and hand,
That calm repose and gallant mien, that courage high and grand?—
O God, who givest nations men to meet their lofty needs,
Vouchsafe another Thomas when our country prostrate bleeds!

They fought with all the fortitude of earnest men and true—
The men who wore the rebel gray, the men who wore the blue;
And those, they fought most valiantly for petty state and clan,
And these, for truer Union and the brotherhood of man.

They come, those hurling legions, with banners crimson-splashed,
Against our stubborn columns their rushing ranks are dashed,
Till 'neath the blistering iron hail the shy and frightened deer
Go scurrying from their forest haunts to plunge in wilder fear.

Beyond, our lines are broken: and now in frenzied rout
The flower of the Cumberland has swiftly faced about;
And horse and foot and color-guard are reeling, rear and van,
And in the awful panic man forgets that he is man.

Now Bragg, with pride exultant above our broken wings,
The might of all his army against "Pap" Thomas brings;
They're massing to the right of him, they're massing to the left,
Ah, God be with our hero, who holds the crested cleft!

Blow, blow, ye echoing bugles! give answer, screaming shell!
Go, belch your murderous fury, ye batteries of hell!
Ring out, O impious musket! spin on, O shattering shot,—
Our smoke-encircled hero, he hears but heeds ye not!

Now steady, men! now steady! make one more valiant stand,
For gallant Steedman's coming, his forces well in hand!
Close up your shattered columns, take steady aim and true,
The chief who loves you as his life will live or die with you!

By solid columns, on they come; by columns they are hurled,
As down the eddying rapids the storm-swept booms are whirled;
And when the ammunition fails—O moment drear and dread—
The heroes load their blackened guns from rounds of soldiers dead.

God never set His signet on the hearts of braver men,
Or fixed the goal of victory on higher heights than then;
With bayonets and muskets clubbed, they close the rush and roar;
Their stepping-stones to glory are their comrades gone before.

O vanished majesty of days not all forgotten yet,
We consecrate unto thy praise one hour of deep regret;
One hour to them whose days were years of glory that shall flood
The Nation's sombre night of tears, of carnage, and of blood!

O vanished majesty of days, when men were gauged by worth,
Set crowned and dowered in the way to judge the sons of earth;
When all the little great fell down before the great unknown,
And priest put off the hampering gown and coward donned his own!

O vanished majesty of days that saw the sun shine on
The deeds that wake sublimer praise than Ghent or Marathon;
When patriots in homespun rose—where one was called for, ten—
And heroes sprang full-armored from the humblest walks of men!

O vanished majesty of days! Rise, type and mould today,
And teach our sons to follow on where duty leads the way;
That whatsoever trial comes, defying doubt and fear,
They in the thickest fight shall stand and proudly answer, "Here"!

KATE BROWNLEE SHERWOOD

CHARGE OF THE MULE BRIGADE

Moore, *The Civil War in Song and Story,* p. 225.

On the night of October 28, 1863, when Gen. Geary's division of the Twelfth corps repulsed the attacking forces of Longstreet at Wauhatchie, Tenn., a number of mules, affrighted by the noise of battle, dashed into the ranks of Hampton's Legion, causing much dismay among the rebels, and compelling many of them to fall back, under a supposed charge of cavalry.

Capt. Thomas H. Elliott, of Gen. Geary's staff, gives the following rendition of the incident, which he gleaned from [a] ... contemporary. Its authorship is not known.

I.

Half a mile, half a mile,
  Half a mile onward,
Right towards the Georgia troops,
  Broke the two hundred.
"Forward, the Mule Brigade,"
"Charge for the Rebs!" they neighed;
Straight for the Georgia troops
  Broke the two hundred.

II.

"Forward, the Mule Brigade!"
Was there a mule dismayed?
Not when the long ears felt
  All their ropes sundered;
Theirs not to make reply;
Theirs not to reason why;
Theirs but to make them fly.
On! to the Georgia troops,
  Broke the two hundred.

III.

Mules to the right of them,
Mules to the left of them,
Mules behind them,
  Pawed, brayed, and thundered.
Breaking their own confines,
Breaking through Longstreet's lines,
Into the Georgia troops
  Stormed the two hundred.

IV.

Wild all their eyes did glare,
Whisked all their tails in air,
Scattering the chivalry there,
    While all the world wondered.
Not a mule back bestraddled,
Yet how they all skedaddled!
    Fled every Georgian.
Unsabred, unsaddled,
    Scattered and sundered,
How they were routed there
    By the two hundred!

V.

Mules to the right of them,
Mules to the left of them,
Mules behind them
    Pawed, brayed, and thundered;
Followed by hoof and head,
Full many a hero fled,
Fain in the last ditch dead,
Back from an "ass's jaw,"
All that was left of them,
    Left by the two hundred.

VI.

When can their glory fade?
O! the wild charge they made!
    All the world wondered.
Honor the charge they made,
Honor the Mule Brigade,
    Long-eared two hundred.

LOOKOUT MOUNTAIN

Historic mount! baptised in flame and blood,
Thy name is as immortal as the rocks
That crown thy thunder-scarred but royal brow.
Thou liftest up thy aged head in pride
In the cool atmosphere, but higher still
Within the calm and solemn atmosphere

Of an immortal fame. From thy sublime
And awful summit, I can gaze afar
Upon innumerous lesser pinnacles,
And oh! my winged spirit lives to fly,
Like a strong eagle, 'mid their up-piled crags.
But most on thee, imperial mount, my soul
Is chained as by a spell of power.
        I gaze
From this tall height on Chickamauga's field,
Where Death held erst high carnival. The waves
Of the mysterious death river moaned;
The tramp, the shout, the fearful thunder-roar
Of red-breath'd cannon, and the wailing cry
Of myriad victims, filled the air. The smoke
Of battle closed above the charging hosts,
And, when it passed, the grand old flag no more
Waved in the light of heaven. The soil was wet
And miry with the life-blood of the brave,
And with a drenching rain; and yon broad stream,
The noble and majestic Tennessee,
Ran reddened toward the deep.
        But thou, O bleak
And rocky mountain, was the theater
Of a yet fiercer struggle. On thy height,
Where now I sit, a proud and gallant host
The chivalry and glory of the South,
Stood up awaiting battle. Somber clouds,
Floating far, far beneath them, shut from view
The stern and silent foe, whose storied flag
Bore on its fold our country's monarch-bird,
Whose talons grasp the thunderbolt. Up, up
Thy rugged sides they come with measured tramp,
Unheralded by bugle, drum, or shout,
And though the clouds closed round them with the gloom
Of double night, they paused not in their march
Till sword and plume and bayonet emerged
Above the spectral shades that circled round
Thy awful breast. Then suddenly a storm
Of flame and lead and iron downward burst,
From this tall pinnacle, like winter hail.
Long, fierce, and bloody was the strife—alas!
The noble flag, our country's hope and pride,
Sank down beneath the surface of the clouds,
As sinks the pennon of a shipwrecked bark
Beneath the stormy sea, and naught was heard
Save the wild cries and moans of stricken men,

And the swift rush of fleeing warriors down
Thy rugged steeps.
                          But soon the trumpet-voice
Of the bold chieftain of the routed host
Resounded through the atmosphere, and pierced
The clouds that hung around thee. With high words
He quickly summoned the brave soldiery back
To the renewal of the deadly fight;
Again their stern and measured tramp was heard
By the flushed Southrons, as it echoed up
Thy bald, majestic cliffs. Again they burst,
Like spirits of destruction through the clouds,
And mid a thousand hurtling missiles swept
Their foes before them as the whirlwind sweeps
The strong oaks of the forest. Victory
Perched with her sister eagle on the scorched
And torn and blackened banner.
                                    Awful mount:
The stains of blood have faded from thy rocks,
The cries of mortal agony have ceased
To echo from thy hollow cliffs, the smoke
Of battle long since melted into air,
And yet thou art unchanged. Ages thou wilt lift
In majesty thy walls above the storm,
Mocking the generations as they pass,
And pilgrims of the far-off centuries
Will sometimes linger in their wanderings,
To ponder, with a deep and sacred awe
The legend of the fight above the clouds.

                                 GEORGE D. PRENTICE

THE BATTLE ABOVE THE CLOUDS

Anonymous, quoted in Morton: *Sparks from the Camp Fire*

By the banks of Chattanooga, watching with a soldier's heed,
In the chilly, autumn morning gallant Grant was on his steed,
For the foe had climbed above him, with the banners of their land,
And the cannon swept the river from the hills of Cumberland.

Like a trumpet rang his orders—"Howard, Thomas to the Bridge!
One brigade aboard the Dunbar, storm the heights of Mission Ridge!
On the left, the ledges, Sherman, charge, and hurl the rebels down.
Hooker, take the steeps of Lookout, and the slope before the town."

Fearless, from the northern summit looked the traitors where they lay,
On the gleaming Union army, marshalled as for muster day,
Till the sudden shout of battle thundered upward from the farms,
And they dropped their idle glasses, in a sudden rush to arms.

Then together up the highlands surely, swiftly swept the lines,
And the clang of war above them swelled with loud and louder signs,
Till the loyal peaks of Lookout in the tempest seemed to throb,
And the star-flag of our country soared in smoke o'er Orchard Knob.

Day and night and day returning, ceaseless shock and ceaseless change,
Still the furious mountain conflict burst and burned along the range.
While the battle's cloud of sulphur mingled heaven's mist of rain,
Till the ascending squadron vanished from the gazers on the plain.

From the boats upon the river, from the tents upon the shore,
From the roofs of yonder city, anxious eyes the clouds explore;
But no rift amid the darkness shows them fathers, brothers, sons,
Where they trace the viewless struggle by the echo of the guns.

Upward! charge for God and country! up! aha! they rush, they rise,
Till the faithful meet the faithless in the never clouded skies,
And the battle-field is bloody, where a dewdrop never falls,
For a voice of tearless justice for a tearless vengeance calls.

And the heaven is wild with shouting; fiery shot and bayonet keen
Gleam and glance where Freedom's angels battle in the blue serene.
Charge and volley fiercely follow, and the tumult in the air
Tells of right in mortal grapple with rebellion's strong despair.

They have conquered! God's own legions; well their foes might be dismayed,
Standing in the mountain temple, 'gainst the terrors of his aid.
And the clouds might fitly echo pæan loud and parting gun,
When from upper light and glory sank the traitor host undone.

They have conquered! Through the region where our brothers plucked the
    palm
Rings the noise with which they won it with the sweetness of a psalm.
And our wounded sick and dying hear it in their crowded wards,
And they whisper, "Heaven is with us! Lo, our battle is the Lord's!"

And our famished captive heroes, locked in Richmond's prison hells,
List those guns of cloudland booming, glad as Freedom's morning bells,
Lift their haggard eyes, and panting with their cheeks against the bars
Feel God's breath of hope and see it playing with the stripes and stars.

Tories still in serpent treason startle at those airy cheers,
And that wild, ethereal war-drum falls like doom upon their ears.
And that rush of cloud-borne armies, rolling back a nation's shame,
Fights them with its sound of judgment and the flash of angry flame.

Widows weeping by their firesides, loyal sires despondent grown,
Smile to hear their country's triumph from the gate of heaven blown;
And the patriot's children wonder in their simple hearts to know
In the land above the thunder our embattled champions go.

YACOB AT LOOKOUT MOUNTAIN

George L. Catlin: *Sparks from a Camp Fire*

"Yah, I shpeaks English a leetle; berhaps you shpeaks petter der German."
"No, not a word." "Vel den, meester, it hardt for to be oonderstandt.
I vos drei yahr in your country, I fights in der army mit Sherman—
Twentiet Illinois Infantry—Fightin' Joe Hooker's commandt."

"So you've seen service in Georgia—a veteran, eh?" "Vel, I tell you
Shust how it was. I vent ofer in sixty, und landt in Nei-Yark;
I sphends all mine money, gets sick, und near dies in der Hospiddal
   Bellevue;
Ven I gets petter I tramps to Shecago to look for some vork."

"Pretty young then, I suppose?" "Yah, svansig apout; und der peobles
Vot I goes to for some work, dey hafe none for to geef;
Efery von laughs: but I holds my head ope shust so high as der steeples.
Only dot var comes along, or I should have die, I belief."

"Ever get wounded? I notice you walk rather lame and unsteady.
Ah! got a wooden leg, eh? What battle? At Lookout! don't say?
I was there too—wait a minute—your beer-glass is empty already.
Call for another. There! tell me how 'twas you got wounded that day."

"Vel, ve charge ope der side of der mountain—der sky vos all smoky und
   hazy;
Ve fight all day long in der clouds, but I never get hit until night—
But—I don't care to say mooch apout it. Der poys called me foolish und
   crazy.
Und der doctor vot cut ofe my leg, he say, 'Goot'—dot it serf me shust right."

"But I dinks I vood do dot thing over again, shust der same, und no matter
Vot any man say." "Well, let's hear it, you needn't mind talking to me,
For I was there, too, as I tell you—and Lor'! how the bullets did patter
Around on that breastwork of boulders that sheltered our Tenth Ten-
   nessee."

"So? Dot vos a Tennessee regiment charged upon ours in de efening,
  Shust before dark; und dey yell as dey charge, und ve geef a hurrah;
  Der roar of der guns, it vos orful." "Ah! yes, I remember, 'twas deafening;
  The hottest musketry firing that ever our regiment saw."

"Und after ve drove dem back, und der night come on, I listen,
  Und dinks dot I hear somepody a callin'—a voice dot cried,
  'Pring me some vater for Gott's sake'—I saw his pelt-blate glisten
  Oonder der moonlight, on der parapet, shust outside.

"I dhrow my canteen ofer to vere he lie, but he answer
  Dot his left handt vos gone, und his right arm proke mit a fall;
  Den I shump ofer, und gife him to drink, but shust as I ran, sir,
  Bang! come a sharp-shooter's pullet; und dot's how it vos—dot is all."

"And they called you foolish and crazy, did they? Him you befriended—
  The 'reb,' I mean—what became of him? Did he ever come 'round?"
"Dey tell me he crawl to my side, und call till his strength all ended,
  Until dey come out mit der stretchers, und carry us off from der ground.

"But pefore ve go, he ask me my name, und says he, 'Yacob Keller,
  You loses your leg for me, und some day, if both of us leefs,
  I shows you I don't vorget'—but he most hafe died, de poor feller;
  I nefer hear ofe him since. He don't get vell, I beliefs,

"Only I always got der saddisfachshun ofe knowin'—
  Shtop! vots der matter? Here, take some peer, you're vite as a sheet—
  Shteady! your handt on my shoulder! my gootness? I dinks you vos goin'
  To lose your senses avay, und fall right off mit der seat.

"Geef me your handts. Vot! der left one gone? Und you vos a soldier
  In dot same battle?—a Tennessee regiment?—dot's mighty queer—
  Berhaps after all you're—" "Yes, Yacob, God bless you, old fellow, I told you
  I'd never—no, never forget you. I told you I'd come, and I'm here."

KELLY'S FERRY

Benjamin F. Taylor: *Songs of Yesterday*

The flowers of battle are not always crimson. Some of them are
white as snow. During the late war, Kelly's Ferry, on the Tennessee,
was a scene of mingled men, mud, profanity and mules, and as deso-
late as Hogarth's "End of All Things;" but no fairer flower ever

blossomed anywhere than when the Third Ohio Blues fed the faint-
ing Fifty-fourth Virginia Grays, captured at the Storming of Mission
Ridge. The flower is called Fraternity, and they had brought it all
the way from Georgia, where those same Grays were hosts, those very
Blues the famished guests, and set it out beside the lazy Tennessee.
It was the writer's fortune to see one of the grandest battles of all
the war, when "Greek met Greek" in a gallantry so splendid that
it lights up that far November day as with the glory of an Easter sun;
but never anything so fine as that.

Those two banquets make a pair of pictures never to be turned to
the wall. And the flower, Fraternity, that, drenched with costly
blood, yet lived—let it be transplanted from Kelly's Ferry far and
near, till it blossoms in all weathers and beautifies the whole land.

KELLY'S FERRY

I.

Have you read in any book, heard anybody tell
Of the gallant Third Ohio, Lieutenant-Colonel Bell,
So like in shaggy ruggedness a mountain full of lairs
That when they cheered, you never knew the Buckeyes from the bears?
Ah! they loved the River Danger as Satan loves to sin,
Just drew their belts another hole, and then they waded in—
Waist-deep, chin-deep, the fellows went, nor drew a doubting breath,
No halting for an order nor touch of hat to Death!
"Go in!" and "Third Ohio!" their battle-cry and faith.

II.

Their talk was rough as bowlders are, and when they named the Flag
They christened it "Old Glory" or just "That blessed rag;"
Somebody fell—"passed in his checks" was all they had to say;
"God's country" was the happy land of "boiled shirts" every day;
They told of "wooden overcoats" and rude board coffins meant,
And thought they were a snugger fit than any Sibley tent;
But count the ragged blouses up, be sure the tale is true,
Each hides a handful of a heart beneath the tattered blue
That always played the Forward, March! and never beat tattoo.

III.

One Derby day they rode a raid and never drew the rein;
They rode as if they never meant to ride that route again.
Like long, clean sweep of trenchant blade where bonny flags burned blue,
And not a rift in all the field to let a star-beam through.
Down came a mantle broad and deep as comes the dusk of night,
In folds of gray and butternut, and swept them out of sight,
And swept them from their saddle-bows, and set their faces South.
And made a Daniel of the troop for Richmond's lion mouth,
And shriveled shut the bannered stars like daisies in a drouth.

IV.

"But why not tell it as it was?" I hear a fellow shout,
"Just make a finish of the thing, and say they bowled us out—
"One swallow, and the regiment was fairly gobbled up—
"Scooped by the blasted Johnny Rebs like water in a cup.
"They brushed us clean of cavalry, the infantry of clothes,
"And left the Third Ohio boys as naked as a nose."
For heavy baggage only hearts, each haversack was lank,
Nor flag nor fife to cheer along the dull, disastered rank;
Ah! deader than the March in Saul a canteen's empty clank.

V.

Along the road the weary miles lay quivering in the sun,
While naked Noon, with brazen blows, did weld them into one,
That naked feet must measure off before the work was done.
The days and boys crept slowly on—'twas thirst and starve and tramp,
Until they tumbled, supperless, beside a Southern camp.
The Fifty-fourth Virginians came, like long-flanked leopard cats,
With dingy pipes of corn-corb in their shapeless, battered hats,
And, lean as stakes, they stood around and watched the novel sight
Of colors struck and empty hands, and Yankees "flying light."

VI.

Not long they gazed, but bolted with an "Old Dominion" whoop,
Promoted in a twinkling to a commissary troop!
You heard the clink of coffee-mills, the merry bayonet stroke,
The camp was turbaned like a Turk with wreaths of cedar smoke;
Then came the clang of frying-pan, the kettle's tambourine,
They routed out the lazy fires and tucked the "dodgers" in;
The marytred bacon made complaint and clouds of incense rose—
Oh! sweeter than the censer's swing to gain a soul's repose,
The Boys in Gray forgot that night the Boys in Blue were foes!

VII.

So sped the night in brotherhood, and when the dawning came,
They tucked two figures in their hearts—two figures and a name—
And hand met hand in soldier grip, no words of courtly thanks,
One said, "Good-by, Virginia," and one, "Light out, you Yanks."
Still war's wild weather ruled the year. November to July,
Deep thunders in the Cumberlands and lightnings in the sky.
The raiders were their own again, to Lookout back they came,
They told the tale a thousand times, it ended all the same;
The "Fifty-fourth Virginia" toast set hearts and cheeks a-flame,
And cheers flew wild, like sparks of fire—two figures and a name!

VIII.

The Hawk's Nest hatched great broods of blue; they chipped the butternut shell,
And fluttered up the rugged Ridge against the gates of hell—
How fierce and grand the flight and swoop let Chattanooga tell.
Lo! 'mid the captives whirling down, their faces to the North,
All wrapped like kittens in a cloak, Virginia's Fifty-fourth!
With bodies lean and faces long, they trailed in straggling rank,
And clustered like bepollened bees upon the river bank.
There, on the lazy Tennessee, the Third Ohio lay,
From Kelly's poor old Ferry a rifle-shot away.
And so the laden caravan went filing down the hill.
The hosts were guests, the guests were hosts, and this alone was new,
The standard blazed with all its stars *above* the "bonny blue."
With winking camp-fires' dancing lights and dewdrops' beaded shine,
The night-air mantled rich and red as old Madeira wine,
Toned down the mellow picture, and made it half divine.
The sturdy boys were "keeping house," amid the mountain glooms,
And smoky cones of Sibley tents, like rainy nights' mushrooms,
Had spread their gray umbrellas, with narrow streets between,
And the flicker of a bayonet, the glitter of canteen
As flitting spots of indigo pinked out the living green.

IX.

A lounging Buckeye took a look, saw "Old Virginia" come,
And broke for camp with lively feet, as drumsticks beat a drum.
Before he struck the picket-line he emptied every tent,
He never stayed for stock or stone, but shouted as he went—
What golden bugles should have blown and made a "joyful noise":
"THE FIFTY-FOURTH VIRGINIA IS AT THE FERRY, BOYS!"

Three minutes and the camp had swarmed: they bought the sutler out,
And brought their treasures to the light, and strewed them round about.
And nothing but a night surprise could raise so wild a rout.

x.

The kettles filled with Araby upon their muskets swung;
A bag of "hard-tack," tough as tiles, upon a shoulder slung;
A slab of bacon, broad and brown, as if it came from mill,
Oh! sweeter than the censer's swing to gain a soul's repose,
The Boys in Blue forgot that night the Boys in Gray were foes!

xi.

Arms won the game at Mission Ridge and played the hand alone;
At Kelly's Ferry hearts were trumps and *everybody* won.
The drifting years, like thistledown, have glittered out of sight;
The boys are mustered out of life, let no man say "good-night!"
The Boys in Blue and Boys in Gray sleep peacefully together,
And God's own stars shine through the flag and make it pleasant weather.
I lay this old love-story down upon the breast of May,
And dare to hope its words are meet for Decoration Day.
I lay this ballad's homely flower upon some soldier's bed,
While Love's sweet rain is falling fast upon the speechless dead.
The rose's stain is not of blood. Are lilies pale with fear?
Then sure this offering of mine will harm nobody here.
At Kelly's Ferry once again let all the people meet,
With blessings clustered round their hearts and blossoms at their feet,
Give thanks the graves have ebbed at last that broke in billowed sod,
And make one grand Red-letter Day for manhood and for God.

SONG OF THE REBEL SIGNAL CORPS

Brown, *The Signal Corps, U.S.A., in the War of the Rebellion,* p. 224.

There is a flag as yet unsung,
  A banner bright and fair,
It moves in waves of right and left,
  That banner in the air.
The wise may look, the scholar con,
  The wondering urchin stare,
But naught can make of the bonnie white flag
  That bears the crimson square.

Chorus:—
>> Hurrah! Hurrah!
>> For the Signal Corps, hurrah,
>> Hurrah for the bonnie white flag
>> That bears the crimson square.

To comrades true, far, far away,
> Who watch with anxious eye,
These secret signs an import bear
> When waved against the sky.
As quick as thought, as swift as light,
> Those airy symbols there,
Are caught and read from the bonnie white flag,
> That bears the crimson square.

When armèd hosts in serried ranks
> Sweep forward to the fray,
The signal flag is waving there
> To point the victorious way,
From hill to hill, from crag to crag,
> The wingèd words to bear
That gave a name to the bonnie white flag
> That bears the crimson square.

When night draws o'er the wearied earth
> Her cloak of sable hue,
And bids us dream of home and friends,
> The soldiers staunch and true.
'Tis then the torch that's burning bright,
> Tells by its meteor glare
That we're on watch with the bonnie white flag
> That bears the crimson square.

Then let us hope when war is o'er
> And great, and good, and free,
We stand and boast ourselves with truth
> A model confederacy,
That midst war's recollection oft
> We too may claim a share
As we fondly think of the bonnie white flag
> That bears the crimson square.

ON THE HEIGHTS OF MISSION RIDGE

When the foes, in conflict heated,
  Battled over road and bridge,
While Bragg sullenly retreated
  From the heights of Mission Ridge—
There, amid the pines and wildwood,
  Two opposing colonels fell,
Who had schoolmates been in childhood,
  And had loved each other well.

There amid the roar and rattle,
  Facing Havoc's fiery breath,
Met the wounded two in battle,
  In the agonies of death.
But they saw each other reeling
  On the dead and dying men,
And the old time, full of feeling,
  Came upon them once again.

When that night the moon came creeping,
  With its gold streaks o'er the slain,
She beheld two soldiers, sleeping,
  Free from every earthly pain.
Close beside the mountain heather,
  Where the rocks obscure the sand,
They had died, it seems, together,
  As they clasped each other's hand.

J. Augustine Signaigo

NEGRO SONG OF MISSION RIDGE

Moore, *The Civil War in Song and Story*, p. 302

Ole massa he come dancin' out,
  And call de black uns roun',
        Oh—O! Oh—O!
He feels so good he couldn't stan'
  Wid boff feet on de groun'.
          Oh!—O—ee!

Say don't you hear dem 'tillery guns
  You niggers? don't you hear?
        Oh—O! Oh—O!

Ole Gen'ral Bragg's a mowin' down
   De Yankees ober dar!
                 Oh!—O—ee!

You Pomp, and Pete, and Dinah too,
   You'll catch it now, I swear,
                 Oh—O! Oh—O!
I'll whip you good for mixin' wid
   Dem Yanks when dey was here.
                 Oh!—O—ee!

Here comes our troops! in crowds on crowds†
   I knows dat red and gray.
                 Oh—O! Oh—O!
But, Lord! what makes dem hurry so,
   And frow dere guns away?
                 Oh!—O—ee!

Ole massa den keep boff feet still,
   And stared wid boff he eyes,
                 Oh—O! Oh—O!
Till he seed de blue-coats jes behin',
   Which cotch him wid surprise!
                 Oh!—O—ee!

Ole massa's busy duckin' 'bout
   In de swamps up to he knees.
                 Oh—O! Oh—O!
While Dinah, Pomp, and Pete, dey look
   As if dey's mighty pleas'.
                 Oh!—O—ee!

THE HEROES AND THE FLOWERS

Benjamin F. Taylor: *Songs of Yesterday*

In Rose Hill, Chicago, stands a monument to the Boys in Blue. It is the Angel Hope, waked by a master from her sleep in the pale tombs of Carrara. A star is over her head, and one hand is lifted toward it as if she had just plucked it fresh from Heaven, or as if she had halted it that it might shine there forever. She keeps watch and ward over the dead soldiers of Bridges' Battery lying at her feet.

Their graves radiate from the base of the monument like the rays that encircle the head of the Madonna.

Standing by the Angel one day in May, and looking down upon those beds of peace, whose occupants I had known, and some of whom I had seen in the grand anger of battle, this was the thought: will nothing wake these cannoneers?

Let us try bugles, and they shall not wake them.

Let the drums beat to arms, but they shall not heed them.

We will wheel out the battery and give the thunder-gusts of battle, and they shall slumber right on.

They are hopelessly dead. They are utterly dumb. We must summon witnesses to testify for them who cannot speak, and among them this marble Angel that came all the way across the sea for their sake. That star above her brow is a star fallen out of the Flag! The Flag? And we never thought of it when we would wake the sleepers! Ah, that's the thing. Over all "the pomp and circumstance" of war, over all constitutions and laws, they will surely heed the Flag, and they do, and the dead soldiers answer the roll-call. So, the poem did not blossom like a flower in a week, but opened like a fan in an instant, and who wonders?

That golden day in May, on the threshold of June, the murmur of the distant city, the hush of the multitude, the air sweet with ten thousand flowers, the marble doors of the enduring houses the grave-digger builds, standing far and near, white and still in the sunshine —doors that shall open to mortal love and longing never more— ah, me, I can never forget it, for I shall never look upon its like again.

THE HEROES AND THE FLOWERS
ROSE HILL

I.

Oh, be dumb all ye clouds
As the dead in their shrouds,
Let your pulses of thunder die softly away,
Ye have nothing to do
But to drift round the blue,
For the emerald world grants a furlough to-day!

II.

Bud, blossom, and flower,
　All blended in shower,
In the grandest and gentlest of rains shall be shed
　　On the acres of God
　　With their billows of sod
Breaking breathless and beautiful over the dead!

III.

They do flush the broad land
　With the flower-laden hand,
Drift the dimples of graves with the colors of even;
　　Where a BOY IN BLUE dreams,
　　A "Forget-me-not" gleams—
No rain half so sweet ever fell out of Heaven!

IV.

From no angel was caught
　The magnificent thought
To pluck daisies and roses, those *bravest* of things,—
　　For they stand all the while
　　In their *graves* with a smile—
And to strew with live fragrance dead lions and kings!

V.

It was somebody born,
　It was Rachel forlorn,
'Twas the love they named Mary, the trust they called Ruth;
　　'Twas a *woman* who told
　　That the blossoms unfold
A defiance to death and a challenge for truth;
　　That the violet's eye,
　　Though it sleep, by and by
Shall watch out the long age in the splendor of youth.

VI.

Ah, she hallowed the hour
　When she gathered the flower;
When she said, "This shall emblem the fame of my brave!"
　　When she thought, "This shall borrow
　　"Brighter azure to-morrow;"
When she laid it to-day on the crest of a grave.

———

A great mart's majestic arterial beat
Throbbed this multitude out, where the graves at our feet
Have so roughened the earth with their motionless surge
That we know we are treading its uttermost verge,
That another step more and life's flag would be furled,
Another step more we are out of the world!

Did ye think we had come to give greeting to June,
Who had opened her gates by a May-day too soon,
Breathed her buds into blossom, her birds into song,
And reached here before us by ever so long?
Stay, reverent feet! Bid the bosom be still!
The campaigning is ended—we halt at Rose Hill.

We are looking for comrades off duty forever!
Do you dream that a handful of ashes can sever
The stout sterling hearts that were beating as one,
And kept time as they beat, to the throb of a gun?

Now summon the sexton, master-builder for man,
Who has worked for the world since its dying began—
Bid him tell if he thinks he ever has crushed
Out the love of a heart that was worth the poor dust
That would hide it. I solemnly tell you, no clod
Tolls the knell of the love as immortal as God,
That is born out of danger and christened with blood;
That can look in the graves of dead valor and say
It was grander than living, that passing away,
For they halted the world for the truth and the right,
Said "Begone, mighty Death, and forever good-night!"
And, shoulder to shoulder, let Batteries tell
How they marched within hail of the borders of hell.

Ah, the brave cannoneers overtaken at last!
Here they went into camp when "the dead line" was passed,
Left the turbulent world with a cadence sublime,
And these born sons of thunder had marched out of time,
Worn away for grand orders their glorious scars,
Here they lie, side by side, front face to the stars!

And I knew we should find them! As ever their wont,
Bridges' Battery Boys always breasted the brunt,
As in life, so in death, they had gone to the "front!"
Will they sleep out their furlough? Blow bugles amain!
Give the old warble breath! Let them hear it again
As they heard it that day when Cumberland's crags
Right up to the sky were a-flutter with flags,

As if eyries of eagles should burst on the sight,
And sweep up the mountain on pinions of might
To meet the gray morning half way in its flight!
Let the sounding recall mock Euroclydon's lips
When it strews the Levant with a million of ships,
And the shout through the roar of the seas as they whelm,
Is "All hands upon deck and two at the helm!"
Oh, ye trumpets give o'er! If the sleepers can hear
They will answer you back with an old-fashioned cheer.

There's a goldfinch aloft on a billow song,
There's the drift of a leaf as it rustles along—
Can nothing bring utterance out of the sod
But the blast of that angel, the Bugler of God?

Bring out the drum-majors! Strike with ague the air,
Bid them sling up the parchment, and tighten the snare,
While the drums of the drummer-boys beat "the long roll,"
And the surges of thunder rumble up to the pole,
Till they jar the dead clod, till they thrill the live soul.
Stormy pulses be dumb! All unheeded, unheard,
As the heart-beat that troubles the breast of a bird.

Wheel the Battery out! Unlimber the guns!
All flashing electric the eyes of its sons,
All glowing the forges, all ready to fire,
The cannon all panting with keenest desire,
The columns all grander and broader and nigher,
For the souls within range, God pardon their sins!
Let all go, Mighty Heart! and the battle begins.
Each throb is the thunder—a bolt for each flash
Rends the air with a howl, smites the earth with a crash,
And the shriek of the shell with the quivering cry
That a demon might utter if demons could die,
Cuts keen through the din like a wing through the sky;—
Till old Kennesaw roars from its mantle of cloud,
And Lookout stands white before God in its shroud,
As if Gabriel's trumpet had sounded that day,
And the mountain had heard and was first to obey!
And the breath of the battery dims the broad noon,
And the heart of the battery quickens its tune,
It is "Stand by the guns!" It is "Right about wheel!"
It is "In with the iron!" It is "Out with the steel!"
As a squadron swoops down with a roar on the flank—
And it reddens the Ridge and it riddles the rank—
It is God and dry powder forever we thank!

Round the turbulent land its sledges have swung,
In a score of grand battles its melody rung,
Atlanta and Franklin have heard its grand chime,
And before Mission Ridge it gave them the time.
Chickamauga's dread Sunday it thundered "amen"
'Mid the gusts of wild fire, when the iron clad rain
Did ripen brown earth to the reddest of stars,
And baptized it anew and christened it Mars.
In that moment supreme, to their bridles in blood,
Like a rock in the wilderness grandly *he* stood
Till the Red Sea was cleft and he rode down the street,
With the fame on his brow and the foe at his feet!
Oh, be muffled ye drums! Let artillery toll!
Cloud up, all ye flags! Earth has lost a great soul.
Gallant THOMAS, good-night, but good-morn to thy glory,
Outranking them all in the charm of thy story!
Like a shadow in sunshine they have borne thee in state
Far across the new world, to the true "Golden Gate"—
Philip Sydney, make room, for thy comrade is late!
Spike the guns! When their tongues of eloquent fire
Sent the crashing old anthem, that ought to inspire
The pale dead in their graves, around the green world,
Not a cheer fluttered up, not a shroud was unfurled.
Did the men of Chaldea, lone watching afar,
Ever hear, in their dreaming, the throb of a star?
Inarticulate earth! Is there nothing can reach
To thy chambers serene? Can unlock the dead speech?

We have come into court, this court of the Lord,
To bear witness for them who can utter no word.
Bare-hearted, bare-browed, in this presence we stand,
For the gift Pentecostal comes down on the land;
To speak for the speechless how witnesses throng,
And the earth is all voice, and the air is all song!
There's a fleet of white ships blown abroad on the deep,
And their courses forever they peacefully keep,
And they toss us a roar and it melts into words,
And they strike to the heart like the sweeping of swords:
"Would ye honor the men you must look in their graves,
Who did score danger out with their wakes from the waves."

There are soft, fleecy clouds fast asleep in the sun,
Like a flock of white sheep when the washing is done,
Not a breath of a battle is staining the blue,
It is nothing but Paradise all the way through!
There are domes of white blossoms where swelled the white tent,

There are plows in the field where the war-wagons went,
There are songs where they lifted up Rachel's lament.
Would you know what this mighty beatitude cost,
You must search in the graves for what Liberty lost!
Has man waited too long that the silence is broken
By beings that God never meant should have spoken
And that never were born—poor inanimate things
All endowed with the accents of creatures and kings?
Oh, ye living, make way! For direct from the tomb
Of Carrara a wonderful witness has come—
As fair as an angel, as free from all sin,
With one whisper from God would her pulses begin!
She had lain there forever in marble repose
But Love spoke the word, she grew human, and rose,
At the touch of the sculptor, awoke from the swoon,
Cast off the cold shroud and stood up in the noon!
Will you see where that hand, pure and pale as a drift,
Has just halted a star with its eloquent lift,
That the heroes who lie in their slumber together
May have it for emblem, whatever the weather?
'Tis a spark from the Flag! Dare ye think they are dead
Without whom the brave star had forever been shed,
And the autumn come down like the night on the world
And our fragment of heaven disaster'd and furled!
Aye! up with the banner and down with the thought!
Fling the "old glory" out till the breezes have wrought
Into billows of beauty its marvelous flame
That can kindle a soul to the color of fame!

Now, Sergeant, the roll! Soft and low, sweet and clear,
The dread silence is cleft, and the answer is "HERE!"
"Here!" Bishop and Seborn! Brave lieutenants, stand fast!
Thanks to God for the flag, we have found you at last!
"Here!" Ferris and Smith! "Here!" Hammond and Brown!
Ye that trod the acanthus and trampled it down,
And it turned at the touch a Corinthian crown.
Here! glorious Score! On our hearts and our lips,
Not a name of ye all can be quenched in eclipse!
Disenthralled from your graves you have left them alone,
We will borrow them now for these dead of our own!
Let us bury all bitterness, passion, and pride,
Lay the rankling old wrong to its rest by their side,
Keeping step to the manhood that marches the zone,
And believe the good GOD will take care of His own!

Appendix F

ARTILLERY IN THE CHICKAMAUGA–CHATTANOOGA NATIONAL MILITARY PARK

Listed by Dr. James C. Hazlett

UNION

City of Chattanooga

5th and Walnut Sts.:	One 20-pound Parrott rifle.
1219 East Terrace St.:	Two 20-pound Parrott rifles.
Oak and Palmetto Sts.:	Two 3″ Ordnance rifles.
849 Vine St.:	Two 30-pound Parrott rifles.
504 McCallie Ave.:	Two 12-pounder Napoleons.
Orchard Knob:	Six 12-pounder Napoleons.
Payne St., River Bluff:	Two 12-pounder Napoleons.

Chickamauga Battlefield

McDonald Field:	Three 12-pounder Napoleons; three 3″ Ordnance rifles.
U.S. Route 27:	Four 12-pounder Napoleons; for 12-pounder field howitzers; three 6-pounder guns; one rifled 6-pounder; * two 3″ Ordnance rifles; two 10-pound Parrott rifles.
Battleline Road:	Six 12-pounder Napoleons; eight 12-pounder field howitzers; four rifled 6-pounder guns.

* The rifled 6-pounder gun is a standard model 6-pounder smoothbore bronze gun which has been rifled into a 12-pounder. In contemporary reports, this is most frequently referred to as a James rifle, because the pieces were rifled according to the James system. This disregards the fact that there were original James guns, both rifled and smoothbore, invented by General James which were entirely different in appearance. When a 6-pounder gun was rifled, there was little material difference in the bore diameter of the piece. Whereas a smoothbore fired a round shot weighing 6 pounds, the resulting rifle fired an elongated projectile which was roughly twice as heavy, or twelve pounds. To differentiate between the true James rifle and the rifled U.S. 6-pounder gun, William Kay, Park Historian, Shiloh National Military Park (1958) suggested that the latter be designated a 6/12.

South end of Kelly Field:	Two 3″ Ordnance rifles.
Poe Road:	Five 12-pounder Napoleons; one 24-pounder howitzer; two 10-pound Parrott rifles.
Field south of Brotherton House:	Four 12-pounder Napoleons; two 6-pounder guns; two 12-pounder mountain howitzers.
Reed's Bridge Road:	Ten 12-pounder Napoleons; two 12-pounder field howitzers; two rifled 6-pounder guns.
West of Jay's Mill:	Two 12-pounder Napoleons.
Winfrey Field:	One 10-pound Parrott rifle.
Mullis Hill:	Two 12-pounder Napoleons.
West of Mullis-Vittetoe Road:	Two 12-pounder Napoleons; one 3″ Ordnance rifle.
Snodgrass House:	Four 12-pounder Napoleons; four 3″ Ordnance rifles.
Snodgrass Hill:	Two 12-pounder Napoleons.
Glen-Kelly Road:	Four 3″ Ordnance rifles; two 10-pound Parrott rifles.
Wilder Tower:	Two 24-pounder howitzers; two 3″ Ordnance rifles.
West of Viniard's:	Four 3″ Ordnance rifles; two 10-pound Parrott rifles.

Total:

12-pounder Napoleons	54
12-pounder field howitzers	14
12-pounder mountain howitzers	2
24-pounder howitzers	3
6-pounder guns	5
Rifled 6-pounder guns	7
3″ Ordnance rifles	24
10-pound Parrott rifles	9
20-pound Parrott rifles	3
30-pound Parrott rifles	2
	123

CONFEDERATE

Missionary Ridge

Sherman Reservation:	Four 12-pounder Napoleons.
Railroad Tunnel:	Two 12-pounder Napoleons.
Crest Road:	Ten 12-pounder Napoleons; nine 12-pounder field howitzers; three 6-pounder guns; four rifled 6-pounders.

Lookout Mountain
  Point Park: Two 12-pounder Napoleons; two 20-pound Naval Parrott rifles; two 12-pounder field howitzers.

  Craven's Reservation: Two 6-pounder guns.

Chickamauga Battlefield
  McDonald Field: Four 12-pounder Napoleons; two rifled 6-pounder guns.

  U.S. Route 27:   Twelve 12-pounder Napoleons; six 12-pounder field howitzers; two 6-pounder guns; two 3" Ordnance rifles.

  Lee Residence (town of
    Chickamauga):   Two 6-pounder guns.

  Battleline Road: Four 3" Ordnance rifles.

  Poe Road: Two 12-pounder Napoleons; two 10-pound Parrott rifles.

  Forrest Road: Two 12-pounder Napoleons.

  South of Helm Monument: Three 12-pounder Napoleons; seven 12-pounder field howitzers; two 6-pounder guns.

  Alexander Bridge
    Road: Two 12-pounder Napoleons; two 12-pounder field howitzers.

  East of Poe Field: Two 12-pounder Napoleons; two 12-pounder field howitzers.

  North of Brock Field: Two 12-pounder field howitzers.

  East edge of Brock
    Field: Two 12-pounder field howitzers.

  Brotherton Road: Three 12-pounder Napoleons; two 12-pounder field howitzers; six 6-pounder guns.

  East of Viniard's: Two 12-pounder Napoleons.

  North-west slope of
    Snodgrass Hill: Two 12-pounder Napoleons; three 12-pounder field howitzers.

  South spur of Snodgrass
    Hill: Two 12-pounder Napoleons; two 12-pounder field howitzers; one 6-pounder gun.

  At South Carolina
    Monument: Two 12-pounder Napoleons.

  Vittetoe-Chickamauga
    Road: One 6-pounder gun.

  Dyer Ridge: One 12-pounder field howitzer; two 6-pounder guns.

Hill overlooking Lytle
    Station: Two 12-pounder Napoleons.
        Total:

12-pounder Napoleons	56
12-pounder field howitzers	38
6-pounder guns	21
Rifled 6-pounder guns	6
3" Ordnance rifles	6
10-pound Parrott rifles	2
20-pound Parrott rifles (Naval)	2
	131

Due to changes being made in Chattanooga for a new highway, part of Cameron Hill has been removed, and the following guns have been taken from the area to the Park Utility Building:

12-pounder Napoleons	6
Rifled 6-pounder guns	4
30-pound Parrott rifles	3

Unmounted gun tubes at the Park Utility Building:

12-pounder Napoleons	1
6-pounder guns	4
Rifled 6-pounder guns	5
Blakely rifles	2
	25

Unmounted tube at Park Headquarters Building:
    12-pounder mountain howitzer   1

NOTE: Mr. Charles Dunn, Superintendent, and Mr. Rock Comstock, Historian at Chickamauga-Chattanooga National Military Park, gave valuable aid in completing these lists.

Appendix G

CIVIL WAR ARTILLERY

The following brief descriptions of the service of the piece and materiel are derived from the War Department manuals of the period.

Duties of the Gun Squad in Loading and Firing.

Gunner. Sights piece for direction and range. Gives commands.

No. 1. Uses rammer staffs for loading and sponging.

No. 2. Receives round from N. 5 and loads.

No. 3. Primes and stops vent. Swings trail right or left with trail handspike in obedience to gunner's order or hand motion for direction of the muzzle.

No. 4. Fastens lanyard hook to friction primer. On command to fire, pulls lanyard.

Nos. 5, 6, and 7. Cut fuses and handle ammunition.

No. 8. In charge of the caisson. Directs and assists other higher numbered cannoneers in resupply of limber ammunition chest or replacement by one from the caisson.

In the event of casualties, the manual prescribed the reapportionment of duties among surviving members of the squad.

Equipment

Friction primer. A small, powder-filled tube inserted through the vent at the cannon's breech into the powder charge of the round in the bore. The primer was ignited when a rough wire running through its composition was jerked out by a pull of the lanyard.

Fuse board. Placed on this board, time fuses were cut at a desired point by fuse gouge. The powder-filled, metal-covered fuse was marked at intervals for regulating time of explosion during the projectile's flight; intervals extended from $\frac{3}{4}$ to $5\frac{1}{4}$ seconds. The cut fuse, screwed into the shell's nose, was ignited by the flame of discharge and burned to the point cut; whereupon it exploded the shell. Percussion fuses burst the shell on impact.

Rammer and sponge staffs. Pushed the load through the bore of the gun to the breech, or swabbed out the bore after firing. The sponge, dipped in a water bucket, cleaned and cooled the bore.

Worm. A corkscrew on a staff to withdraw clogged or unexploded charges.

Prolonge. A stout rope hooked to the lunette of the gun carriage or the pintle hook of the limber to move them short distances without the horses.

Vent punch or pick. Used for cleaning out the vent.

Two hooks. For removal of the tight packing around ammunition in the chests; also used in tamping down the packing.

Pendulum-hausse. A sliding-scale range instrument placed in a seat at the base of the breech and used in conjunction with the muzzle sight. They were aligned on the target by turning the elevating screw beneath the breech. A gunner's quadrant was employed in the bore at the muzzle. A gunner's level was used on the tube near the breech.

Thumbstall. A padded piece of leather, fastened on a thumb as protection from hot metal, for covering the vent while the piece was being loaded. If the vent were not thus stopped, the new charge might be ignited by lingering particles of the old, and the loader be injured.

Notes and References

CHAPTER 1. The Mountain

1. Beatty, *Memoirs of a Volunteer*, p. 271.

2. King's Mountain of the Revolution, where American mounted riflemen defeated the British in 1780.

3. Taylor, *In Camp and Field*, p. 20.

Benjamin Franklin Taylor (1819–87) was a war correspondent for the *Chicago Evening Journal*. Though he was less known than such noted reporters for papers in the East as Dana, Greeley, and Reid, he rated high in his profession and was so widely quoted as to win a national reputation. While mindful of the newspaper axiom that names make news and of the deeds of troops from his paper's state, his great quality was his gift as a poet, exemplified in his magnificent descriptions of the Battles of Lookout Mountain and Missionary Ridge. Those won him a national audience. During the Atlanta campaign he incautiously disclosed the position of the Union lines in a dispatch to his paper. General Sherman, as in other similar instances, erupted and ordered Taylor's trial as a spy, but the correspondent escaped arrest by leaving the front. Later, avoiding Sherman's jurisdiction, he returned to write a brilliant account of Jubal Early's advance on Washington. After the war three books of his poetry and three of travel were published, and he delivered many popular lectures.

For two of Taylor's poems, inspired by the Chattanooga Campaign, see Appendix E.

4. Byron, *Don Juan*, Canto III.

5. "Maybe the real trouble was that the battle was too theatrical. People could see too much; most particularly the Confederates could see too much. They were up in the balconies and all the Federals were down in the orchestra pit, and when the fighting began, every move down on the plain was clearly visible to the Southerners on the heights. Perhaps just watching it did something to them." Catton, *This Hallowed Ground*, p. 294.

6. "As we came through some camps, I inquired at different places, 'Whose are those tents I see away off there? Looks like a division;' receiving reply repeatedly to this effect: 'Why, don't you know? Ha, Ha! That's Joe Hooker who has brought a lot of Potomac soldiers down here to show us Western boys how to fight. Why, those fellows can't do anything but turn out for dress parade, with white gloves on, and want to break ranks and go home if they can't get butter and cheese along with their rations. But, whoosh, just you wait! Fight, is it? What do they know about that? They'll learn a thing or two before we get through with 'em!' This was hard for me to bear, for I loved the Army of the Potomac and had once been part of it, knowing something of its tragic history and hard endurance." Notes by Capt. E. H. Russell, Signal Corps, quoted in Brown, *The Signal Corps, U.S.A.*, p. 489.

275

7. Catton, *op. cit.*, p. 292.

8. "Neither in armament, equipment, or organization was the Western army in even nearly as good shape as the Army of Northern Virginia. About one-third of the infantry was still armed only with the smooth-bore musket, calibre .69. Only a few batteries of the artillery were formed into battalions, and their ammunition was all of inferior quality." Alexander, *Military Memoirs of a Confederate*, p. 451.

9. Fiske, *The Mississippi Valley in the Civil War*, pp. 248f.

10. Jones, *An Artilleryman's Diary*, p. 124. Henry S. Muchmore, 11th New Hampshire Infantry, also makes grateful mention of bountiful foraging in his unpublished diary (courtesy of its owner, Colonel Mather Cleveland). "Killed a hog weighed 400 lbs. Had for supper beans and fresh pork.... Picked 6 qts. of blackberries; sold 5 qts. for $1."

CHAPTER 2. "For I Am a Man Under Authority, Having Soldiers Under Me"

11. U. S. Grant in *Battles and Leaders of the Civil War* (hereinafter referred to as B.&L.), III, p. 710, recalls this story.

12. Fort Bragg, North Carolina, designated as having been named for him as a United States captain, not as a Confederate general.

13. "Bragg was a fantastic character, as singular a mixture of solid competence and bewildering ineptitude as the war produced. He distrusted democracy, the volunteer system, and practically everything except the routine of the old regular army, and just before Shiloh he had complained that most of the Confederate soldiers had never fired a gun or done a day's work in their lives.... A ferocious disciplinarian, he shot his own soldiers ruthlessly for violations of military law, and his army may have been the most rigidly controlled of any on either side." Catton, *This Hallowed Ground*, p. 156.

Another interesting characterization is Mitchell's in *Decisive Battles of the Civil War*, p. 116. "Braxton Bragg ... was a conscientious, hard-working officer, wholeheartedly devoted to the Confederate cause. He was also possessed of a natural aggressiveness. He believed in attacking first but, if he was not immediately successful he became dispirited and lost his temper, blaming his subordinates for things that went wrong. In fact, he was a hard taskmaster who was not at all liked by the men who served under him. On important occasions he saw only too clearly the things that had gone wrong while forgetting the successes of his own troops. He found it difficult, if not impossible, to look confidently forward to what could be eventual success. The net result might perhaps be summed up by saying that he was an intelligent, skillful planner but, in the execution of his plans, he was his own worst enemy."

14. Quoted by Cleaves in his *Rock of Chickamauga*, p. 45.

15. Taylor, *In Camp and Field*, pp. 192f.

16. Henry, *The Story of the Mexican War*, p. 251.

17. Foote, *The Civil War Narrative*, p. 283.

18. One critic was U. S. Grant, who would succeed Rosecrans and Thomas in command. "He felt that Rosecrans should have followed up his Corinth victory by destroying Van Dorn's army; any battle that left the enemy with any appreciable number of survivors was apt to strike Grant as imperfect." Catton, *op. cit.*, p. 177.

19. *Ibid.*, p. 285.

20. Beatty, *Memoirs of a Volunteer*, pp. 176f.

21. Freeman, *Lee's Lieutenants*, III, 176f.

22. Hood died of yellow fever in 1879.

23. Morton, *The Artillery of Nathan Bedford Forrest's Cavalry*, pp. 130f., quoting Dr. J. B. Cowan, Forrest's chief surgeon, who was present at the meeting. Forrest subsequently confirmed Cowan's report of his words as substantially correct.

24. Wyeth, *Life of Lieutenant-General Nathan Bedford Forrest*.

25. Address at the U.S. Army Command and General Staff School, March 7, 1949.

CHAPTER 3. The Volunteers

26. Enlistments expired for 455 out of 956 Union infantry regiments; for 81 of 158 artillery batteries. *The War of the Rebellion: Official Records* (hereinafter referred to as *O.R.*), V, Ser. 3, 650.

27. Ganoe, *The United States Army*, p. 290, observes that the draft law was still not effective. Congress, instead of modifying it to be so, on December 23, 1863, appropriated $23,000,000 for bounties and advance pay. The states failed to curb the fraud payment by brokers of bounties to recruiting agents, who, to avoid draft of local citizens, paid sums many times in excess of those offered by the Federal government. Not until February 24, 1864, did Congress give the President power to call for the men required, proportioning calls on the number of men liable to military duty, with exemption only for the physically and mentally unfit and those who had served two years honorably.

28. *Ibid.*, p. 291.

29. *O.R., op. cit.*, pp. 649, 651. In 1864 there were 26,000 re-enlistments in the Army of the Potomac, at least 50 per cent of the time-expired troops. The record in the western armies was better.

30. Catton, *This Hallowed Ground*, p. 319.

31. While many officers of the Regular ante-bellum army resigned to join their seceded states, very few enlisted men left to serve the South.

32. For example, the black slouch hats of the Iron Brigade of the Army of the Potomac.

33. Coulter, *The Confederate States of America*, pp. 313ff.

34. *Augusta Weekly Constitutionalist*, January 29, 1864.

35. Wiley, *The Life of Johnny Reb*, p. 132.

36. McMurray, *History of the Twentieth Tennessee Regiment Volunteer Infantry*, pp. 500f.

CHAPTER 4. "This Is the Arsenal"

37. "At the outbreak of the war, the infantry arms in the possession of the Federal Government consisted of 560,000 smoothbore muskets and 49,000 rifles. Of those 300,000 muskets and 27,000 rifles were in the Northern arsenals; the remainder were in Southern arsenals and were appropriated for the use of the Confederate army." *Selected Readings in American Military History*, I, 211.

Distinction must be made between rifled muskets and rifles. The latter had been manufactured in Federal armories since 1803 and were always considered separately. Information from Harold L. Peterson.

38. Exceptions were the massed artillery fire that won the day at Malvern Hill and played a vital part in the repulse of Pickett's charge at Gettysburg. Second Manassas and Stone's River also saw effective concentrations.

39. It was long before the Civil War's dearth and confusion of munitions were remedied. The U.S. Armed Forces did not adopt the Industrial Mobilization program for munitions manufacture until after World War I. NATO standardization of ammunition was an achievement of 1959.

40. *Selected Readings, op. cit.*, I, 211.

41. Major Samuel B. Smith, "Military Small Arms" in *Sketches of War History*, Military Order of the Loyal Legion, Ohio Commandery.

Further fouling after a few more shots nullified that interchange of ammunition, and cleaning the piece could no longer be delayed.

42. The usual efficiency in loading is pointed up by comparatively infrequent mischances. In battle excited soldiers sometimes rammed a bullet into the barrel before the powder—might leave the ramrod in the barrel, fire it off and lose it— might load the cartridge without breaking the paper. Any one of those mistakes could render the gun useless for the rest of the battle. "On the field of Gettysburg more than 24,000 loaded muskets and rifles were found. Six thousand of them had one load apiece, twelve thousand had two loads, and six thousand had from three to ten loads. One famous specimen had twenty-three loads rammed down in regular order." Bruce, *Lincoln and the Tools of War*, p. 100.

The Civil War soldier's handicaps have been emphasized for modern riflemen by the shoots of the North-South Skirmish Association, armed with the weapons of the sixties.

See Appendix A for manual of loading.

43. Bruce, *op. cit.*, p. 101.

44. *Ibid.*

45. The Springfield, altered to a breechloader but still a single-shot gun, was the U.S. Army standard arm through the Indian wars in spite of the fact that the enemy were not infrequently armed with Winchester and other repeaters, sold them by traders "for hunting."

In 1939 the author fired one of the new Garand semiautomatic rifles at Springfield Armory. The Garand was under test as a replacement for the Springfield, Model of 1903. As the M-1 of World War II and Korea, the Garand served well, thereafter giving way to present-day improvements in shoulder firearms, still basic despite atomic warfare.

For an inventive and enterprising nation the repeated time lags in weapons development seem as incomprehensible as their tardy adoption is culpable.

46. Buckeridge, *Lincoln's Choice*, pp. 43, 46f.

47. Upson, *With Sherman to the Sea*.

48. Connolly, *Letters to His Wife*, pp. 262, 285.

49. Bruce, *op. cit.*, pp. 285f.

50. *Ibid.*, p. 67.

51. Fuller and Steuart in *Firearms of the Confederacy* and the latter in *The Confederate Veteran*, Vol. 32 (1924), pp. 166f., give the following interesting figures. By conservative estimate arms seizures from United States arsenals, excluding Harper's Ferry, where valuable machinery also was carted away, amounted to 150,000 stands. Battlefield yields: Wilderness, 35,000; Second Manassas, 20,000; Fredericksburg, 9,000; Antietam and Shiloh, 15,000; the Tennessee campaign of late 1862, 27,500; Chancellorsville and Chickamauga, 35,000.

52. Tennent, *The Story of the Guns*, pp. 52ff., 64.

53. Fuller and Steuart, *op. cit.,* p. 229.

54. Green, *Johnny Green of the Orphan Brigade,* pp. 105f.

55. McClellan, *Manual of Bayonet Exercise.*

56. Bruce, *op. cit.,* pp. 119, 282.

57. Taylor, *op. cit.,* p. 166.

58. En route to the fatal field of the Little Big Horn, Custer "was offered three Gatling guns but refused them because their teams were condemned cavalry horses (one more shameful Government economy) and because he thought wheeled vehicles might not be able to negotiate the broken country he must traverse." Downey, *Indian-Fighting Army,* p. 198. Gatlings waited for their vindication until the Spanish-American War, when they were tellingly employed at San Juan Hill. See Downey, *Sound of the Guns,* pp. 182ff.

59. Longfellow, "The Arsenal."

CHAPTER 5. "The Diapason of the Cannonade"

60. *Selected Readings in American Military History,* I, 213.

61. The experience of Benjamin Huger and other United States ordnance officers who joined the South was undoubtedly valuable in cannon founding.

62. Birkhimer, *Historical Sketch of the . . . Artillery, U.S. Army.*

Difficulties with the variety of ammunition furnished the Confederate artillery at Chickamauga are noted in the ordnance report of Major John A. Cheatham, *O.R.,* Ser. I, Pt. 2, XXX, p. 82. Some guns, Cheatham stated, were put out of action by the clogging of balls in their bores. He recommended more careful inspection of ball sizes, use of sufficient grease, and wrapping of balls too small for a tube with thick paper.

63. With the exception of two features, cannon had not greatly changed since bombards were touched off at Crécy. Since John Zizka mounted them on carts, the first gun carriages, in the fifteenth-century Hussite wars of Bohemia. Since Gustavus Adolphus of Sweden, Frederick the Great of Prussia, and France's Napoleon Bonaparte turned the tide of battle on many a field with them. A gun crew of the American Revolution, manning a 6-pounder or a 12-pounder, could have handled as readily a Civil War smoothbore. The first great innovation of the mid-nineteenth century was rifling, and the second was the breech-loading cannon.

64. For cannon and batteries and their positions in the National Military Park see Appendix F.

65. Rifled pieces had to be made of iron or steel, since lands in bronze barrels would not stand up under the stress of firing rifle projectiles. Bronze barrels had the advantage, however, of being far less liable to burst.

66. Howitzer barrels were shorter and the walls of their tubes thinner because they used reduced powder charges. Those features account for their light weight. Civil War models could fire higher trajectories than guns but were of course less capable in that respect than modern howitzers. High-angle fire long remained the particular province of mortars.

67. *O.R.,* Ser. I, Pt. 1, XXX, 457.

68. "Secretary Cass had, in 1836, added the French mountain howitzer to the field system through a belief, which events confirmed, that this gun would be of practical utility against the Indians, with whom at that time we were commencing the tedious and not very glorious Seminole war." Birkhimer, *op. cit.,* p. 282.

69. Wise, *The Long Arm of Lee*, pp. 174f.

70. Cf. warfare in the Korean mountains when the rears of tanks were dug in, deep in the ground, to give their guns greater elevation than their mechanism permitted. But it must be remembered, in the case of the Union guns firing up at Lookout that, while they could obtain a higher angle of fire by placing trails on lower ground (and consequently raising muzzles), the degree was limited by the necessity of allowing for recoil of five or six feet or more. Recoil likewise had to be considered for Alexander's down-firing guns; he could depress them only so far and could not reduce powder charges below the quantity necessary to obtain the range desired.

Recoil mechanism, permitting the tube to slide back on the gun carriage and then returning it into battery, was a twentieth-century invention, notably exemplified by the French .75 mm. with its hydraulic (oil) cylinder.

71. Alexander, *Memoirs of a Confederate*, p. 746.

72. *Ibid.*, p. 748.

73. Taylor, *In Camp and Field*, pp. 10f.

74. The implication here that there were Napoleons heavier than 12-pounders is poetic license (unless Taylor means howitzers when he mentions the larger calibers).

75. Canister was issued in World War II and effectively used by 37-mm. cannon, mounted on armored cars, for sudden, close-range attacks; also for 75-mm. mountain howitzers in light tanks.

Civil War caissons often carried a larger proportion of canister than was called for by regulations, when they could draw it from the train. It was backs-to-the-wall ammunition, making a cannon into "a huge sawed-off shotgun."

A desperate and successful defense of a battery with canister was that by Wheeler's 13th New York during the Atlanta campaign. The 13th, however, had previously served at Chattanooga. Lieutenant Edward Baldwin tells the story in *New York at Gettysburg*, III, 1320ff.

"On July 20th, we crossed Peach Tree Creek, and went into position along the edge of some woods with a large clear field on its front. Shortly after taking position, the pickets came running in. We looked for the enemy, but seeing none we laughed at the boys for running. A little later, without firing a shot or making a sound of any kind, a heavy force of infantry was in our front and coming on the double-quick for our guns. The command was given, 'Load with canister quick!' and the guns poured canister into the advancing ranks so rapidly and accurately that the enemy's line wavered and broke. But it was quickly rallied and again advanced only to be driven back again. But, twice again he came and was repulsed, all except a few, bolder than the rest, who reached the right section. But some of our men seized handspikes, and the sergeants using revolvers drove them back. A force now came through the woods on our right flank, and gave us a volley, which killed two men, mortally wounded two, and severely wounded two. The captain, as soon as he saw this new danger, ordered the left section to change front to the right and open on the enemy on our right. This was quickly done and a charge of canister, *together with a stocking full of minié balls, of which we had probably thirty or forty stowed in our limber chests for close work (the men having gathered them at different times from fields of battle),*—these were poured into them three times in rapid succession. Reinforcements of infantry came to us at this time and drove the enemy from our right."

For the Napoleon 32 rounds were carried in the gun limber chest and 96 rounds in each caisson and limber chest. The content of each chest was as follows:

	Number	Weight
Shot, fixed	12	184.8
Spherical case, fixed	12	176.4
Shells, fixed	4	48.7
Canister, fixed	4	76.6
Spare cartridges, 2½ lbs.	2	5.
Friction primers	48	.4
Slow match	2	.5
Portfires	4	.7
		493.1 lbs.

76. The grapeshot mentioned was provided for siege guns. An authority, Harold L. Peterson, in a letter to the author, states: "I doubt that grapeshot was ever used in field guns except possibly to use up old stocks made before the idea had been abandoned. We have checked the reports of ammunition expended which were made after every battle and engagement from the time the use of such reports started early in the war for the Army of the Potomac, and not one stand of grape is listed as having been shot. Also there are the statements in the manuals that it is not to be used, and the categoric statements by Hunt [Chief of Artillery, Army of the Potomac], etc., in the testimony before the Committee on the Conduct of the War that 'grape is not used in field guns.' After all, canister served the same purpose; it was undoubtedly easier on the bore of the gun, and it was packaged much better to withstand the vicissitudes of transport over rough ground."

Regardless, grapeshot seems to have captured the imaginations of war correspondents and others and is frequently referred to, although the ammunition in each instance was almost certainly canister. That inaccuracy has a parallel in repeated references in World War II to shrapnel, which had then been superseded by high-explosive shell.

77. Taylor, *op. cit.*, pp. 8ff.

78. For the method of firing a Civil War cannon see Appendix G.

79. There were, of course, similar instances in both World Wars I and II—in the Argonne, at Kasserine Pass, in the Battle of the Bulge, and elsewhere. Among factors accounting for the diminution of such crises from the Civil War's high average were: longer ranges permitting the placement of artillery farther to the rear; indirect fire enabling concealment; superior communications; better armament for a battery's defense such as machine guns on its flanks. Numbers of those advantages were nullified in Korea by the mountainous terrain and the infiltration tactics of the Red Chinese.

80. Information from General Barnett's granddaughter, Mrs. Stanton Garfield.

81. Jones, *An Artilleryman's Diary*, p. 137.

CHAPTER 6. Your Move, General

82. Polk was killed at the Battle of Kenesaw Mountain.

83. Mme. Turchin, daughter of a Russian colonel, married one of her father's subalterns, a Crimean War veteran, and took an active part in his career, studying with him. After their democratic ideas caused banishment of the couple to the United States, Turchin became colonel of the 19th Illinois. When the regiment entrained for the front, Mme. Turchin went right along, in defiance of the regulations: "No woman, whether wives of officers or soldiers, shall be permitted

to remain in camp or accompany the troops in the field." With cool indifference to fire, she served as a nurse and on occasion rallied wavering lines in battle.

It was during the Tennessee campaign of 1862 that she took over her husband's command when he fell ill, issuing orders to battalion commanders and adjutants with great competence. Colonel Turchin ordered Athens, Alabama, burned in retaliation for its townsfolks' resistance when his brigade marched into town. His superior, General Buell, thereupon sent him before a court-martial, which sentenced him to dismissal from the service. Hastily Mme. Turchin journeyed to Washington where she appealed direct to Lincoln. The President, admiring a good fighting man—and woman—not only ordered Turchin restored to duty but promoted to brigadier general. "The Mad Cossack" continued in command through the Chattanooga campaign, about which he wrote a book. His wife ("with all the refinements of a lady, she had the energy and self-reliance of a man") was seldom far from his side.

84. Buck's "An Epick" is part of the Ezra R. Rickett Collection, Ohio State Museum. For full text, except for lines indecipherable in the manuscript, see Appendix E.

85. *Selected Reading in American Military History*, I, 224.

86. Taylor, *In Camp and Field*, pp. 103ff.

87. See Appendix E.

88. Colonel David Urquhart in *B.&L.*, III, 608.

89. Green, *Johnny Green of the Orphan Brigade*, p. 61.

90. *B.&L.*, III, 609.

91. Beatty, *Memoirs of a Volunteer*, p. 233.

92. *Ibid.*, p. 174.

93. Reminiscences of Harry Adney, courtesy of his grand-nephew, L. G. Delay. *Connolly Letters*, Illinois State Historical Society (1928), XXXV, 321f.

94. Good details on the Tullahoma operation are found in Fitch, *The Chattanooga Campaign*, pp. 39–50.

95. From the journal of David H. Haines, quoted by Wiley, *The Life of Billy Yank*, p. 165.

96. Fiske, *The Mississippi Valley in the Civil War*, p. 258.

97. Cist (Brevet Brigadier General, of Rosecrans' and Thomas's staffs), *The Army of the Cumberland*, pp. 175–177.

98. W. S. Furey in the *Cincinnati Gazette*, 1888.

99. Calkins, *History of the 104th Regiment of Illinois Volunteer Infantry*, p. 98.

100. Govan and Livingood, *The Chattanooga Country*, pp. 217, 219f.

101. Fitch, *Annals of the Army of the Cumberland*, p. 236. McGee, *History of the 72nd Indiana Volunteer Infantry*, p. 108.

102. *O.R.*, Ser. I, Pt. 3, XXX, 123.

CHAPTER 7. Jaws of a Trap

103. Steele, *American Campaigns*, I, 440.

104. Bircher, *A Drummer-Boy's Diary*, p. 11.

105. *B.&L.*, III, 641n.

106. Hill in *B.&L.*, III, 639.

107. *Ibid.*

108. *O.R.*, Ser. I, Pt. 2, XXX, 49.

109. *Ibid.*, pp. 54ff.

110. *B.&L.*, III, 641f.

CHAPTER 8. The Iron Horsemen

111. Fiske, *The Mississippi Valley in the Civil War*, pp. 266f.

112. Sorrel, *Recollections of a Confederate Staff Officer*, p. 189. Dickert in his *History of Kershaw's Brigade*, p. 264, adds: "The cars on all railroads in which troops were transported were little more than skeleton cars; the weather being warm, the troops cut all but the framework loose with knives and axes. They furthermore wished to see outside and witness the fine country and delightful scenery that lay along the route; nor could those inside bear the idea of being shut up in a box car while their comrades on top were cheering and yelling themselves hoarse at the waving of handkerchiefs and flags in the hands of pretty women and the hats thrown in the air by old men and boys along the roadside as trains sped them through the Carolinas and Georgia."

113. Chesnut, *A Diary from Dixie*, p. 308.

114. Fiske, *op. cit.*, p. 267.

115. Leech, *Reveille in Washington*, p. 271 .

116. Bryant, *History of the Third Regiment of Wisconsin Volunteer Infantry*, p. 217.

117. Howard in *The Atlantic Monthly*, XXXVIII (1876), 204, 206.

118. *Ibid.*, p. 205.

119. Williams, *Lincoln Finds a General*, II, 765.

120. Turner, *Victory Rode the Rails*, p. 293. See also Black, *The Railroads of the Confederacy*.

121. Turner, *op. cit.*, pp. 302f.

122. Taylor, *In Camp and Field*, p. 146.

CHAPTER 9. Battle in the Woods

123. Govan and Livingood, *The Chattanooga Country*, p. 21.

124. Perry, *History of the 38th Regiment Indiana Volunteer Infantry*, pp. 89-91.

125. Polley, *Hood's Texas Brigade*, p. 200.

126. Polley, *A Soldier's Letters to Charming Nellie*, pp. 146f.

127. Steele, *American Campaigns*, I, 432.

128. Morton, *The Artillery of Nathan Bedford Forrest's Cavalry*.

129. *Army Register* for January, 1886; Heitman, *Historical Register and Dictionary of the United States Army;* Wiley, *The Life of Billy Yank*, pp. 296ff.; Wittenmeyer, *Under the Guns;* Taylor, *In Camp and Field*, pp. 168f.; *Who's Who in America*, 1912–1913; *Outlook*, CVII (1914), 546f. A novel by James A. Rhodes and Dean Jauchius based on Clem's life, *Johnny Shiloh*, was published in 1959.

130. *O.R.*, Ser. I, Pt. 2, XXX, 108.

131. Watkins, "*Company Aytch*," pp. 114f.

132. Green, *Johnny Green of the Orphan Brigade*, pp. 93, 95.

133. Fletcher, *Rebel Private, Front and Rear*.

134. *O.R.*, Ser. I, Pt. 1, XXX, 317; also Medal of Honor citations, for which see Appendix D.

135. *Ibid., et seq.*

136. Dana, *Recollections of the Civil War*, p. 114.

137. Eckenrode and Conrad, *James Longstreet, Lee's War Horse*, p. 227. One of the officers, Sorrel, states that they wheeled and galloped away under fire by the picket.

CHAPTER 10. "Hell Broke Loose in Georgia"

138. Letter of W. C. Athay to his sister, quoted in Wiley, *The Life of Johnny Reb*, p. 33.

139. McGee, *History of the 72d Indiana Volunteer Infantry*, pp. 176f.

140. Watkins, *"Company Aytch,"* p. 117.

141. *Ibid.*, p. 114.

142. *O.R.*, Ser. I, Pt. 2, XXX, 47.

143. *Ibid.*

144. *B.&L.*, III, 656.

145. Catton, *This Hallowed Ground*, p. 282.

146. *O.R.*, Ser. I, Pt. 1, XXX, 103. For other references see same source, pp. 59, 101ff., 645ff.

147. Brevet Brigadier General Gates P. Thurston in *B.&L.*, III, 663f.

148. Bierce, *Battle Sketches*, pp. 41f.

149. *O.R.*, *op. cit.*, pp. 413f.

150. *Ibid.*, p. 800.

151. *Ibid.*, p. 676.

152. *Ibid.*, p. 597.

153. *Ibid.*, p. 467. The references to limbering indicate that Lilly's Battery was equipped with the prairie carriage for its mountain howitzers. Benton in *Ordnance and Gunnery* (1862), p. 238, describes the carriage as follows: "The necessity for a small carriage for the mountain howitzer, when used on our western prairies, has led to the adoption of a special carriage for that service, with a limber attached as in a field carriage. This gives a carriage less liable to overturn, and preferable in many ways for that service to the two-wheeled one. The limber is furnished with two ammunition-boxes, placed over the axletree and parallel to it, and just wide enough for one row of shells and their cartridges.

"The caisson for this new carriage is a two-wheeled cart with shafts, on which are fixed four boxes for ammunition, similar to those on the limber, but placed perpendicular to the axletree, and a fifth box for equipment, etc., in front of the other boxes, perpendicular to them, and resting against their ends."

154. *B.&L.*, III, 664.

155. Dana, *Recollections of the Civil War*.

156. *O.R.*, *op. cit.*, p. 192.

157. Heartsill, *Fourteen Hundred and 91 Days in the Confederate Army*.

158. *Ibid.*, p. 159.

159. Owen, *In Camp and Battle with the Washington Artillery of New Orleans*.

CHAPTER 11. "Rock of Chickamauga"

160. Catton, *This Hallowed Ground*, p. 283.

161. *Ibid.*, p. 284.

162. Brevet Major General Emerson Opdycke in *B.&L.*, III, 671.

163. Fullerton in *B.&L.*, III, 666.

164. *Ibid.*

165. *Ibid.*, p. 667.

166. *Ibid.*

167. Cist, *The Army of the Cumberland*.

168. Bierce, *Battle Sketches*, pp. 146f.

CHAPTER 12. Tarnished Stars

169. Livermore, *Numbers and Losses in the Civil War in America*, p. 106.

170. *Ibid.*, p. 105.

171. *Southern Historical Society Papers*, XII, 223.

172. *O.R.*, Ser. I, Pt. 2, XXX, 56. Longstreet's words become somewhat ironic in the light of his criticisms of Lee's tactics at Gettysburg.

173. General Rosecrans was frequently referred to (either flippantly or unknowingly) as Rosencrantz, the name of one of Hamlet's courtier friends.

174. Chesnut, *Diary from Dixie*, pp. 316, 307. After beating off Bragg's attacks at Murfreesboro, Rosecrans is said to have declared, "Bragg's a good dog, but Hold Fast's [referring to himself] a better."

175. Sorrel, *Memoirs of a Confederate Staff Officer*, p. 196.

176. *Ibid.*, pp. 196f.

177. Horn, *The Army of Tennessee*, pp. 239ff.

CHAPTER 13. At All Hazards

178. Quoted in Wiley, *The Life of Billy Yank*, p. 228.

179. Kansas. Office of the Adjutant General. *Report for 1861–1865*, I, 132.

180. Grant in *B.&L.*, III, 683.

181. Thatcher, *A Hundred Battles in the West*, pp. 30, 276ff.

182. Downey, *Famous Horses of the Civil War*, pp. 66f.

183. *B.&L.*, III, 684.

184. Belknap, *Michigan at Chickamauga* (etc.), pp. 156ff.

185. Taylor, *In Camp and Field*, pp. 146f.

186. *Pennsylvania at Chickamauga and Chattanooga*, p. 374.

187. *Ibid.*

188. For details on the service of Civil War cannon see Appendix G.

189. For full text see Appendix E.

190. *B.&L.*, III, 678.

191. Fiske, *The Mississippi Valley in the Civil War*, p. 292.

CHAPTER 14. Sound of the Guns

192. Quoted in Moore, *The Civil War in Song and Story*, p. 439.

193. Fire from the Federal guns, with trails sunk when necessary for the elevation required, was more effective than that of the Confederate guns firing downward.

194. Little and Maxwell, *A History of Lumsden's Battery*.

195. Lewis, *Sherman, Fighting Prophet*, p. 316.

196. Fiske, *The Mississippi Valley in the Civil War*, pp. 293f.

197. *Ibid.*, p. 295. "From the tone of some of the despatches one would gather that neither Lincoln, Stanton, nor Halleck had a particle of confidence in Burnside's ability to take care of himself, and the question is forcibly suggested, why was he kept so persistently in important commands?"

198. *B.&L.*, III, p. 694.

199. Lewis, *op. cit.*, p. 315.

200. Grant in *B.&L.*, III, 691.

201. Boatner, *The Civil War Dictionary*, p. 144. "These unglamorous provisions for his logistical support have a little-understood or appreciated importance not only in Grant's victory at Chattanooga, but also in the clearing of east Tenn. and in Sherman's subsequent Atlanta campaign."

202. Lewis, *op. cit.*, p. 316.

203. *B.&L.*, III, 721.

CHAPTER 15. "Battle Above the Clouds"

204. Taylor, *In Camp and Field*, p. 24.

205. Brown, *The Signal Corps, U. S. A., in the War of the Rebellion*, PH, VIII, 312–340.

206. "Among the writers for the *New York Herald* following the army was one DeBow Randolph Keim, a journalist of singular immodesty, who left three scrapbooks of his writings to the Library of Congress upon his death, and once confided to a group of his fellow correspondents that he never read Shakespeare for fear of its interfering with his own style. Keim made an interesting discovery, namely, that Union cryptanalysts had unraveled the code in which the Confederates were signaling to each other by flags waved from high platforms in the wooded mountains towering over the route of advance. The news appeared in the *New York Herald* of June 23rd, causing an apoplectic reaction in headquarters, for if the news got to the 'rebels' it would mean a change in the system and the slamming of a shutter over a helpful window into enemy plans. Sherman sent a scorching note down through channels, and conceivably thought once more about gibbets, but the actual handling of the case rested with the less inflammable General George H. Thomas, who sent Keim on the reporters' road to exile northward." Weisberger, *Reporters for the Union*, p. 122.

207. See Appendix E for full text.

208. Connolly, *Letters to His Wife*.

209. Fiske, *The Mississippi Valley in the Civil War*, p. 302.

210. Brown, *op. cit.*, p. 490.

211. Lancaster in his novel, *No Bugles Tonight*, p. 310, describes such an incident, adapted from another battlefield.

212. *O.R.*, Ser. I, Pt. 2, XXXI, 716f.

213. Taylor, *op. cit.*, p. 45.

214. *O.R., loc. cit.*

215. Fiske, *op. cit.*, p. 306.

216. Taylor, *op. cit.*, p. 47.

217. *O.R., op. cit.*, p. 163.

CHAPTER 16. The Last Rampart

218. An actual cyclorama was painted, and several scenes from it are reproduced in *B.&L.*, III. However, the canvas has disappeared, reported destroyed.

219. Bragg was still convinced that Missionary Ridge was invincible, and Grant was close to sharing the belief that it could not be taken, not by frontal assault at any rate. It was only after the Ridge had been successfully stormed that Grant remarked, "Well, it *was* impregnable."

Also Bragg realized it was imperative that he make a stand on the Ridge. If he did not, he was finished as commander of the Army of Tennessee, Jefferson Davis regardless. He could not have failed to sense the effect of his guarded dispatch of November 24 to Richmond. Lack of confidence in him was summed up by Jones in *A Rebel War Clerk's Diary*, II, 104. "November 25th.—We have had an unintelligible dispatch from Gen. Bragg, saying he had, yesterday, a prolonged contest with the enemy for the possession of Lookout Mountain, during which one of his divisions suffered severely, and that the maneuvering of the hostile army was for position. . . . There is no indication of probable result—no intimation whether the position was gained. But the belief is general that Bragg will retreat, and that the enemy, may, if he will, penetrate the heart of the South! To us it *seems* as if Bragg has been in a fog ever since the battle of the 20th of September. He refused to permit—to move on the enemy's line for nearly two months, and finally consented to it when the enemy had been reinforced by 30,000 from Meade, and by Sherman's army from Memphis, of 20,000, just when he could not spare a large detachment! In other words, lying inert before a defeated army, when concentrated; and dispersing his forces when the enemy was reinforced and concentrated! If disaster ensues, the government will suffer the terrible consequences, for it assumed the responsibility of retaining him in command when the whole country (as the press says) demanded his removal."

220. Jones, *An Artilleryman's Diary*.
221. Cleburne's Report, *O.R.*, Ser. I, Pt. 2, XXXI, 745–753.
222. *B.&L.*, III, 713.
223. Lewis, *Sherman, Fighting Prophet*, p. 231.
224. *Ibid.*, p. 321.
225. *Ibid.*
226. Hazen, *Narrative*.
227. Taylor, *In Camp and Field*.
228. Upson, *With Sherman to the Sea*.

CHAPTER 17. Charge Without Orders

229. Taylor, *In Camp and Field*, pp. 61f.
230. *Ibid.*, p. 64.
231. Kansas. Office of the Adjutant General. *Report for 1861–1865*, I, 136.
232. *B.&L.*, III, 725.
233. Lewis, *Sherman, Fighting Prophet*, p. 323.

CHAPTER 18. "Terrible as an Army with Banners"

234. Taylor, *In Camp and Field*, pp. 69ff.
235. See Appendix D.
236. *O.R.*, Ser. I, Pt. 2, XXXI, 224.
237. Connolly, *Letters to His Wife*, p. 302.
238. Kansas. Office of the Adjutant General. *Report for 1861–1865*, I, 137.

CHAPTER 19. Race for the Crest

239. Briant, *History of the 6th Regiment Indiana Volunteer Infantry*, p. 275.
240. Taylor, *In Camp and Field*, p. 75.
241. Lewis, *Sherman, Fighting Prophet*, p. 324.
242. Kansas. Office of the Adjutant General. *Report for 1861–1865*, I, 137.

243. Prisoners of the 38th Alabama, captured *en masse*, spent the rest of the war in a Union stockade.

244. *O.R.*, Ser. I, Pt. 2, XXXI, 742.

245. *B.&L.*, III, 726.

246. Mitchell, *Decisive Battles of the Civil War*, p. 180.

247. Kansas, *op. cit.*, 137f.

248. Briant, *op. cit.*

249. Taylor, *op. cit.*, p. 73.

250. McMurray, *History of the Twentieth Regiment Tennessee Volunteer Infantry*, p. 137.

251. Watkins, *"Company Aytch,"* p. 125.

252. *Ibid.*, p. 126.

253. Livermore, *Numbers and Losses in the Civil War*, pp. 107f.

254. Fitch, *The Chattanooga Campaign*, p. 224.

CHAPTER 20. Clasped Hands

255. Told the author by John S. Fletcher.

256. Speech of Vice-President Adlai E. Stevenson.

257. See Appendix F.

258. Shakespeare, *Julius Caesar*, Act II, Scene ii.

BIBLIOGRAPHY

Alexander, General E. P. *Military Memoirs of a Confederate.* New York: Charles Scribner's Sons, 1907.

American Historical Association. *Annual Reports.* Washington: 1885–1954.

Andrews, J. Cutler. *The North Reports the Civil War.* Pittsburgh: University of Pittsburg Press, 1955.

Andrews, R. Snowden. *Andrew's Mounted Artillery Drill.* Charleston: Evans and Cogswell, 1863.

Battles and Leaders of the Civil War. Robert Underwood Johnson, ed. 4 vols. New York: The Century Company, 1884–87.

Beatty, John. *Memoirs of a Volunteer, 1861–1863. (The Citizen-Soldier).* New York: W. W. Norton & Co., 1946.

Belknap, Charles E. *History of the Michigan Organizations at Chickamauga, Chattanooga and Missionary Ridge.* Lansing, Michigan: Robert Smith Printing Co., 1897.

Bierce, Ambrose. *Battle Sketches.* London: Shakespeare Head Press, 1930.

Bircher, William. *A Drummer-Boy's Diary.* St. Paul: St. Paul Book and Stationery Co., 1889.

Birkhimer, Wm. E. *Historical Sketch of the Organization, Administration, Matériel, and Tactics of the Artillery, United States Army.* Washington: 1884.

Black, Robert C., III. *The Railroads of the Confederacy.* Chapel Hill: The University of North Carolina Press, 1952.

Blay, John S. *The Civil War, a Pictorial Profile.* New York: Thomas Y. Crowell Co., 1958.

The Blue and the Gray: the Best Poems of the Civil War. Claudius Meade Capps, ed. Boston: Bruce Humphries, Inc., 1943.

Boatner, Mark Mayo, III. *The Civil War Dictionary.* New York: David McKay Company, Inc., 1959.

Boynton, H. V. *Dedication of the Chickamauga & Chattanooga National Military Park.* Washington: Government Printing Office, 1896.

Brown, J. Willard. *The Signal Corps, U.S.A., in the War of the Rebellion.* Boston: U. S. Veteran Signal Corps Association, 1896.

Bruce, Robert V. *Lincoln and the Tools of War.* Indianapolis: The Bobbs-Merrill Co., 1956.

Bryant, Edwin E. *History of the Third Regiment of Wisconsin Veteran Volunteer Infantry, 1861–1865.* Madison: Wisconsin Veteran Association of the Regiment, 1891.

Buck, Irving A. *Cleburne and His Command.* New York and Washington: The Neale Publishing Co., 1908.

Calkins, William Wirt. *History of the 104th Regiment of Illinois Volunteer Infantry.* Chicago: 1891.

Carter, Colonel William H. *Horses, Saddles, and Bridles*. Baltimore: The Lord Baltimore Press, 1902.

Casey, Brigadier General Silas. *Infantry Tactics*. 3 vols. New York: D. Van Nostrand Co., 1862.

Catton, Bruce. *This Hallowed Ground*. New York: Doubleday & Company, Inc., 1956.

Chesnut, Mary Boykin. *A Diary from Dixie*. Boston: Houghton Mifflin & Co., 1949.

Cist, Henry M. *The Army of the Cumberland*. New York: Charles Scribner's Sons, 1882.

Civil War Centennial Commission. *Facts about the Civil War*. Washington: 1959.

Civil War Papers Read before the Commandery of the State of Massachusetts, Military Order of the Loyal Legion of the United States. Boston: Printed for the Commandery, 1900.

Cleaves, Freeman. *Rock of Chickamauga, the Life of General George H. Thomas*. Norman: University of Oklahoma Press, 1948.

Commager, Henry Steele, ed. *The Blue and the Gray*, 2 vols. Indianapolis: Bobbs-Merrill Company, 1950.

The Confederate Soldier in the Civil War. Ben La Bree, ed. Louisville: The Prentice Press, 1897.

Confederate Veteran, The, 40 vols. Nashville, Tennessee: 1893–1932.

Connolly, James Austin. *Letters to His Wife*. In Illinois State Historical Library. Publication No. 35. Transactions of the Illinois State Historical Society for the Year 1928. Springfield, Illinois, 1928.

Cooke, Philip St. George. *Cavalry Tactics*. 2 vols. Philadelphia: J. B. Lippincott & Co., 1862.

Coulter, E. Merton. *The Confederate States of America*. Baton Rouge: Louisiana State University Press, 1950.

———. *Travels in the Confederate States: a Bibliography*. Norman, Oklahoma: University of Oklahoma Press, 1948.

Cox, Jacob Dolson. *Military Reminiscences of the Civil War*, 2 vols. New York: Charles Scribner's Sons, 1900.

Crozier, Emmet. *Yankee Reporters, 1861–1865*. New York: Oxford University Press, 1956.

Cullum, George W. *Biographical Register of the Officers and Graduates of the U. S.Military Academy*. 7 vols. Boston: 1891–1930.

Cunningham, W. H. *A History of the Battle of Chickamauga*. Evergreen, Alabama: Press of the Orphans' Call (n.d.).

Downey, Fairfax. *Sound of the Guns*. New York: David McKay Company, Inc., 1956.

———. *The Guns at Gettysburg*. New York: David McKay Company, Inc., 1958.

———. *Indian Fighting Army*. New York: Charles Scribner's Sons, 1941. New York: Bantam Books, 1957.

———. *Famous Horses of the Civil War*. New York: Thomas Nelson & Sons, 1959.

———. *Clash of Cavalry: The Battle of Brandy Station*. New York: David McKay Company, Inc., 1959.

Duke, Basil W. *History of Morgan's Cavalry*. Cincinnati: Miami Printing and Publishing Co. 1867.

Dyer, Frederick H. *A Compendium of the War of the Rebellion*. Des Moines, Iowa: The Dyer Publishing Co., 1908.

Field Artillery Journal. Washington: 1911–45.

Fiske, John. *The Mississippi Valley in the Civil War.* Boston and New York: Houghton, Mifflin & Co., 1900.

Fitch, John. *Annals of the Army of the Cumberland.* Philadelphia: J. B. Lippincott & Co., 1864.

Fitch, Michael Hendrick. *The Chattanooga Campaign.* Wisconsin History Commission. Original Papers No. 4: Democrat Printing Co., 1911.

————. *Echoes of the Civil War as I Hear Them.* New York: R. F. Fenno & Co., 1905.

Fletcher, William Andrew. *Rebel Private, Front and Rear.* Austin: University of Texas Press, 1954.

Foote, Shelby. *The Civil War Narrative.* New York: Random House, 1958.

Forbes, Edwin. *Thirty Years After.* New York: Fords, Howard, & Hulbert, 1890.

Foster, John Y. *New Jersey and the Rebellion.* Newark, New Jersey: Martin R. Dennis & Co., 1868.

Fox, Lieutenant Colonel, William T. *Regimental Losses in the American Civil War.* Albany: Albany Publishing Co., 1889.

Freeman, Douglas Southall. *Lee's Lieutenants, a Study in Command.* 3 vols. New York: Charles Scribner's Sons, 1942–44.

————. *R. E. Lee, A Biography.* 4 vols. New York: Charles Scribner's Sons, 1934–35.

Fuller, Claud E., and Richard D. Steuart. *Firearms of the Confederacy.* Huntington, West Virginia: Standard Publications, Inc. 1944.

Ganoe, William Addleman. *The History of the United States Army.* New York: D. Appleton-Century Co., Inc., 1942.

Gaskill, J. W. *Footprints Through Dixie.* Alliance, Ohio: 1919.

Govan, Gilbert E., and James W. Lingood. *The Chattanooga Country, 1540–1951.* New York: E. P. Dutton & Co., Inc., 1952.

Gracie, Archibald. *The Truth about Chickamauga.* Boston and New York: Houghton Mifflin Co., 1911.

Green, John W. *Johnny Green of the Orphan Brigade.* A. D. Kirwan, ed. Lexington, Kentucky: University of Kentucky Press, 1956.

Guernsey, Alfred H. and Henry M. Alden. *Harper's Pictorial History of the Great Rebellion.* Chicago: McDounell Bros., 1868.

Guild, George B. *A Brief Narrative of the Fourth Tennessee Cavalry Regiment.* Nashville, Tennessee: 1913.

Hard, Abner. *History of the Eighth Cavalry Regiment, Illinois Volunteers.* Aurora, Illinois: 1868.

Haupt, General Herman. *Reminiscences of General Herman Haupt.* Milwaukee: Wright & Joys Co., 1901.

Hazen, William B. *A Narrative of Military Service.* Boston: Ticknor & Co., 1885.

Hazlett, Dr. James Cummins. *Field Artillery on the Gettysburg Battlefield.* Notebook, 1957.

Heartsill, W. W. *Fourteen Hundred and 91 Days in the Confederate Army.* Jackson, Tennessee: McCowat-Mercer Press, 1954.

Hedrick, Mary A. *Incidents of the Civil War.* Lowell, Massachusetts: Vox Populi Press, 1888.

Heitman, Francis B. *Historical Register and Dictionary of the United States Army.* 2 vols. Washington: 1900.

Henry, Robert Selph. *The Story of the Confederacy.* Indianapolis: The Bobbs-Merrill Co., 1931.

————. *The Story of the Mexican War.* Indianapolis: The Bobbs-Merrill Co., 1950.

————. *"First with the Most" Forrest.* Indianapolis: The Bobbs-Merrill Co., 1944.

Henry, Robert Selph. *Campaign Sketches of the War with Mexico.* New York: Harper & Brothers, 1847.

Hoale, W. Stanley. *Vizetelly Covers the Confederacy.* Tuscaloosa, Alabama: Confederate Publishing Co., 1957.

Horn, Stanley F. *The Army of Tennessee.* Indianapolis: The Bobbs-Merrill Co., 1941.

Instruction for Field Artillery. Philadelphia: J. B. Lippincott & Co., 1861.

Jones, J. B. *A Rebel War Clerk's Diary.* 2 vols. New York: Old Heritage Bookshop, 1935.

Jones, Jenkin Lloyd. *An Artilleryman's Diary.* Wisconsin History Commission, 1914.

Kansas. Office of the Adjutant General. *Report for 1861–65,* I.

Koller, Larry. *The Fireside Book of Guns.* New York: Simon & Schuster, 1959.

Lancaster, Bruce. *No Bugles Tonight.* Boston: Little, Brown & Co., 1948.

Leech, Margaret. *Reveille in Washington.* New York & London: Harper & Brothers, 1941.

Lewis, Colonel Berkeley R. *Small Arms & Ammunition in the United States Service.* Washington: Smithsonian Institution, 1956.

———. *Notes on Ammunition of the American Civil War, 1861–65.* Washington: American Ordnance Association, 1959.

Lewis, Lloyd. *Sherman, Fighting Prophet.* New York: Harcourt, Brace & Co., 1932.

Little, Dr. George, and James R. Maxwell. *A History of Lumsden's Battery, C.S.A.* Tuskaloosa, Alabama: R. E. Rhodes Chapter, United Daughters of the Confederacy, 1905.

Livermore, Thomas L. *Numbers and Losses in the Civil War in America, 1861–65.* Boston and New York: Houghton, Mifflin & Co., 1901.

Lonn, Ella. *Foreigners in the Union Army and Navy.* Baton Rouge: Louisiana State Press, 1951.

———. *Foreigners in the Confederacy.* Chapel Hill: University of North Carolina Press, 1940.

McClellan, George Brinton. *Manual of Bayonet Exercise.* Philadelphia: Grambo & Company, 1852.

McMurray, Dr. W. J. *History of the Twentieth Tennessee Regiment Volunteer Infantry.* Nashville, Tennessee: 1904.

Massachusetts Historical Society. *Proceedings.*

Meigs, General M. C. *The Three Days' Battle of Chattanooga.* Washington: McGill & Witherow, 1864.

Military Collectors and Historians. *Journal.* Files.

Military Historical Society of Massachusetts. *Papers.* Boston: 1908 and 1910.

Military Order of the Loyal Legion. Ohio Commandery. *Sketches of War History, 1861–65.* Cincinnati: Robert Clarke & Co., 1883.

Millis, Walter. *Arms and Men.* New York: G. P. Putnam's Sons, 1956.

Mitchell, Lieutenant Colonel Joseph B. *Decisive Battles of the Civil War.* New York: G. P. Putnam's Sons, 1955.

Moore, Frank, ed. *The Civil War in Song and Story.* New York: P. F. Collier, 1892.

Morton, John Watson. *The Artillery of Nathan Bedford Forrest's Cavalry.* Nashville: Publishing House of the Methodist Episcopal Church, 1909.

Morton, Joseph W., Jr., ed. *Sparks from the Camp Fire.* Philadelphia: The Keystone Publishing Co., 1890.

O'Connor, Richard. *Thomas: Rock of Chickamauga*. New York: Prentice-Hall, Inc., 1948.

Owen, William Miller, *In Camp and Battle with the Washington Artillery of New Orleans*. Boston: Ticknor & Co., 1885.

Paris, Louis Philippe Albert d'Orléans, Comte de. *History of the Civil War in America*. 4 vols. Philadelphia: Porter and Coates, 1875–88.

Patten, George Washington. *Cavalry Drill and Sabre Exercises*. Richmond: West and Johanston, 1862.

Pennsylvania at Chickamauga and Chattanooga. Harrisburg: 1901.

Perry, Henry Fales. *History of the Thirty-Eighth Regiment Indiana Volunteer Infantry*. Palo Alto. California: F. A. Stuart, 1906.

Peterson, Harold L. *Notes on Ordnance of the American Civil War, 1861–1865*. Washington: The American Ordnance Association, 1959.

Photographic History of the Civil War. Francis Trevelyan Miller, ed. 10 vols. New York: 1911.

Pickerill, W. N. *History of the Third Indiana Cavalry*. Indianapolis: 1906.

Polley, J. B. *Hood's Texas Brigade*. New York and Washington: The Neale Publishing Co., 1910.

————. *A Soldier's Letters to Charming Nellie*. New York and Washington: The Neale Publishing Co., 1908.

Ramsdell, Charles M. "General Robert E. Lee's Horse Supply, 1862–1865." *American Historical Review*, XXXV (1930), 758–777.

Robertson, John. *Michigan in the War*. Lansing, Michigan: W. S. George & Co., 1880.

Rodenbough, Theophilus F., and William L. Haskin, eds., *The Army of the United States, Historical Sketches of Staff and Line*. New York: Maynard, Merrill & Co., 1896.

Rogers, J. L. *The Civil War Battles of Chickamauga and Chattanooga*. Chattanooga, Tennessee: Andrews Printing Co. (n.d.).

Schaff, Morris. *The Spirit of Old West Point*. Boston and New York: Houghton, Mifflin & Co., 1907.

SeCheverrell, J. Hamp. *Journal History of the Twenty-Ninth Ohio Veteran Volunteers*. Cleveland: 1883.

Seitz, Don C. *Braxton Bragg, General of the Confederacy*. Columbia, South Carolina: The State Co., 1924.

Shannon, Fred Albert. *The Organization and Administration of the Union Army, 1861–1865*. 2 vols. Glendale, California: Arthur H. Clark Co., 1928.

Sheridan, Philip H. *Personal Memoirs of P. H. Sheridan*. 2 vols. New York: Charles L. Webster & Co., 1888.

Sketches of War History. Military Order of the Loyal Legion, Ohio Commandery. Vol. I. Cincinnati: Robert Clarke & Co., 1883.

Skinner, Captain George W. *Pennsylvania at Chickamauga and Chattanooga*. (n.p.) William Stanley Ray, 1897.

Smith, Justin H. *The War with Mexico*. 2 vols. New York: The Macmillan Company, 1919.

Smith, Theodore Clarke. *The Life and Letters of James Abram Garfield*. 2 vols. New Haven: Yale University Press, 1925.

Sorrel, General G. Moxley. *Recollections of a Confederate Staff Officer*. New York. The Neale Publishing Co., 1917.

Southern Historical Society. *Papers*, vols. 1–50. Richmond: 1914–53.

Spaulding, Colonel Oliver Lyman, Jr. *The United States Army in War and Peace*. New York: G. P. Putnam's Sons, 1937.

Starr, Louis M. *Bohemian Brigade: Civil War Newsmen in Action.* New York: Alfred A. Knopf, 1954.

Steele, Major Mathew Forney. *American Campaigns.* 2 vols. Washington: War Department Document No. 324, 1943.

Stern, Philip Van Doren. *They Were There.* New York: Crown Publishers, Inc., 1959.

Sullivan, James R. *Chickamauga and Chattanooga Battlefields.* Washington: National Park Service Historical Handbook Series No. 25, 1956.

Taylor, Benjamin F. *Pictures of Life in Camp and Field.* Chicago: S. C. Griggs & Co., 1875.

Tennent, Sir J. Emerson. *The Story of the Guns.* London: Longman, Green, Longman, Roberts, and Green, 1864.

Thatcher, Captain Marshall P. *A Hundred Battles in the West. St. Louis to Atlanta, 1861–65. The Second Michigan Cavalry.* Detroit, Michigan: Published by the Author, 1884.

Turchin, John B. *Chickamauga.* Chicago: Fergus Printing Co., 1888.

Turner, George Edward. *Victory Rode the Rails.* Indianapolis: The Bobbs-Merrill Co., 1953.

U.S. Department of the Army. U.S. Military Academy. *Summaries of Selected Military Campaigns.* West Point: 1953.

U.S. Department of the Army. The Infantry School. *Selected Readings in American Military History.* 3 vols. Fort Benning, Georgia: 1953.

U.S. Department of the Army. Public Information Division. *The Medal of Honor of the United States Army.* Washington: Government Printing Office, 1948.

U.S. Department of the Army. *R.O.T.C. Manual No. 145-20. American Military History, 1607–1953.* Washington: Government Printing Office, 1956.

U.S. Department of the Army. The Infantry School. *Selected Readings in American Military History,* 3 vols. Fort Benning, Georgia: 1953.

U.S. War Department. *Bibliography of State Participation in the Civil War, 1861–1866.* Washington: Government Printing Office, 1913.

U.S. War Department. *Instruction for Field Artillery.* 2 vols. Philadelphia: 1860.

U.S. War Department. *The War of the Rebellion: Official Records.* 130 vols. Washington: 1880–1901.

Upson, Theodore F. *With Sherman to the Sea.* Baton Rouge: Louisiana State University Press, 1943.

Van Horne, Thomas B. *History of the Army of the Cumberland.* 2 vols. and atlas. Cincinnati: Robert Clarke & Co., 1873.

――――. *The Life of Major General George H. Thomas.* New York: Charles Scribner's Sons, 1882.

Waddle, Angus L. *Three Years with the Armies of the Ohio and the Cumberland.* Chillicothe, Ohio: Scioto Gazette, 1889.

Walker, Robert Sparks. *Lookout Mountain, Battles and Battlefields.* Chattanooga, Tennessee: George C. Hudson & Co., 1952.

――――. *Lookout, the Story of a Mountain.* Kingsport, Tennessee: Southern Publications, Inc., 1941.

Watkins, Sam R. *"Company Aytch."* Jackson, Tennessee: McCowat-Mercer Press, 1952.

Weisberger, Bernard A. *Reporters for the Union.* Boston: Little, Brown & Co., 1953.

Westrate, E. V. *Those Fatal Generals.* New York: Knight Publications, Inc., 1936.

Weller, Jac. "The Field Artillery of the Civil War." *Journal of the Company of Military Collectors and Historians.* Vol. V, Nos. 2, 3, and 4, 1953.

The West Point Atlas of American Wars, 1689–1900. Colonel Vincent J. Esposito, chief ed. 2 vols. New York: Frederick A. Praeger, 1959.

Wiley, Bell Irwin, *The Life of Johnny Reb.* Indianapolis: The Bobbs-Merrill Company, Inc., 1943.

————. *The Life of Billy Yank.* Indianapolis: The Bobbs-Merrill Company, Inc., 1943.

Williams, Kenneth P. *Lincoln Finds a General.* 5 vols. New York: The Macmillan Co., 1949–52.

Wittenmyer, Annie. *Under the Guns, a Woman's Reminiscences of the Civil War.* Boston: E. B. Stillings & Co., 1895.

Wood, Major Bradford R., Jr. *Chattanooga or Lookout Mountain and Missionary Ridge from Moccasin Point.* Albany, New York: U.S. Veteran Signal Corps Association, 1907.

Wood, William, and Ralph Henry Gabriel. *In Defense of Liberty. Pageant of America.* Vol. VII, New Haven: Yale University Press, 1928.

Wyeth, John Allen. *Life of Lieutenant General Nathan Bedford Forrest.* New York and London: Harper & Brothers, 1899.

INDEX

Military Organizations

General

Alexander, Col. E. Porter, 51 f., 108, 147 f., 159, 173
Alexander's Bridge, 39, 97
Ammunition, artillery, 50, 52 ff.
Ammunition, infantry, 35 ff.; *see also* Minié bullets ("minnie balls")
Anderson, Sgt. Eli W., 120
Andersonville Prison, 171
Appomattox, 16, 194
Arms; *see under names, as* Colt revolvers, Sharps carbines, Spencer carbines and rifles, *etc.*
Artillery, 45 ff.; *see also makes of cannon, as* Napoleons, Parrotts, Whitworth, *etc.*
Artillery, equipment, 50
Artillery, weights and ranges, 49
Atlanta, Ga., 66, 84
Austrian rifles, 35

Baird, Gen. Absalom, 101 f., 183
Banks, Sgt. George L., 183 f.
Barnett, Gen. James, 55
Bayonets, 34, 41 f.
Beatty, Gen. John, 18, 25, 63
Belgian rifles, 35
Bell, Sgt. James B., 184
Benét, Col. Stephen V., 38
Benning, Gen. Henry L., 122
Bickerdyke, "Mother" Mary A., 62
Bierce, Capt. Ambrose, 117 f., 128 f.
Birch, Billy, 77
Bragg, Gen. Braxton, 8, 10 ff., 20 ff., 56 ff., 62 f., 70, 73 ff., 94, 97, 107 f., 113, 130 ff., 137 f., 143, 149 f., 160, 167 f., 178, 180, 192 f.

Brandy Station, battle, 9
Brannan, Gen. John M., 102
Breckinridge, Gen. John C., 73, 104, 131
Bridgeport, Ala., 67, 88, 90, 136, 138, 141 f., 152
Bridges, Capt. Lyman, 174
Brotherton House, 115 f., 198
Brown's Ferry, 142, 146, 152 f.
Buck, E. S., 58 f.
Buckner, Gen. Simon Bolivar, 70, 80 f.
Buena Vista, battle, 10, 15
Buford, Gen. John, 38
Bull Run or Manassas, battles, 60, 124
Burnside, Gen. Ambrose, 19, 70, 85, 88, 150 ff., 194
Butler, Gen. Benjamin F., 18
Butler, Pvt. Benjamin F., C.S.A., 104
Byers, Capt. S. H. M., 171

Cagle, George, 111, 122
Caperton's Ferry, Ala., 73
Carson, Bugler William J., 105
Chancellorsville, battle, 8, 19, 35, 65, 88, 153
Chaplains, 112
Chapultepec, 10
Chase, Kate, 101
Chattanooga, Tenn., 4 f., 6, 23, 52, 57, 66 ff., 69 ff., 73 ff., 78, 82, 84, 87, 91, 107, 135 ff., 147 ff., 153, 172, 196 ff.
Chattanooga Creek, 168
Chattanooga, The, 145 f.

Date Due

E   3.25 +   19888
475.97
D6   Downey

AUTHOR

Storming of the gateway

TITLE

DATE DUE	BORROWER'S NAME
NOV 7 '69	Junde Bowers Box 391 Jockey
DEC 2 '69	Joal Cotton 0375
	Bobby Brown
NOV 16 '71	241-90-3916
	T A. W. D. 742

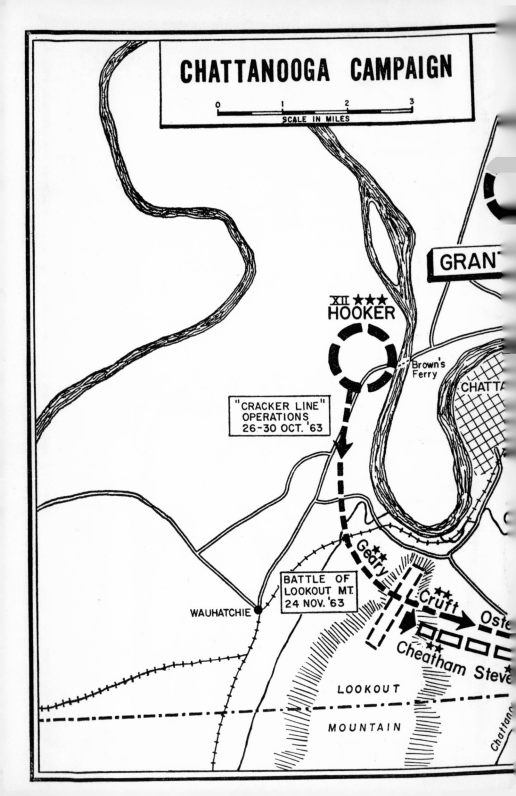